THE MARIAN MANIFESTO

How Devotion to the Immaculate Heart
will Renew the World

LAWRENCE MAGINOT

foreword by Monsignor Charles M. Mangan

BLUE ARMY PRESS

Washington, New Jersey

ISBN: 978-0-578-52664-5

Cover and text design by Sundae Graphic Design

Published in the United States by Blue Army Press,
World Apostolate of Fatima, USA,
P.O. Box 976, Washington, NJ 07882
www.bluearmy.com

Printed and bound in the United States of America

DEDICATION

To my mother,
Elizabeth "Betty" Dawson Maginot,
(June 16, 1931 – April 27, 2014)
who taught me from my childhood,
both by word and example,
the habits of praying the Rosary every day
and of gratefully surrendering my will to God's will and providence
in all situations and circumstances.

Contents

ACKNOWLEDGEMENTS

It would be an impossible task to acknowledge everyone who had an influence upon me in the formation of this book. I can only mention those who have had a more direct and immediate influence. This book has been several years in the making, and I must first acknowledge Patrick Sabat, who I have worked with for a number of years with the International Pilgrim Virgin Statue of Our Lady of Fatima. He was the first to tell me that I should write down my thoughts into the form of a book. Then I must also mention my lovely wife, Chimgee, who never stopped believing that the time I was spending on putting it together was not in vain.

There are a number of people who helped me by reading over my early drafts and providing valuable feedback: My brother, Fr. Michael Maginot; my aunt, Sr. Lorraine Maginot of the Ursuline Sisters; my niece, Angela Hughes, who was an English major in college; Sharon Staley, a devout friend who never stopped praying for this work to see its completion; Lt. Col. Gerald Pearman, (U.S.Army, Ret.); and Michael Gibson.

Special mention must be made of Fr. Edward O'Connor, CSC, Professor (emeritus) of Theology at the University of Notre Dame, who carefully examined the work in its latter stage and provided some invaluable insights. Also, Msgr. Charles Mangan, director of the Office of the Marian Apostolate in the Diocese of Sioux Falls, SD, who also provided some invaluable insights and wrote the Foreword for the book.

A tremendous thank you to David Carollo, executive director of the World Apostolate of Fatima, USA, for agreeing to publish the book.

I cannot thank enough Barb Ernster, editor and head of communications for the World Apostolate of Fatima, USA, for laboring hard to make the manuscript more readable and knocking down every barrier to see this work through to publication.

Finally, I thank my bishop, His Excellency, Donald Hying, DD, Bishop of Gary, IN (at the time he granted his imprimatur; now Bishop of Madison, WI), and Sean Martin, Director of Religious Education, Evangelization and Family Life for the Diocese of Gary, for faithfully fulfilling their duty to examine the doctrinal integrity of the manuscript. Sean went above and beyond his call of duty and provided me with helpful insights which helped to improve the final draft.

FOREWORD

The volume before you presents realities that are simultaneously challenging and comforting.

The challenge to love God, come what may – to venerate His Ever-Virgin Mother, to form our lives upon the tenets of the Holy Gospels, to go forward always united to Holy Mother Church – challenges all, to be sure.

But what unspeakable comfort it is to follow Jesus Christ! This comfort does not derive from a transitory, "Oh, whatever!" kind of feeling that too often seems to represent an avoidance of effort. Rather, it hails from the persistent desire to embrace the Redeemer's cross, thereby experiencing the comforts of soul that only God Himself can affect.

Lawrence Maginot's useful text does not shy away from these challenges or these comforts.

The author grants to us a careful look at the meaning of the Apparitions of Our Lady of Fatima and invites us to consider anew our response to the Church's cherished, longstanding devotion to the Immaculate Heart of Mary.

More than ever, having commemorated in 2017 the centenary of Holy Mary's visits to Lucia, Francisco and Jacinta – a significant date in the life of the Church and of the world that certainly had an influence on what Mr. Maginot now shares with us – we note the importance of Our Lady's words. She reminded us that conversion of heart is a must, just as it was when Jesus spoke of it two millennia earlier; it is not optional. It is time to walk without hesitation on the path of Christ, keeping our eyes fixed on the Father and surrendering to the inspiration of the Holy Spirit.

The recitation of the Most Holy Rosary, the frequent and worthy reception of the Sacraments, the offering of our sacrifices in reparation for sinners and the performance of our "daily duty" are recurring themes over the six months during which Our Lady came to Fatima as well as during the three appearances of the Angel of Peace in 1916. We must not underestimate the value of these great "works." How consoling they are for those who seek to love and imitate the Savior of the human race and the Woman who unfailingly cooperated in all His plans.

On the first Holy Saturday, when the friends of Jesus were disturbed and discouraged, it was Mary at Nazareth who believed that what her Son promised would be fulfilled. Centuries later, may we hold fast to the Word of Life and experience Our Lady's ceaseless joy in her Son's decisive victory over sin and death.

We thank the author for his contribution, and we pray that the readers of the work will ponder the indescribable riches of the Hearts of Jesus and Mary that were conveyed by the Mother of God at Fatima to the young trio and, by extension, to each of us more than 100 years ago.

Monsignor Charles M. Mangan
Office of the Marian Apostolate
Diocese of Sioux Falls
Holy Saturday
March 31, 2018

INTRODUCTION

Surely the Lord God does nothing without
revealing his secret to his servants the prophets.
(Am 3:7)

When prefacing the official commentary of the Third Secret of Fatima for its initial release on June 26, 2000, Cardinal Joseph Ratzinger (the future Pope Benedict XVI) stated, "Fatima is undoubtedly the most prophetic of modern apparitions."[1] As someone of his theological stature understands in making this claim about Fatima, the message of Fatima has proved to be not just accurate in predicting future world events and conditions, but solidly grounded in the fullness of truth in the whole range and scope of its message.

The capacity of a truly prophetic witness to predict accurately certain future events or conditions is dependent upon the degree to which that source is grounded in the full truth about God, His creation and His concern for human beings and their salvation. Though some parts of a prophetic message may concern matters of only a provincial or temporal scope, true prophecy is never concerned with merely trivial matters, as might be the case of claims coming from a fortuneteller attempting to impress and captivate an audience.

Rather, like the hub of a wheel to which its spokes are firmly attached in order to maintain the wheel's integrity and equilibrium, so, too, the weighty historic events and conditions to which prophecy draws attention must firmly attach to God's revealed truth and providential concern and care for all humanity. Such prophecy can then help us to see and understand all such things in the wisdom of the true light of God.

The Fatima message was given at the dawn of the most stunning of revolutions in the advancement of science and technology.

---

[1] Congregation for the Doctrine of the Faith. *The Message of Fatima.* Accessed July 11, 2015. www.vatican.va/.../rc_con_cfaith_doc_20000626_message-fatima_en.html

This revolution, with all its impressive accomplishments, is often referenced as a premise for many in their efforts to dislodge Western Civilization from its stable anchoring in the hub of God's truth and goodness. This world view that was once the common subject of conversation around dinner tables and fireplaces, has now become the object of ridicule and mockery by elites in entertainment, media, education and government, who view it as an archaic relic of a pre-scientific, superstitious past.

Though the basis of this contempt is not grounded upon true premises, from which the certainty of logical conclusions can be drawn, the dizzying historic upheaval brought about by the scientific revolution has emboldened many to feel justified in an attitude of contempt for all former ways of thinking, including theological, philosophical, moral and social. In this intellectual atmosphere, Fatima, as "undoubtedly the most prophetic of modern apparitions," holds a capacity to recall millions of people back to a renewed confidence in the ever-abiding truths of God's revelation in Scripture, Tradition and His created works.

The central topic of this book is the concluding prophecy spoken of by Our Lady at Fatima: **"In the end my Immaculate Heart will triumph. ... and a certain period of peace will be granted to the world,"**[2] which seems to defy every movement and trend taking place in the world today. But what developed within the nation of Portugal in the years following the supernatural events at Fatima provides a microcosm for this prophecy. The one unique event at Fatima that, more than any other, challenges the intellectual complacency of the modern secularist worldview is the event that occurred on October 13, 1917, commonly known as the great *miracle of the sun*. Like the miraculous event that occurred on Mount Carmel as chronicled in the pages of the Old Testament, this event stands out like no other event documented in modern times.

---

[2] Lucia dos Santos, *Fourth Memoir* (Words of Mary to Lucia during the third apparition, July 13, 1917), *Documents on Fatima & Memoirs of Sr. Lucia,* Edited by Fr. Antonio Maria Martins, S.J. 2nd English ed. (Hanceville, AL: Fatima Family Apostolate, 2002), 440.

Lucia dos Santos had promised for months that, "in October, [the "beautiful lady" who was appearing to her and her two cousins] will perform a miracle that everyone will see in order to make them believe."[3] On October 13, tens of thousands had gathered at the site of the apparitions in Fatima in anticipation of this predicted miracle. It is reminiscent of the tale of the prophet Elijah who gathered around himself a great throng of Israelites and four hundred and fifty prophets of the pagan god, Baal, for a decisive duel of divine power (cf. 1 Kgs 18:17-40). Elijah proposed a contest where he and the false prophets of Baal would prepare separate offerings to their respective deities; the deity who responded in an obvious display of power was to be acknowledged as the true God and worshiped by Israel. The prophets of Baal called upon their god for hours but failed to produce any reaction. Then Elijah took his turn and prayed aloud:

> "O Lord, God of Abraham, Isaac, and Israel, let it be known this day that thou art God in Israel, and that I am thy servant, and that I have done all these things at thy word. Answer me, O Lord, answer me, that this people may know that thou, O Lord, art God, and that thou hast turned their hearts back." Then the fire of the Lord fell, and consumed the burnt offering, and the wood, and the stones, and the dust, and licked up the water that was in the trench. And when all the people saw it, they fell on their faces; and they said, "The Lord, he is God; the Lord, he is God" (1 Kgs 18:36-39).

At Fatima something quite similar happened, which, because it happened so recently in modern times, cannot be denigrated as merely a pious fable. Rather than being a showdown between the prophet Elijah and four hundred and fifty prophets of Baal, however, the Mother of God confronted ministers of the modern secular worldview by the faith and witness of three children.

In 1910, only seven years before the miracle of the sun, a revolution sent the Portuguese royal family into exile, and the people

---

[3] *ibid.* 439

of Portugal found themselves governed by revolutionaries who possessed a vision that was both radically secularist and anti-clerical. The online encyclopedia, *Wikipedia*, provides some details of the revolutionary government's anti-clerical policies:

> The Church's property and assets were expropriated by the State. Bishops were persecuted, expelled or suspended from their activities in the course of the secularization. All but one were driven from their dioceses. The property of clerics was seized by the state, wearing of the cassock was banned, all minor seminaries were closed and all but five major seminaries. A law of 22 February 1918 permitted only two seminaries in the country, but they had not been given their property back. Religious orders were expelled from the country, including 31 orders comprising members in 164 houses. Religious education was prohibited in both primary and secondary school.[4]

It was in the midst of this politically repressive atmosphere that the *beautiful lady* had promised to perform a miracle that everyone will see in order to make them believe. The government-aligned, secular media were extremely critical of the hysteria that had developed around the rumored events in Fatima over the summer months and were well prepared to mock the gullibility of all who fell for the fanciful imaginings of the little children. Immediately following the event, though, news outlets found no basis on which to ground an assertion of mass gullibility on the part of those who testified with certainty to what they had witnessed. An article in the Lisbon newspaper, *O Seculo*, reported the scene this way:

> From beside the parked carriages and where many thousands stood, afraid to descend into the muddy soil of the Cova da Iria, we saw the immense crowd turn toward the sun at its highest, free of all clouds. The sun seemed to

---

[4] Wikipedia, *5 October 1910 Revolution*, Accessed July 11, 2015. https://en.wikipedia.org/wiki/5_October_1910_revolution.

us like a plate of dull silver. It could be seen without the least effort. It did not blind or burn. It seemed as though an eclipse were taking place. All of a sudden a tremendous shout burst forth, "Miracle, miracle!"

Before the astonished eyes of the people, whose attitude carried us back to Biblical times, and who, white with terror, heads uncovered, gazed at the sun which trembled and made brusque and unheard of movement beyond all cosmic laws, the sun seemed literally to dance in the sky.

Immediately afterward the people asked each other if they saw anything and what they had seen. The greatest number avowed that they saw the sun trembling and dancing; others declared they saw the smiling face of the Blessed Virgin herself. They swore that the sun turned around on itself as if it were a wheel of fireworks and had fallen almost to the point of burning the earth with its rays. Some said they saw it change colors successively.[5]

Though the author of this article, Avelino de Almeida, reported the event as though he were just conveying the testimonies of others, in private correspondence with a high public official and childhood friend, Antonio de Bastos, president of the Municipal Council of Santarem, Avelino left no doubt of the position of his own testimony:

> Your rationalism suffered a formidable blow, and wishing to establish a definite opinion, you make use of unprejudiced evidence, such as mine, since I was there only in fulfillment of a very difficult mission, that of reporting impartially for *O Seculo* facts which might develop before me.
>
> It may not satisfy you, but certainly what your eyes saw and what you heard was no different from what I saw and heard, and there were few who were insensible to the grandeur of this spectacle, unique and worthy of thought and study from every viewpoint.[6]

---

[5] John M. Haffert, *Meet the Witnesses*. (Asbury, NJ: 101 Foundation, Inc., 2002), 106.
[6] *ibid*, 107.

One would like to think that immediately following such an overwhelming display of divine power, the nation of Portugal would have witnessed an almost instantaneous reversal of its government's anti-clerical and anti-religious policies. But just as Elijah had to face threatening hostility following the indisputable display of divine power on Mount Carmel, so too, with matters that followed the Fatima event, the political powers of the day began to step up their religious persecution and purge from their own ranks those who had become sympathetic towards the Church and faithful believers. Like Pharaoh, who had hardened his heart in defiance against the unquestionable display of God's power working through Moses, the secularists doubled down in their anti-clerical policies over the next decade. During that same time period, though, Portugal witnessed its own form of *exodus* as pilgrimages to Fatima continued to grow year after year, despite the government's best efforts to dissuade the people. Finally, the year 1927 saw the beginning of a peaceful political transformation in Portugal, when people with some religious sensitivity were granted political power to put in place reforms to help Portugal convert from the police state it had become to one that dutifully protects the religious liberties of its citizens.

There is an important lesson to be learned in the political transformation that emerged only patiently, and serves as an example of how a real societal transformation may be expected to take place on a greater, global scale in association with the predicted *triumph of the Immaculate Heart*. Though God is truly capable of performing "a miracle that everyone will see in order to make them believe,"[7] the conversion of human hearts and, especially, the mass conversion of entire societies and cultures involve a grace of a much greater depth and reach than merely that resulting from an unquestionable display of God's power.

It is difficult to breach the subject of this book in some depth without presuming that the reader has at least some knowledge about the events and message of Fatima, which can be gained easily from other sources. Though many conflicting interpretations of the events

---

[7] July 13, 1917 Apparition, *Fourth Memoir, Documents,* 439

of Fatima and its message have been presented by varied sources, it is my intention here to help the reader pierce through any confusion, gain a better appreciation of this remarkable, divine intervention in our recent history, and better understand what it means for us, our Church and our world today.

As a divine intervention with a very prophetic component, much of what can be ascertained from the events of Fatima is not always conveyed explicitly by spoken or written word. Rather, like some of the prophets of the Old Testament, much is often implied by the symbolism of the described actions of the prophet. The events of Fatima are richly packed with symbolic references and meaning, and by drawing particular attention to these it is my hope to better convey some of its spiritual wealth.

Elements of the events will be referred to as they tie in thematically to the interpretation. By so doing, the overall meaning of the message of Fatima should become clearer to all who read and make the connections. Nevertheless, for those who have little knowledge of the apparitions, some brief background about Fatima is needed.

.   .   .

Fatima is the name of a town in Portugal where, in 1917, the Blessed Virgin Mary appeared to three children six times during six consecutive months, May through October. The name itself holds some weighty significance, which should not be overlooked; Fatima was the name of the beloved daughter of the prophet Mohammed, and along with her father, she is revered by Muslims to this day. Fatima is actually a popular female name in Muslim cultures. Thus, it is of interest to consider why Our Lady chose to appear in a remote village that carries the name of the daughter of Mohammed.

Portugal, a nation that shares with Spain the landmass of the Iberian Peninsula, was an area of Europe where, for centuries, Muslims and Christians lived in relative coexistence. The militantly masculine religion of Islam has an unusually tender openness for the mother of Jesus and, because of this, we should have all the more confidence to entrust the future peace of the world to her. The late, Archbishop Fulton J. Sheen (1895-1979) covers the topic of Mary in the religion of Islam in his book *The World's First Love*, in a chapter entitled "Mary and the Muslims." As he explains it:

> Mary, then, is for the Muslims the true Sayyida, or Lady. The only possible serious rival to her in their creed would be Fatima, the daughter of Mohammed himself. But after the death of Fatima, Mohammed wrote: "Thou shalt be the most blessed of all the women in Paradise, after Mary." In a variant of the text, Fatima is made to say: "I surpass all the women, except Mary."[8]

Because Islam is a religion founded some six centuries after Christianity in areas once evangelized by Christians and home to Jewish communities, Mohammad's writings are influenced by these older religious traditions. Though the Koran views Jesus as merely a prophet who preceded and prepared the way for Mohammed, it retains very lofty praise for Mary, the mother of Jesus. In the Christian Tradition, this esteem for Mary is logically based upon the realization of the complete identity of Jesus. In Islam, the appeal is a bit more curious and testifies to the general, high regard that the Arab populations retained for the mother of Jesus at the time of Islam's founding. By retaining this high esteem for Mary, though obscuring the theological reasoning for the singular graces bestowed upon her, the writings of Mohammed were able to hold some appeal to many in the Arab world who had already developed some devotion to her. The Koran supports Mary's Immaculate Conception and perpetual virginity. It contains verses descriptive of the Annunciation of the Angel Gabriel to Mary, Mary's visitation to Elizabeth, and the Birth of Jesus. Because of this exaltation of Mary within Islam, Archbishop Sheen expressed his particular hope of Mary's intervention at Fatima:

---

[8] Archbishop Fulton J. Sheen, *The World's First Love: Mary, the Mother of God.* (San Francisco: Ignatius Press, 2010), 206-207.

Since nothing ever happens out of heaven except with a finesse of all details, I believe that the Blessed Virgin chose to be known as "Our Lady of Fatima" as a pledge and a sign of hope to the Muslim people and as an assurance that they, who show her so much respect, will one day accept her Divine Son, too.[9]

We can thus see in heaven's "finesse" of this detail that the Blessed Virgin Mary, in her appearance at Fatima in 1917, was expressing the great love that God has for Muslims and His desire that all come to a saving knowledge of His Son (cf. 1 Tm 2:4).

Interestingly, that year was also the fourth year of what was known then as "The Great War." World War I had much to do with the scrambling of nations determined to fill the vacuum of power left behind by the declining influence of the Turkish Muslim Ottoman Empire. In this rapidly changing world, Mary appears to three shepherd children and speaks to them about being able to end the war by praying the Rosary. She never utters the words *Islam* or *Muslims*, but rather speaks about the need for prayer and sacrifice for the conversion of sinners and to make reparation to God, who is *offended* by sin; that wars and persecutions are a result of sin and are, thus, a form of punishment for sin; and that, united with Christ by grace as members of His mystical body, we can by our prayer and sacrifices repair the damages caused by sin and help bring peace to the world.

The three children to whom the Blessed Virgin appeared were Lucia dos Santos, age ten, and her two cousins, Francisco Marto, age nine, and his younger sister, Jacinta Marto, age seven. Prior to Mary's apparitions, an angel visited the children three times the year before in 1916. As Mary had prophesied to the children,[10] Francisco died of the Spanish flu epidemic on April 4, 1919, and Jacinta of tuberculosis on February 20, 1920. In contrast, Lucia went on to live until February 13, 2005. Consequently, it is primarily through Lucia's testimony that we know many of the inner details of the events that took place at Fatima.

---

[9] *ibid.*, 207.
[10] June 13, 1917 Apparition, *Fourth Memoir, Documents*, 438.

·   ·   ·

As mentioned above, the subject of this book receives its primary impetus from the well-known words spoken by Mary at Fatima on July 13, 1917: "In the end, my Immaculate Heart will triumph…" These words were recorded by Lucia in her fourth memoir, when she became confident that the time had come for her to make known the first two parts of "the secret" entrusted to her that day. This includes the horrifying vision of hell and the warning about Russia's future path, which if not converted "will scatter her errors throughout the world, provoking wars and persecutions of the Church."[11]

In relation to the first part of the secret, Our Lady told the children, "You have seen hell where the souls of poor sinners go. To save them **God wishes to establish in the world the devotion to my Immaculate Heart.** If they do what I will tell you, many souls will be saved, **and there will be peace.**"[12] Notice here the direct correlation between the general state of souls and the overall condition of peace in the world. One can also recognize the broad implication that devotion to the Immaculate Heart of Mary has the potency to tip the scale of events favorably for both the salvation of souls and peace in the world. That same correlation in the second part of the secret becomes a remarkably uncanny prophecy about particular events, which we now know from hindsight have decisively shaped the world and its recent history. Our Lady's words are quoted here as recorded by Sister Lucia, with information in brackets to point out their prophetic fulfillment:

> The war is going to end [The First World War ended the following year]. But if they do not stop offending God, another even worse war will begin in the reign of Pius XI [WWII: This statement is very insightful, considering that WW I was called both, "The Great War" and, "The war that would end all wars"].

---

[11] *ibid.*, 440.

[12] *ibid.*

When you see a night illumined by an unknown light, know that it is the great sign that God gives you that He is going to punish the world for its crimes by means of war, hunger and persecutions of the Church and of the Holy Father [This event occurred on January 24, 1938, and has become known as the "Fatima (solar) storm," not to be confused with the miracle of the sun.[13] It occurred when Japan was already expanding its imperial thrust into China and only weeks before Hitler made his move to occupy Austria.].

To prevent this I will come to ask for the consecration of Russia to my Immaculate Heart and the Communion of reparation on the first Saturdays. If they listen to my requests, Russia will be converted and there will be peace. If not, she will scatter her errors throughout the world, provoking wars and persecutions of the Church. The good will be martyred, the Holy Father will have much to suffer, and various nations will be annihilated. **In the end my Immaculate Heart will triumph**. The Holy Father will consecrate Russia to me, and it will be converted **and a certain period of peace will be granted to the world**. (Emphasis mine) [It is interesting to note that in July the Bolshevik Communists had not yet seized control of the Russian government. The Czar had already been overthrown but, at that time, the country was being governed by a provisional parliament. The Bolsheviks would seize control in the weeks which followed the miracle of the sun, October 13, 1917. The Bolshevik's great campaign of spreading counter intelligence and disinformation propaganda "throughout the world" was one of their most notable modes of foreign operation and strategy for achieving

---

[13] cf. www.solarstorms.org/SRefStorms.html.

their hope of eventual world domination.][14] [15]

Many details of this prophetic message have rightly received much attention in various circles within the Church. Unfortunately, some of that attention has been less than conducive to building up a generous response to God's desire "to establish in the world the devotion to [the] Immaculate Heart" of Mary. Some questions arising from certain details of Our Lady's message have taken on such a life of their own as to almost completely detract from and obscure the greater meaning and intention of the expressed global mission assigned to Lucia by Our Lady. This was made abundantly clear to Lucia on June 13, 1917, as noted above.

Lucia's mission deserves greater attention and closer examination. In so many respects, we are utterly dependent upon the commentary that Sister Lucia has provided about the events at Fatima and Our Lady's words to the children, most of which she wrote under obedience to Church authority. Yet, in this regard, she herself stated in a letter to her spiritual director that, "The mission God has given me in this world, I believe is not that of a prophet, but rather that of a voice in the desert where only God hears."[16] In her third memoir, she expounds upon this sense of her mission in greater detail (again the quote is bracketed with some helpful commentary):

> Maybe, your Excellency, it might seem to some that I should have told all these things [that is, the things she is now revealing in the *Third Memoir*] a long time ago [This *Third Memoir* was dated August 31, 1941, twenty four years after the apparition events, and when WWII was already executing its horrifying destruction all over Europe. Though the message of the first two parts of the secret given by Our

---

[14] cf. Lt. Gen. Ion Mihal Pacepa and Prof. Ronald J. Rychlak, *Disinformation: Former Spy Chief Reveals Secret Strategies for Undermining Freedom, Attacking Religion, and Promoting Terrorism,*; and, Christopher Andrew and Vasili Mitrokhin, *The Sword and the Shield: The Mitrokhin Archive and the Secret History of the KGB*, Chapter 14, "Political Warfare: Active Measures and the Main Adversary"

[15] July 13 Apparition, *Fourth Memoir, Documents*, 440.

[16] Sr. Lucia, *Letter to Very Rev. Fr. Aparicio from Tuy, Spain, 9/1/1940, Documents*, 387.

Lady was not revealed in its complete wording until this *Third Memoir*, Sr. Lucia persistently warned of its essence to her confessors and superiors (all the way up to the pope), in private correspondence, in obedience to our Lord's request upon her to ask for the promotion of the *Five First Saturdays of Communions of Reparation* and the *collegial consecration of Russia to the Immaculate Heart of Mary,* long before she had written her *Third Memoir.*] In their opinion, it would have been worthwhile some years ago. That would have been true, if God had wanted to present me to the world as a prophet, but I believe this wasn't His intention in revealing these things to me. If it had been, I think that in 1917 He would have ordered me to speak. Instead, He told me to be silent, and His order was seconded by those who acted for Him. Then, your Excellency, I believe that God intended to use me only to remind the world of the necessity of avoiding sin and making reparation to God by prayer and penance. Where could I have hidden myself to avoid answering endless questions which would have been asked if this matter had been disclosed? Even now I am afraid just thinking about the possible results. And I confess that the repugnance of disclosing it is such that, in spite of your letter before me ordering me to write everything I can remember and also in spite of my interior sentiment that this is the time willed by God to do so, I hesitate and am in a real conflict whether to deliver the letter or burn it.

I still don't know the outcome. May what God wills be done. Keeping silent has been a great grace for me. What about the revelation of hell? I can't even find the exact words to explain its reality. What I say is nothing, it only gives a vague idea of it. What would have happened if I had said one thing this time and another that time trying in vain to explain myself. I might have caused such a confusion of ideas as, perhaps, to hinder God's work. For this very reason I thank God and find that He does everything well.

Ordinarily God causes an interior and exact discernment of their meaning to accompany His revelations. But I don't dare speak about this for fear of being led by my imagination, which, in my opinion, can very easily happen.[17]

Lucia's own perception of her role in mediating the message given at Fatima should not be dismissed. To hear Lucia claim that it was not God's intention "to present [her] to the world as a prophet" may seem incredible to anyone at all familiar with the impact Fatima has had in helping the Church to maintain at least some equilibrium amidst a torrent of countless challenges, both from within her own ranks and from the world at large. She has fulfilled the role that the Blessed Mother gave her: **"Jesus wishes to make use of you to have me acknowledged and loved. He wishes to establish in the world the devotion to my Immaculate Heart."**[18]

If Lucia did not view her role so much as that of a prophet, but more as "a voice in the desert where only God hears," then we are presented with a challenge. Rather than scrutinize the details of a prophetic message, a message amendable and mutable according to the degree of response made to it, we are to probe ever more deeply her 'voice," for it is a voice that **"Jesus wishes to make use of ... ,"** a "voice" that expresses intimately the devotion which **"He wishes to establish in the world ..."**

John Haffert, co-founder of The Blue Army / World Apostolate of Fatima, spent a great deal of his lifetime researching the events at Fatima and testified to the extraordinary gifts Lucia had in accurately conveying Fatima's message:

After the apparitions, because of her lively intelligence and extraordinary memory, Lucia learned to read and write very quickly. Concerning her memory, one can only say that it was absolutely remarkable. As she wrote one section of the Memoirs after the other under obedience,

---

[17] Lucia, *Third Memoir, Documents*, 408-409.

[18] June 13, 1917 Apparition, *Fourth Memoir, Documents*, 438.

she had *the power of total recall*. She rarely changed a single word. When she wrote the very last Memoir, as she came to a point about which she had written previously, she simply stated that she had already recorded this![19]

Despite these extraordinary gifts, Lucia felt incapable of conveying well an accurate description of what she experienced, and she worried that people would misunderstand her and get confused. We know now, from hindsight, that many of Lucia's concerns about being misunderstood or misinterpreted were justified.

A common desire of those who become familiar with Our Lady's words spoken to Lucia is not all that unlike that of the first disciples who, just before our Lord's Ascension, asked Him, "Lord, will you at this time restore the kingdom to Israel?" (Acts 1:6). Like our Lord's first followers, who were close to Him and His gospel message, we eagerly seek the coming "triumph" that she promised. It can be fascinating to be privy to a prophetic message about the future victory of God's saving grace in the world. What we too often fail to grasp is the heart of the message and the needed correspondence of our own hearts to it. It is to this penitential way of the Cross that the grace and mercy of God responds and upon which any hoped for victory in the end is contingent. The *triumph* that Our Lady conveyed to us through Lucia is accomplished by a particular devotion grounded in the mystery of Mary's Immaculate Heart, a heart moved by the suffering of her Son and His disciples, and for the purposes for which He suffered.

Some people who have read the story of Fatima look at the present situation in the world and cast a great deal of blame upon the Church's hierarchy for not responding more rapidly or thoroughly enough to the requests of Our Lady at Fatima. Taken out of context, some words conveyed to us through Sister Lucia may seem to justify this attitude, but it was not Sister Lucia's attitude. Some even make the accusation that Sister Lucia was intentionally kept away from the

---

[19] John M. Haffert, *Her Own Words*, (Asbury, NJ: The 101 Foundation, Inc., 1993), 57.

public by the hierarchy and ordered to remain silent. But, as we saw above, it was the hierarchy that asked Sister Lucia for clarity and details about the apparitions, and this was always the case. Throughout her life, Lucia always approached speaking and writing about the events of Fatima with great trepidation for fear that her words would create confusion rather than clarity.

Even if one holds the opinion (despite Sister Lucia's own stated position)[20] that the collegial consecration performed by St. John Paul II and all the bishops of the world united with him on March 25, 1984, did not satisfy Our Lady's requests, we must still hold that the collegial consecration, asked for at Fatima, whether completed or not, is still merely an ancillary or preparatory act (though an essential one) meant to awaken the Church to a better awareness and practice of devotion to the Immaculate Heart of Mary. This devotion is the more direct means by which our Lord intends to accomplish and maintain in the world a triumph of grace and enduring peace, which is the way Sister Lucia presented it.

During the apparition of July 13, 1917, Our Lady confided to the three children that she would return, "to ask for the consecration of Russia to my Immaculate Heart and the Communion of reparation on the first Saturdays."[21] Our Lady first returned to Lucia on December 10, 1925, to ask for the "first Saturdays" devotion.[22] Then later, on June 13, 1929,[23] our Lady again returned and said to Lucia,

> The moment has come in which God asks the Holy Father, in union with all the Bishops of the world, to consecrate Russia to my Immaculate Heart, promising to save it by this means. There are so many souls that the Justice of

---

[20] cf. *Documents*, 13, 14, and a letter written from Sr. Lucia on August 29, 1989, 122 – 123.

[21] July 13, 1917 Apparition, *Fourth Memoir, Documents*, 440.

[22] Document written by Sr. Lucia at the request of Fr. Jose Aparicio da Silva, S.J., who had been her confessor at her convent in Tuy, Spain, *Documents*, 279.

[23] This date is just four months before the 1929 stock market crash and the beginnings of the Great Depression, which brought economic conditions that made some of the errors of Communism more appealing to many.

God condemns for sins committed against Me, that I have come to ask for reparation: Sacrifice yourself for this intention and pray.[24]

It is instructive that Our Lady first returned asking for the "first Saturday" devotion, a devotion formed precisely to make reparation to the Immaculate Heart of Mary, then, only later (by some three and a half years), said that the moment had come for the consecration of Russia. Lucia always understood that prayer and sacrifice would be required to obtain the grace needed to move the Holy Father [the Pope] to take the action needed to fulfill the consecration. In 1936, Sister Lucia related in a letter to Fr. Jose Bernardo Gonzalves, S.J., her own concerns about the consecration of Russia. She wrote:

Intimately I have spoken to Our Lord about the subject, and not too long ago I asked Him why He would not convert Russia without the Holy Father making the consecration?

"Because I want my whole Church to acknowledge that consecration as a triumph of the Immaculate Heart of Mary in order to later extend its cult and to place the devotion to the Immaculate Heart alongside the devotion to my Sacred Heart."

"But my God, the Holy Father probably won't believe me, unless You Yourself move him with a special inspiration"

"The Holy Father. Pray very much for the Holy Father. He will do it, but it will be too late. Nevertheless the Immaculate Heart of Mary will save Russia. It has been entrusted to Her."[25]

There are a number of things to take note of in Sister Lucia's correspondence. First, we should recognize the expressed need of prayer for the pope that he might gain the inspiration needed to carry

---

[24] Notes by Fr. Gonzalves, taken at Tuy, Spain on April 24, 1941, *Documents*, 394.

[25] Lucia, *Letter to Fr. Gonzalves about the Consecration of Russia*, (Pontevedra, May 18, 1936), *Documents*, 324.

out the requested consecration. Grace is interconnected; it is like a current that flows and can move things, with the ultimate hope of moving human hearts. By this current of grace, God desires that we recognize both its source and channel. Through prayer and reparation the pope is moved to make the consecration, which in turn draws attention to the devotion. This brings us to a second major point to recognize in the words of our Lord. Although He speaks about the consecration as "*a* triumph of the Immaculate Heart of Mary," in this context it is clearly intended to serve as a preliminary (though essential) stage toward a later, greatly expanded awakening within the Church to the efficacy of true devotion to the Immaculate Heart of Mary and its intimate relationship with devotion to the Sacred Heart of Jesus. We can rightly assume then that it is this later extension of the devotion that has the hope of gaining "a certain period of peace [being] granted to the world."[26]

Sister Lucia was always consistent when commenting on what would be the more immediate result of the collegial consecration. Though a reunion of the Russian Orthodox Church with the Papacy would truly be a remarkable grace for the world, something we might see fulfilled in the *era of peace,* which Our Lady promised would be an eventual outcome of the triumph of her Immaculate Heart, Sister Lucia had always spoken about the *conversion of Russia* in the limited moral terms of its ending its policies of deliberate and organized persecution of Christianity.[27] She was also consistent in expecting that, "in response to the end of this persecution, His Holiness is to promise to approve of and recommend the practice of" the Five First Saturdays Communions of Reparation, a devotion formed precisely for making reparation to the Immaculate Heart of Mary in order to counter the ill effects in the world due to the very negligence of devotion to her.[28]

---

[26] July 13, 1917, apparition, *Fourth Memoir, Documents,* 440.

[27] cf. Sr. Lucia, "Letter to Fr. Jose Bernardo Gonzalves, S.J.," *Documents,* 281; and notes taken by Fr. Gonzalves, *ibid.,* 284.

[28] *ibid.*

Complicating the problem of this negligence was the erosive effect of the more than half-century delay fulfilling the collegial consecration. In a set of notes compiled by Father Gonzalves, the priest quotes Lucia telling him that sometime after the June 13, 1929, request for the collegial consecration, Our Lord made known to her by an interior communication that the consecration would eventually be done, "but it will be late. Russia will have already spread her errors throughout the world, provoking wars and persecutions of the Church; the Holy Father will have much to suffer."[29] Thus, we can surmise that between June 13, 1929, when Our Lady said that "the moment had come," and March 25, 1984, when the consecration was finally fulfilled, there had already developed in the world many obstructions to God's grace erected by these errors of Russia in the form of laws, policies, institutions and general attitudes of the culture. All this must now be overcome by the conversion of hearts. We can safely conclude, then, that the "certain period of peace" was not promised as an *immediate* result of the collegial consecration. Rather, that the conversion of Russia, resulting from the consecration, would help to awaken within the Church a much greater hope and trust in the maternal intercessory power and witness of Mary, "to guide our feet into the way of peace" (Lk 1:79).

The Church is now in a position to look back and marvel, in gratitude, at the miraculous series of events that have followed as a result of the collegial consecration to the Immaculate Heart of Mary, and now ought to seek in every way to "extend its cult and to place the devotion to the Immaculate Heart alongside the devotion to the Sacred Heart."[30] If Our Lady was able to accomplish such a remarkable transformation of the geopolitical landscape within the less than six years that followed the 1984 consecration, then should any limitation be placed on the hoped-for results from a greater extension and depth of understanding of this devotion to her Immaculate Heart and its intimate proximity to the Sacred Heart of her divine Son?

---

[29] Notes of Fr. Gonzalves (Tuy, 4/24/1941), *Fatima in Lucia's Own Words*, (Fatima, Portugal: Postulation Centre, 1976), 199.

[30] Sr. Lucia, Letter to Fr. Gonzalves about the Consecration of Russia (May 18, 1936) *Documents*, 324

Some of the well-known events that preceded the collegial consecration can be discerned as the providential hand of God. As noted above, Sister Lucia had confided to her spiritual director about her intimate conversation with our Lord, where she pleaded with God to move the pope with a special inspiration.[31] That special inspiration came following the assassination attempt on the life of St. John Paul II on the 64th anniversary of Our Lady's first appearance at Fatima, May 13, 1981. In the months that followed the near fatal shooting in St. Peter's Square, the pope reflected on the significance of Fatima while various documents were read to him as he lay recovering in Rome's Gemelli Hospital. Exactly one year later on May 13, 1982, he went to Fatima to thank Our Lady for sparing his life and to make an effort to fulfill the collegial consecration as requested.

Unfortunately, Sister Lucia said that not enough of the world's bishops joined in this first attempt. Reports indicated that some bishops did not receive their invitation in time to spiritually join with His Holiness.[32] The pope, thus, arranged to make another attempt on the feast of the Annunciation, March 25, 1984. This time he sent his invitation to all the bishops well in advance. After this consecration attempt, both the papal nuncio and the bishop of Fatima asked Sister Lucia if the request was now fulfilled, and she replied, "Yes."[33] The nuncio responded, "Now we await the Miracle," and Sister Lucia professed, "God will keep His word."[34]

Some events that took place in Russia and its satellite countries following the collegial consecration are truly deserving of our attention. Sister Lucia said, even of John Paul II's first attempt in 1982 that, although it did not quite fulfill the collegial requirements requested by Our Lady, it "will have its effect."[35]

It is interesting to note that during the 60 years from 1922 to 1982, the Communist Party in the Soviet Union had only three gen-

[31] ibid.

[32] cf. Fr. Robert J. Fox, "A Review: 85 Years after Fatima," Documents, 43.

[33] "Interview with Sr. Lucia" published in Fatima Family Messenger, October – December 1989, 7. Documents, 43.

[34] ibid.

[35] Her Own Words, 348

eral secretaries. Joseph Stalin ruthlessly amassed power to this tyrannical office, which he held from 1922 to 1952. Following his death, Nikita Khrushchev reigned from 1953 to 1964. From 1964, Leonid Brezhnev reigned until his death on November 10, 1982. Between John Paul II's 1982 collegial consecration and the first anniversary of the 1984 consecration, the Soviet Union saw four different men holding the office of general secretary. Following Leonid Brezhnev's death, Yuri Andropov was elected general secretary on November 12, 1982. Because Mikhail Gorbachev had a close association with the new leader, he was launched to a position that made him the second most powerful man in the Soviet Union, and during Andropov's successor's reign, his powers only increased.[36]

Andropov died on February 9, 1984, mere weeks before the decisive consecration. On February 13, Konstantin Chemenko was elected to the post. Then, following the fulfillment of the collegial consecration, a flood of unforeseen events precipitated rapid changes within the Soviet Union. Some of the more well-known events have been documented. On the feast of Our Lady of Fatima, May 13, 1984, an explosion took place at the Severomorsk Naval Base in the Soviet Union, which destroyed two-thirds of all the missiles of the Soviet's Northern Fleet stockpile,[37] by far the greatest of the Soviet Union's four fleets. Another explosion is said to have taken place in Siberia on December 13, 1984, destroying their largest ammunition base. Then on December 20, the man who was Soviet defense minister since 1976, Marshal Ustinov, died very unexpectedly from cardiac arrest (maybe from the stress compounded by such great losses).[38] These events combined with others to demoralize the Soviets' sense of their own military readiness in the face of the growing strength of the U.S. Military under the presidency of Ronald Reagan. Time was ripening for major shifts in Soviet policy and leadership.

[36] "Mikhail Gorbachev," *Britannica Encyclopedia*, accessed July 28, 2015, www.britannica.com/biography/Mikhail-Gorbachev.

[37] Wayne LeBaron, *America's Nuclear Legacy*, (Commack, NY: Nova Science Publishers, Inc., 1998) 192 – 194.

[38] "Dmitriy Ustinov," Wikipedia, accessed July 28, 2015, https://en.wikipedia.org/wiki/Dmitriy_Ustinov.

On March 10, 1985, less than a year after the collegial consecration, Konstantin Chemenko died, opening the way for the election of Mikhail Gorbachev on the following day. He would later introduce sweeping changes within the Soviet system, which led to the eventual end of religious persecution both within Russia and its satellite countries, precisely what our Lord had promised Lucia would be the result of the consecration. Sister Lucia made it clear, "In response to the end of this persecution, His Holiness is to promise to approve of and recommend the practice of the already mentioned devotion of reparation."[39]

The time is now long overdue for the whole Church to respond generously to our Lord's request for devotion and reparation to the Immaculate Heart of Mary.

Lucia spent the 87 years of her life following the apparitions, mostly as she stated, "a voice in the desert where only God hears." Knowing what awaited many if they did not convert, and knowing that there was little she could say or do to affect a change, aside from offering the pain in her heart to God, she experienced something of that paradoxical power of the seeming helplessness of the heart of the Mother of God at the foot of the cross (cf. 1 Cor 1:18-25, 2:2-3, 2 Cor 12:9-10, 13:4).

In the chapters that follow, we will see how devotion to the Immaculate Heart of Mary helps us to tap into this paradoxical power of Mary's heart. Devotion to the Immaculate Heart of Mary holds within itself the secret to bursting wide open the floodgates of Divine Mercy. On the cross, the Heart of Jesus was audaciously pierced by a lance that well represents the flagrant guilt of every sinful act ever committed against God's infinite justice. But in God's infinite mercy, that very wound is transformed and transubstantiated into a fountain through which the substance of Divine Mercy gushes forth and is made accessible to every person for the cleansing of their sins and the sanctification of their souls.

The Immaculate Heart of Mary is, in itself, a most profound mystery of union with "the tender compassion of our God" (Lk

---

[39] Notes taken by Fr. Gonzalves interview of Sr. Lucia, *Documents*, 284.

1:78). It extends and expands the reach of that grace and mercy of the Sacred Heart of Jesus to penetrate the callous surfaces of the most hardened of hearts: "A sword will pierce through your own soul also, that thoughts out of many hearts may be revealed" (Lk. 2:35). The very etymology and definition of the term *compassion* means, "The deep feeling of *sharing the suffering of another*, together with the inclination to give aid or support or to show mercy."[40] At the foot of the cross, Our Lady was the prototype, the exemplar of all human compassion for the *Passion*, the suffering of her Divine Son; she thus helps communicate the very rationale for that suffering: the salvation of all who would come to believe in Him and abandon themselves in trust to this outpouring of His mercy.

The Church is called to continue to bear witness to the fullness of truth in a world that has been largely influenced by the errors already spread throughout it by a formerly godless Russia. The weight of witnessing to a world so thoroughly deceived by these errors truly causes the Holy Father to have "much to suffer," along with everyone else united with him in heart and mind. In the face of such a predominant worldview, tenaciously bonded by errors which rationalize a rebellion of heart against God and His natural law, it is truly worth pondering more deeply the devotion to the Immaculate Heart of Mary. It is the remedy for exposing and correcting the influence of these corrupting errors, with the hope that, "In the tender compassion of our God the dawn from on high [might] break upon us, to shine on those who dwell in darkness and the shadow of death, and to guide our feet into the way of peace" (Lk 1:78-79).

In the chapters that follow, we will reflect on how Fatima fulfills, at least in part, this prophetic message of the Gospel of how God intends to and is guiding "our feet into the way of peace," particularly by His desire "to establish in the world devotion to [Mary's] Immaculate Heart. In Chapter One we will look at the doctrinal basis of the message of Fatima as presented in the sources of Revelation, Sacred Scripture and Tradition, and as further developed in the history of

---

[40] "Compassion," *The American Heritage Dictionary*, Second College Edition, (Boston: Houghton Mifflin Company, 1985), 300.

the Church up to the time of Fatima. In Chapter Two we will see how Fatima fits well with the further development of the Church's teaching about Mary, especially as expounded upon by St. Maximilian Kolbe. In Chapter Three we will examine closely the vision of the *third secret* of Fatima to see how it helps to illumine for the Church the way of the Cross that will "guide our feet into the way of peace." Finally, in Chapter Four, we will focus on the details of devotion to the Immaculate Heart of Mary, as the precise way in which God intends to "guide our feet . ."

Therefore, in the first chapter we will look at the message of Fatima with full respect to the authority that the deposit of faith holds for Catholics in relation to private revelations like Fatima. Cardinal Ratzinger expounded thoroughly upon the relationship that private revelations have to the authority of public Revelation in his commentary on the third secret given during its release in June of 2000. There he pointed out that:

> The term "public Revelation" refers to the revealing action of God directed to humanity as a whole and which finds its literary expression in the two parts of the Bible: the Old and New Testaments. ... It is valid for all time, and it has reached its fulfilment in the life, death and resurrection of Jesus Christ. In Christ, God has said everything, that is, he has revealed himself completely, and therefore Revelation came to an end with the fulfilment of the mystery of Christ as enunciated in the New Testament. To explain the finality and completeness of Revelation, the *Catechism of the Catholic Church* quotes a text of Saint John of the Cross: In giving us his Son, his only Word (for he possesses no other), he spoke everything to us at once in this sole Word - and he has no more to say... because what he spoke before to the prophets in parts, he has now spoken all at once by giving us the All Who is His Son. Any person questioning God or desiring some vision or revelation would be guilty not only of foolish behavior but also of offending him, by

not fixing his eyes entirely upon Christ and by living with the desire for some other novelty" (No. 65; Saint John of the Cross, The Ascent of Mount Carmel, II, 22). ...

The authority of private revelations is essentially different from that of the definitive public Revelation [which consists of the deposit of faith]. ... Private revelation is a help to this faith, and shows its credibility precisely by leading me back to the definitive public Revelation. ... The criterion for the truth and value of a private revelation is therefore its orientation to Christ himself. When it leads us away from him, when it becomes independent of him or even presents itself as another and better plan of salvation, more important than the Gospel, then it certainly does not come from the Holy Spirit, who guides us more deeply into the Gospel and not away from it. This does not mean that a private revelation will not offer new emphases or give rise to new devotional forms, or deepen and spread older forms. But in all of this there must be a nurturing of faith, hope and love, which are the unchanging path to salvation for everyone.[41]

We will see in this examination of Fatima's message that this call for devotion to the Immaculate Heart of Mary does not present a new revelation. In fact, it is precisely a devotion to one who, public Revelation says, "kept all these things, pondering them in her heart" (Lk 2:19). Christ through His Apostles entrusted to the whole Church the deposit of faith, but this is not to say that in this endowment the Apostles were also graced with full understanding of the Revelation they were handing down to the Church. The Church understands that the Holy Spirit guides her in a process of doctrinal unfolding of the original deposit, where, "thanks to the assistance of the Holy

---

[41] Congregation for the Doctrine of the Faith, *The Message of Fatima*, Accessed July 11, 2015 from http://www.vatican.va/.../rc_con_cfaith_doc_20000626_message-fatima_en.html.

Spirit, the understanding of both the realities and the words of the heritage of faith is able to grow in the life of the Church."[42]

---

[42] *Catechism of the Catholic Church*, (*CCC*), 2nd Ed. English Trans. (Washington, D.C.: United States Catholic Conference, 1997), 94.

CHAPTER I

DEVOTION TO THE IMMACULATE HEART OF MARY IN THE DEPOSIT OF FAITH

This chapter will examine the sacred deposit of faith – Sacred Scripture and Sacred Tradition – with the purpose of identifying the solid, but rudimentary, foundation upon which rests the devotion to the Immaculate Heart of Mary, requested at Fatima. This examination will give us a better appreciation for the Church's teaching regarding the Blessed Virgin Mary and the reasons for cultivating devotion to her.

As we make this examination, we ought to keep in mind an often quoted Latin axiom of theology, *Lex orandi, lex credendi* ("The rule of prayer is the rule of faith"), which implies that there exists a strong and immediate correlation between the way we pray and the content of what we believe, each impacting and shaping the other. Gaining a better appreciation for the foundation of this devotion in the sacred deposit handed on to us by the Apostles, will help inspire us to make room for this devotion in our own daily lives and encourage others to do the same.

We will also begin to see how this devotion holds the key to correcting our minds and consciences of any errors that have become common in our culture.

Recalling to mind Mary's warning at Fatima that Russia "will scatter *her errors* throughout the world, provoking wars and persecutions of the Church,"[43] we are assured that God's strategy for reversing this very disturbing trend is to "establish in the world devotion to [Mary's] Immaculate Heart."[44] Not only does this mean that she is powerful at defusing potentially caustic political situations and

---

[43] July 13, 1917 Apparition, *Fourth Memoir, Documents*, 440.
[44] *Ibid.*

pacifying hostilities, she also obtains for all her devoted children the graces and mercy needed to respond more decidedly to the truth in all its forms, so that the abiding gifts of the Holy Spirit — wisdom, understanding, knowledge, right judgment, fortitude, piety and fear of the Lord — will grow within each of her devotees.

This look at Revelation may feel like a gathering and sorting through seemingly disparate pieces of a puzzle, but in the subsequent chapters an image should emerge that helps set all the pieces into an organic whole. It is important not to get discouraged if at first it all appears so confusing. Just proceed forward, content to become a bit more familiar with the various pieces as they are presented. You can always return to this chapter as a reference after the developing image emerges into focus.

In this chapter, we will look at only the most significant parts of the sacred deposit that relate, in some way, to devotion to Mary. In the New Testament, those parts are found primarily in the canonical writings of St. Luke and St. John.

St. Luke graphically depicts the physical indications of the Holy Spirit's interaction in the lives of those who are open to His action, in order to draw attention to the underlying, but imperceptible, supernatural interaction taking place. For instance, in his depiction of Mary's visit to her cousin, Elizabeth, one can almost trace the movement of the Holy Spirit from Mary's spoken greeting to Elizabeth, through Elizabeth's ears (and heart), to the excited reaction of the baby (John the Baptist) within her womb: "For behold, when the voice of your greeting came to my ears, the child in my womb leaped for joy" (Lk 1:44). St. Luke depicts the relationship between the Holy Spirit and Mary as being singularly unique and presents her as a supreme model of discipleship.

St. John makes this same living connection between God's Spirit and the human heart that is open to His actions. He draws attention especially to symbolic representations of the sacraments that Christ institutes, or by making analogies to other spiritual realities. In Jesus' discussion with Nicodemus, for example, His use of the image of "wind" to describe the effects of the Spirit is especially illustrative:

"Do not marvel that I said to you, 'You must be born anew.' The wind blows where it wills and you hear the sound of it, but you do not know where it comes from or where it goes; so it is with everyone who is born of the Spirit" (Jn 3:7-8).

The life and movement of the Holy Spirit in His interaction with human hearts is filled with mystery, but His actions can be perceivable by their effects upon the soul.

Mary's role in John's Gospel, in anticipating and mediating certain sacramental symbols, and even Christ's own sacrifice on the cross, reveals that she provides the Church with much more than a supreme example of discipleship, as drawn from Luke's Gospel. When the symbolic dimensions and references to the sacraments made in John's Gospel are understood, Mary's *maternal role in the intercession of grace* with her Son in His Paschal mystery can be more clearly seen. After the death of the Apostles, some of the early writers and fathers of the Church already began alluding to this special role of Mary, which helped to foster a growing appreciation of and devotion to her.

Such a development is exactly what ought to be expected, for the *Catechism* tells us, "Even if Revelation is already complete, it has not been made completely explicit; it remains for Christian faith gradually to grasp its full significance over the course of the centuries."[45]

The history of the development of this devotion is a prime illustration of how the Holy Spirit has fulfilled Christ's promise to "guide [the Church] into all the truth" (Jn 16:13). The Church retains from Christ an authority [called by its Latin name, *Magisterium*] to preserve, expound upon and proclaim the deposit of truth entrusted to it by Christ through His Apostles.[46] Assured of this foundation, let us take a closer look at those portions of the deposit of faith that present to us the apostolic teaching about the mother of Jesus, so that we might better understand the development of the Church's teaching regarding devotion to her.

---

[45] *CCC*, 66.

[46] cf. *CCC*, 85 – 86.

Mary in the Gospel of St. Luke

The essential roots and foundation of devotion to the Immaculate Heart of Mary are present in the very first intimations of the proclamation of the Gospel, the *protoevangelium* of the first book of the Bible, Genesis 3:15, where God says to the serpent, "I will put enmity between you and the woman, and between your seed and her seed."

Israel's expectant longing for the Messiah cannot be separated from the expectation of the great favor that would be bestowed upon the woman who would bear Him into the world. This expectation is expressed well in the inspired words of Elizabeth to Mary, when Mary hastened to visit her upon hearing of her pregnancy:

> Blessed are you among women, and blessed is the fruit of your womb! And why is this granted me, that the mother of my Lord should come to me? For behold, when the voice of your greeting came to my ears, the child in my womb leaped for joy. And blessed is she who believed that there would be a fulfillment of what was spoken to her from the Lord. (Lk 1:42-45)

Here we see expressed in Elizabeth's joy some of the most rudimentary elements of devotion to Mary. Intuiting in her own heart and mind the dramatic weight of the singular favor bestowed upon her cousin by God, and for which the expectation among the faithful of Israel had grown very keen,[47] Elizabeth cries out with words that will be repeated for centuries in the prayer of the *Hail Mary*: "Blessed are you among women, and blessed is the fruit of your womb!"

As Elizabeth exclaims, Mary is blessed because she "believed that there would be a fulfillment of what was spoken to her from the Lord." That fulfillment was none other than that hope awaited by the "daughter of Zion" (cf. Zec 9:9) to be fulfilled in "the fullness of time" (Gal 4:4), in that "child to be born [of her], ... the Son of God" (Lk 1:35). All history pivots on this event, the Incarnation of the Son

---

[47] cf. *CCC*, 711-716

of God within the womb of Mary, which allows for the subsequent saving acts of God in Christ, her Son. The acceptance in faith of this revealed divine mystery is central to the acceptance of the Gospel (cf. 1 Jn 4:2).

We will later see that the full integrity of this mystery of the Incarnation and of the *hypostatic union* (the union of the two distinct natures, divine and human, in Christ), will be effectively preserved by the Church's dogmatic title of Mary as "Mother of God," proclaimed in essence in the Gospel by Elizabeth:[48] "And why is this granted me, that the *mother of my Lord* should come to me?" (Lk 1:43).

The Church acts in the authority granted to her by Christ (cf. Mt 16:18-19) when it acts to clarify revealed truth. The effort involved in engaging our minds in the study of theology has been succinctly summarized by St. Anselm of Canterbury as *faith seeking understanding*. Our faith in the various mysteries of Revelation is rarely easily articulated and often escapes any attempt to describe what, ultimately, is beyond description. It is the duty of the teaching authority of the Church to correct potentially misleading formulations, which have often arisen.

In Luke's Gospel, we see our Lord performing this duty Himself, when a woman in a crowd shouted out, "Blessed is the womb that bore you, and the breasts that you sucked!" (Lk 11:27). This expression, we can say, contains something of that *sensus fidei,* or sense of the faithful,[49] that was expressed by Elizabeth. This sense is not to be confused with sentimentality; rather, it is a supernatural sense of the implications of revealed truth. The Church will often perform the duty of defining, in precise formulation, truths about which the faithful have always had a sense. In this instance, in Luke's Gospel, there is an expressed awareness of the greatness and phenomenal benefit of the mystery of our Lord's presence with us human beings. However, left unchecked in the form spoken by the anonymous woman, it can mislead to what precisely Mary's blessedness ought to ultimately be attributed. For this reason, our Lord seized this teaching moment and exclaimed, "Blessed rather are those who hear the word of God and

---

[48] Council of Ephesus in the year 431

[49] cf. CCC, 91 – 93

keep it!" (cf. Lk 11:27, 28), thereby affirming that, if Mary is to be called "blessed," her blessedness is due, primarily, to her acceptance of God's will in her life; an aspiration that is, by God's grace, within the grasp of every living person.

It was not only our Lord who seized upon this teaching moment. St. Luke, as an inspired evangelist, selected this story and these words out of countless stories and words he doubtlessly must have heard while investigating the events of Christ's life and ministry. This activity of the evangelist indicates that the formation of Sacred Scripture is integrally united to that of Sacred Tradition – an oral tradition handed on by the Apostles through "the spoken word of their preaching, by the example they gave, by the institutions they established, what they themselves had received – whether from the lips of Christ, from his way of life and his works, or whether they had learned it at the promptings of the Holy Spirit."[50]

St. Luke was not one of the Twelve Apostles, but he was a contemporary and companion of theirs, one who was gifted with literary skills. From the living Tradition proposed to him by the Apostles, St. Luke was inspired to record this particular event and our Lord's responding words some decades after the event. We should remember that St. John the Evangelist completed his own Gospel by stating, "there are also many other things which Jesus did; were every one of them to be written, I suppose that the world itself could not contain the books that would be written" (Jn 21:25). We can be confident that, by the inspiration of the Holy Spirit, the evangelists carefully selected the events and the words they did record precisely to help clarify the revealed truths entrusted to their care.

People commonly focus on the incident of Christ's "rebuttal" of the anonymous woman's expression in order to disparage any expression of devotion to His mother. An honest examination of the whole of Luke's Gospel, however, reveals that the author presents the mother of Christ as a supreme model of discipleship.[51] Though

---

[50] *Dei Verbum*, 7.

[51] cf. Frederick M. Jelly, *Madonna: Mary in the Catholic Tradition*, (Eugene, OR: Wipf and Stock Publishers, 1986), 38.

Mary's *womb* was truly blessed to be made a living tabernacle of the Lord for those nine months in which He grew within her, and though her *breasts* were likewise truly blessed to have fed our Lord, the anatomical feature of hers, which St. Luke most unmistakably highlights, is her *heart*.

On two separate occasions he recorded that, as Mary observed all that providentially converged and unfolded in regard to the life of her Son, "Mary kept all these things, pondering them in her *heart*" (Lk 2:19; also cf. 2:51). It is not insignificant that the same evangelist recorded, later in his Gospel, Jesus saying "where your *treasure* is, there will your *heart* be also" (Lk 12:34). Of course, we know that the usage of the word "heart" in these contexts means much more than merely the physical organ of the body that pumps blood throughout its vascular system. The *Catechism of the Catholic Church* speaks about the human heart as the integral center of the human person, where each person possesses a capacity for maintaining a real and vital communion with God:

> Where does prayer come from? Whether prayer is expressed in words or gestures, it is the whole man who prays. But in naming the source of prayer, Scripture speaks sometimes of the soul or the spirit, but most often of the heart (more than a thousand times). According to Scripture, it is the *heart* that prays. If our heart is far from God, the words of prayer are in vain.
>
> The heart is the dwelling-place where I am; according to the Semitic and Biblical expression, the heart is the place "to which I withdraw." The heart is our hidden center, beyond the grasp of our reason and of others; only the Spirit of God can fathom the human heart and know it fully. The heart is the place of decision, deeper than our psychic drives. It is the place of truth, where we choose life or death. It is the place of encounter, because as image of God, we live in relation: it is the place of covenant.[52]

---

[52] *CCC*, 2562 – 2563

We thus see in Mary someone whose life – heart, mind and soul – is totally and decidedly invested in that of her divine Son. Unlike the anonymous woman, Elizabeth does not rest in attributing Mary's blessedness only to her divine maternity. Elizabeth concludes her praise with the words, "And blessed is she who believed that there would be a fulfillment of what was spoken to her from the Lord" (Lk 1:45). Mary thus truly falls into that category of those whom our Lord calls blessed, "... those who hear the word of God and keep it!" (Lk 11:28).

In Luke's Gospel, Mary's blessedness reaches a degree and quality beyond that of any other who might hear the word of God and keep it. She is the personal embodiment of the faithful "remnant of Israel" (Mi 2:12, cf. 5:7-8, Zep 2:7, Zec 8:6), "a people humble and lowly... [who] seek refuge in the name of the Lord ..." and "Sing aloud" and "rejoice" heartily over God's approaching salvation (cf. Zep 3:12, 14). This remnant became prophetically known as the "Daughter of Zion" (cf. Is 62:11, Mi 4:8, Zec 9:9), all who remained faithful, waiting in joyful hope for the coming of their Savior.

Vatican II applies these prophetic scriptural references specifically to Mary when it states that "after a long period of waiting the times were fulfilled in her [Mary], the exalted Daughter of Zion ..."[53] Certainly, she does not stand alone in this capacity. There remained many others who were "looking for the consolation of Israel" (Lk 2:25), like Simeon in the temple, and Anna, the daughter of Phanuel, with him, who gave thanks at Christ's coming "and spoke of him to all who were looking for the redemption of Jerusalem" (Lk 2:38).

But in Mary's own heart and flesh, this hopeful anticipation is personified like no other. Her response to Elizabeth's praise of her at the visitation was to humbly (though not quietly) rejoice in the great saving work of him "who is mighty" in that great canticle, which is recited every evening during the Church's prayer of Vespers, the *Magnificat*:

---

[53] *Lumen Gentium*, Dogmatic Constitution on the Church (*LG*), 55, *Vatican Council II: The Conciliar and Post Conciliar Documents*, Edited by Austin Flannery, (Collegeville, MN: The Liturgical Press, 1975), 415.

My soul magnifies the Lord, and my spirit rejoices in God my Savior; for he has regarded the low estate of his handmaiden. For behold, henceforth all generations will call me blessed; for he who is mighty has done great things for me, and holy is his name. And his mercy is on those who fear him generation to generation. He has shown strength with his arm, he has scattered the proud in the imagination of their hearts, he has put down the mighty from their thrones, and exalted those of low degree; he has filled the hungry with good things, and the rich he has sent empty away. He has helped his servant Israel, in remembrance of his mercy, as he spoke to our fathers, to Abraham and his posterity forever. (Lk 1:46-55)

The rejoicing of her heart is not confined to glorying in her own blessedness, as if she alone is the one for whom the Almighty has done great things; she clearly recognizes that God's mercy is on all those who fear Him. Therefore, what God has done for her fulfills, according to His plan of salvation, precisely, an extension of his mercy to everyone who will accept it. In this great saving act, God has kept His promise of mercy.

"Hail, Full of Grace, the Lord is with You."

The specific words spoken to Mary by the angel Gabriel at the Annunciation, St. Luke records just prior to the visitation of Mary to her cousin Elizabeth:

In the sixth month [of Elizabeth's pregnancy] the angel Gabriel was sent from God to a city of Galilee named Nazareth, to a virgin betrothed to a man whose name was Joseph, of the house of David; and the virgin's name was Mary. And he came to her and said, "Hail, full of grace, the Lord is with you!" But she was greatly troubled at the saying, and considered in her mind what sort of greeting this might be. And the angel said to her, "Do not be afraid, Mary, for you have found favor with God. And behold, you will conceive in your womb and bear a son, and you shall call his name Jesus.

He will be great, and will be called the Son of the Most High; and the Lord God will give to him the throne of his father David, and he will reign over the house of Jacob forever; and of his kingdom there will be no end."

And Mary said to the angel, "How can this be, since I have no husband?"

And the angel said to her, "The Holy Spirit will come upon you, and the power of the Most High will over-shadow you; therefore the child to be born will be called holy, the Son of God.

And behold, your kinswoman Elizabeth in her old age has also conceived a son; and this is the sixth month with her who was called barren. For with God, nothing will be impossible."

And Mary said, "Behold, I am the handmaid of the Lord, let it be to me according to your word." And the angel parted from her. (Lk 1:26-38)

The last statement of Mary to the angel has come to be known in Christian Tradition as Mary's *fiat* to God. The word *fiat* is Latin for "let it be done", and it expresses Mary's total self-surrender to God and His will for her life, despite whatever suffering this surrender may cost her. Recognition of this total self-surrender to the will of God in the heart of Mary is an integral part of devotion to Mary. This will be examined more closely later in Mary's first appearance to the three Fatima children when Mary asks them for their *fiat*.[54]

For any person to overcome the strong natural inclination of the human will toward self-preservation and answer such a request for total self-surrender to God affirmatively requires more than just a determination of the human will. This interior self-surrender to God's will attests to the action of supernatural grace within the soul, moving it with a willing desire to appease God's justice and medi-

---

[54] "1st Apparition, May 13, 1917," *Forth Memoir, Documents,* 437.

ate His mercy. In the case of the Annunciation, Mary's response was exemplary to virtuous perfection, for she was not simply *moved by grace*; the angel Gabriel greeted her with the venerable title of *"full of grace."* In the original Greek, the term St. Luke chose is *kecharitomene*. There is something lost in the effort to translate this word from Greek into English. As a title spoken to her by the very messenger of God, it is helpful to look closer at the meaning of this term in its original Greek, especially since St. Luke attempts to impress upon his audience some interest about its meaning by mentioning Mary's own reaction to it: "But she was greatly troubled at the saying, and considered in her mind what sort of greeting this might be" (Lk 1:29). The Ignatius Catholic Study Bible's commentary on the selection of this term is enlightening:

> This is the only biblical instance where an angel addresses someone by a title instead of a personal name. Two considerations help to clarify its meaning. (1) The expression *full of grace* is rooted in Catholic tradition and traced to St. Jerome's translation of this verse in the Latin Vulgate. Although fundamentally accurate, it lacks some of the depth of the Greek original. Luke could have described her with the words *full of grace* (Gk. *Pleres charitos*) as he did of Stephen in Acts 6:8, yet here he uses a different expression (Gk. *kecharitomene*) that is even more revealing than the traditional rendering. It indicates that God has already "graced" Mary previous to this point, making her a vessel who "has been" and "is now" filled with divine life. (2) Alternative translations like "favored one" or "highly favored" are possible but inadequate. Because of the unparalleled role that Mary accepts at this turning point in salvation history, the best translation is the most exalted one. For God endowed Mary with an abundance of grace to prepare her for the vocation of divine motherhood and to make her a sterling example of Christian

holiness (CCC 490-93, 722).[55]

Based upon the totality of the fullness of grace implied here, Christian Tradition moved toward acknowledging that this singular grace granted uniquely to Mary extends right from the very first moment of her existence, her conception. The universal conviction of this doctrine eventually led to the solemn dogmatic definition of the "Immaculate Conception" by Pope Pius IX in 1854.

The Doctrine's Early Development in Church Tradition

Very early in Church history certain prominent Christian writers began expounding upon the significance of Mary's grace-filled response of *fiat* to the will of the Father and saw it as accomplishing a universal reversal of the action taken by Eve at the dawn of Creation. The name, Eve, etymologically means "Mother of all the living," but by her action she had, in fact, become *the mother of the dead*. Very significant comparisons and contrasts were drawn already by the second century between the actions taken by these two monumental matrons, paralleling St. Paul's references to Christ as the *new Adam* in Romans 5:12-21 and 1 Corinthians 15:45-50. St. Justin Martyr (d. 165) wrote,

> [The Son of God] became man through the Virgin that the disobedience caused by the serpent might be destroyed in the same way in which it had originated. For Eve, while a virgin incorrupt, conceived the word which proceeded from the serpent, and brought forth disobedience and death. But the Virgin Mary was filled with faith and joy when the Angel Gabriel told her the glad tidings ... And through her was he born ... [56]

And St. Irenaeus of Lyon (d. after 193) wrote,

---

[55] *Ignatius Catholic Study Bible, New Testament, Revised Standard Version*, 2nd Catholic ed. (San Francisco: Ignatius Press, 2001), 105.

[56] St. Justin Martyr, *Dialogue with Trypho*, ch. 100, *Patrologia Graeca* (PG) Migne, 6, 709-712. Miravalle, Mark, *Introduction to Mary: The Heart of Marian Doctrine and Devotion*. 3rd ed. (Santa Barbara, CA: Queenship Publishing Company, 2006), 43.

Just as Eve, wife of Adam, yet still a virgin, became by her disobedience the cause of death for herself and the whole human race, so Mary, too, espoused yet a Virgin, became by her obedience the cause of salvation for herself and the whole human race. And so it was that the knot of Eve's disobedience was loosed by Mary's obedience. For what the virgin Eve bound fast by her refusal to believe, this the Virgin Mary unbound by her belief.[57]

Tertullian (d. after 220) also made a similar contrast. The written evidence these three have left behind helps to serve as an historical record to affirm that Mary's active participation in our universal salvation was very likely commonly taught already by the end of the second century. Fr. Frederick M. Jelly, O.P., in his work *Madonna: Mary in the Catholic Tradition* states that,

The writings of all three are significant, since they are together a witness to the faith of the universal Church during the latter half of the second century concerning Mary. St. Justin, native of Palestine who was converted to Christianity in 133, came into touch with the religious belief of Ephesus and Rome. St. Irenaeus, a native of Asia Minor, was a priest in the Church of Lyon (modern France) from at least 177 and became bishop there. Tertullian, a convert from paganism and the first of the Latin Fathers, represents the faith of the African Churches at the time. The fact that these three used the Eve-Mary parallelism as a proof of their testimony to basic Christian truths, without trying to prove its own validity, is an indication that this Marian theme had already been a part of the Tradition.[58]

That last sentence deserves special attention. All three writers were comparing and contrasting Eve and Mary in order to defend cer-

---

[57] St. Irenaeus, *Adversus haereses*, Bk. 3, pg. 32, I; *PG* 7, 958-959. *Introduction to Mary*, 43.

[58] Frederick M. Jelly, O.P., *Madonna: Mary in the Catholic Tradition*. (Eugene, OR: Wipf and Stock Publishers, 1986), 70 – 71.

tain teachings of the Catholic faith, but what they were saying about Mary in contrast with Eve appears to have required no defending. It was very likely already a well- established teaching in the Church's oral tradition, one that helped clarify many others. Its rudimentary form can already be discerned in the careful selection of Greek terminology and phrasing which St. Luke employed in his Gospel, but, as we will see, his Gospel was not the only source for this development.

Among the early writers mentioned above who made reference to the Eve–Mary parallelism, it was St. Irenaeus who most developed this theme, and it is possible to draw the inference that he gained much of his insight from what was handed down by the Apostle and Evangelist, St. John, through Irenaeus' venerated mentor, St. Polycarp (69 – 155).

It was to St. John that Christ entrusted the care of His mother, as St. John recorded the event in his Gospel in the scene where "the beloved disciple" remains with "the mother of Jesus" at the foot of the cross (cf. Jn 19: 26-27). Some stories even hold that Mary may have resided for a time with St. John in Ephesus, a city of Asia Minor near Smyrna, where St. Polycarp later became bishop. During his formative years as a youth, St. Irenaeus lived in Asia Minor, where he became a disciple of St. Polycarp, who was himself in his earlier years a direct disciple of St. John. In one letter, St. Irenaeus describes with great affection his time spent learning the Apostolic Tradition from his beloved mentor. His description is helpful for gaining a better sense of that historical process of the Apostles' actions of passing on the Church's living Tradition:

> … when I was yet a boy, in lower Asia, with Polycarp … I remember indeed what then happened better than more recent occurrences, for the lessons of boyhood grow with the mind and become one with it. Thus I can name the place where blessed Polycarp sat and conversed, and his goings out and comings in, and the fashion of his life, and the appearance of his person, and his discourses to the people, and his familiarity with John, which he used to

tell of, and with the rest who had seen the Lord, and how he used to repeat their words, and what it was that he had learned about the Lord from them. ... Polycarp, whom we have seen in our first youth, ever taught those lessons which he learned from the Apostles, which the Church also transmits, which alone are true. All the Churches of Asia bear witness to them; and the successors of Polycarp down to this day.[59]

By this testimony of St. Irenaeus we gain a sense of how immensely he himself treasured and pondered "those lessons" from St. Polycarp, "which alone" he held to be "true." Such statements seem to preclude any possibility that he would ever have entertained any kind of novelty in teaching. Rather, from the sentiments expressed here, it is clear that St. Irenaeus treasured and sought passionately to understand and develop precisely "those lessons" that he learned from St. Polycarp, who himself must have absorbed like a sponge the words he heard from the Apostle John while sitting at the evangelist's feet.

It is traditionally held, well-grounded historically and maintained by popes and bishops alike, that St. John the Apostle is the inspired author of the *fourth Gospel*, the three *Letters of John*, and the *Book of Revelation* (also called the *Apocalypse*) of the New Testament.[60] John includes the "mother of Jesus" in two very important scenes in his Gospel: once, near the beginning, at the wedding feast in Cana, where Jesus changes water into wine; and again, near the end, at the Crucifixion, where Jesus entrusts His mother to "the beloved disciple" shortly before expiring. These two scenes are integrally linked in the structure of his Gospel.

In Chapter 12 of the *Apocalypse*, St. John describes a vision he has of Mary in glorious fashion, as "a great sign [that] appeared in heaven, a woman clothed with the sun ... [who] brought forth a male child,

---

[59] *An Essay on the Development of Christian Doctrine*, John Henry Cardinal Newman, taken from *Conscience, Consensus, and the Development of Doctrine*, (Image Books, New York, 1992), 308-309.

[60] cf. *Navarre Bible, Gospel of St. John*, 2nd ed. (Dublin, Ireland: Four Courts Press, 1992), 21.

one who is to rule all the nations with a rod of iron" (Rv 12:1,5). Each of these three sections of his inspired writings provides firm support for the other two, like a tripod of a painter's easel. Upon this easel, the artistic hand of the Holy Spirit inspired the heart and mind of St. John to compose the loftiest words of Scripture that reference the mother of Jesus. This same Holy Spirit has, throughout the centuries, further developed the Church's teaching about Mary as the *new Eve* and *helpmate* (*Cooperatrix, Collaboratrix, Adjutrix, Associate, Co-Redemptrix*) of her Son, and continues to draw the implications of this teaching toward its fruitful and glorious conclusions. In this light, we now turn to examine more closely those sections of St. John's writings.

Mary in the Canonical Writings of St. John

The canonical writings of St. John the Apostle present a more developed understanding of Christ's teaching about His mother than that which is found in Luke's Gospel, since they were written later.[61] Also, the providential arrangement of our Lord entrusting the care of His mother to John at his Crucifixion (cf. Jn 19:26-27) surely put John in a special relationship with Mary, allowing him privileged access to the depths of her holiness, wisdom and understanding. Implications of what is written in the Gospel of Luke and the other Synoptic Gospels can be drawn from John's careful choice and arrangement of words, phrases, events, etc.

To appreciate the inspired scriptural writings of St. John requires a willingness to dive below the surface of what is written and allow its many elements to unfold before the mind. St. John's writings are packed with rich thematic and sacramental symbolism, all of which is meant to open the believer up to the depths of the inexhaustible mysteries of God's Revelation. Actions, events, words and symbols very often hold some metaphorical or allegorical value, without undermining the historical truth of the event being described. In the third chapter of John's Gospel, Jesus instructs Nicodemus about this, when Nicodemus fails to grasp Christ's allegorical use of human ter-

---

[61] cf. *ibid.*, 20; and *Navarre Bible, Gospel of St. Luke*, 2nd ed. (Dublin, Ireland: Four Courts Press, 1991), 18.

minology like "wind" and "born anew" (cf. Jn 3:1-21). Jesus asks him, "Are you a teacher of Israel, and yet you do not understand this? ... If I have told you earthly things and you do not believe, how can you believe if I tell you heavenly things? No one has ascended into heaven but he who descended from heaven, the Son of man" (Jn 3:10, 12-13).

Within the narrative of John's Gospel, the Evangelist invites the reader to probe ever more deeply into these mysteries of faith by showing how Christ was routinely misunderstood by those who heard Him (cf. Jn 2:19-22; 3:4-10; 4:10-15; etc.). Very often, His own disciples failed to understand Him until after He explained things further, or the unfolding of events helped to clarify His meaning to them, particularly when it came to the earth-shattering events involving the Paschal Mystery: His Passion, Death, Resurrection and Ascension.

Those who remained with Him, even though they did not understand all that He told them, had already become convinced by His works that He has "the words of eternal life" (Jn 6:69). It is the work of His heavenly Father, through the action of the Holy Spirit, that allows a person to come to Jesus and listen to His teaching (cf. Jn 6:44). Any growth of understanding about the meaning of His words and deeds reveals the action of the Holy Spirit working within both the individual and collective memories of His disciples, which is itself presented as a major theme of the fourth Gospel (cf. Jn 14:26; 16:12-13).

In the various scenes narrated in the fourth Gospel, the reader can often recognize in what sense certain characters in the stories who are listening to Christ's words may be confused. Interestingly though, in the scene where Christ's mother first appears in the Gospel, the wedding feast at Cana in Chapter 2, the situation is reversed. The conversation between Jesus and His mother bewilders everyone else – including scripture scholars even in our own day – while Jesus and Mary seem to understand each other perfectly well. Maybe this is intentional on the part of John, maintaining a unique consistency with this theme of his Gospel. The mother of Jesus seems to share a spiritual symbiosis with her Son to an extent to which we can only marvel. Together they share a *communion of hearts* of which human history knows no equal.

Reflecting on this scene at Cana in his Encyclical Letter, *Redemptoris Mater* ("Mother of the Redeemer"), St. John Paul II expresses this wonder with open-ended, rhetorical questions: "What deep understanding existed between Jesus and his mother? How can we probe the mystery of their intimate spiritual union?"[62] Though the depths of their "intimate spiritual union" is truly beyond our full comprehension, we must, at least, make an attempt to "probe the mystery" here, that we might grow in our appreciation of their *communion of hearts,* by examining this scene as the beloved disciple has presented it:

> On the third day there was a marriage at Cana in Galilee, and the mother of Jesus was there; Jesus also was invited to the marriage, with his disciples. When the wine failed, the mother of Jesus said to him, "They have no wine." And Jesus said to her, "O woman, what have you to do with me? My hour has not yet come." His mother said to the servants, "Do whatever he tells you." Now six stone jars were standing there, for the Jewish rites of purification, each holding twenty or thirty gallons. Jesus said to them, "Fill the jars with water." And they filled them up to the brim. He said to them, "Now draw some out, and take it to the steward of the feast." So they took it. When the steward of the feast tasted the water now become wine, and did not know where it came from (though the servants who had drawn the water knew), the steward of the feast called the bridegroom and said to him, "Every man serves the good wine first; and when men have drunk freely, then the poor wine; but you have kept the good wine until now." This, the first of his signs, Jesus did at Cana in Galilee, and manifested his glory; and his disciples believed in him. (Jn 2:1-11)

The first thing to notice here is how St. John labels this event: He calls it "the first of his signs." Though Jesus performed a miracle here, to St. John it is much more than that; it is a "sign," and as a sign, it

---

[62] *Redemptoris Mater (RM)*. (Eugene, OR: Wipf and Stock Publishers, 1987), 21.

bears significance and meaning beyond what is described happening at the surface level. It was precisely in order to draw attention to that greater significance and meaning that St. John chose to record this event, that we too might believe (cf. Jn 20:31). Jesus' response to His mother cannot be simply dismissed as a rebuke since He responds to her concern. Jesus will later state that He never acts arbitrarily, but does only "what he sees the Father doing":

> Truly, truly, I say to you, the Son can do nothing of his own accord, but only what he sees the Father doing; for whatever he does, that the Son does likewise. For the Father loves the Son, and shows him all that he himself is doing; and greater works than these will he show him, that you may marvel. (Jn 5:19-20)

Thus, the first sign Jesus did at Cana in Galilee manifested his glory, and his disciples believed in him (cf Jn 2:11).

We can certainly *marvel* that, despite Jesus' apparent objection to His mother's request – "O woman, what have you to do with me? My hour has not yet come." He must have discerned in His mind and acted upon "what he [saw] the Father doing;" and somehow, despite His words, His mother carried on as though assured that her Son would concern Himself with her request, for she went to the servants of the feast and said to them, "Do whatever he tells you" (Jn 2:5). It may be that His question and statement here were less a questioning of His mother's request than an inquiry concerning the will of His Father into the handling of this concern of hers.

If we consider here the bold insight of St. Maximilian Kolbe about the implications of the *fullness of grace* possessed by the Blessed Virgin Mary – "that she is, in a certain sense, the 'incarnation' of the Holy Spirit"[63] – then we may have the hermeneutical key to unlocking the true sense of our Lord's response to His mother and their subse-

---

[63] Conference given by St. Maximilian Kolbe, Feb. 5, 1941, recorded in *Immaculate Conception and the Holy Spirit: The Marian Teachings of St. Maximilian Kolbe.* Translated from French by Br. Richard Arnandez. (Libertyville, IL: Prow Books / Franciscan Marytown Press, 1977), 50

quent actions.[64] St. Maximilian's Marian teaching will be considered more fully in the next chapter. For now let's look a little closer at this particular point he makes. St. Maximilian Kolbe wrote that,

> The third Person of the Blessed Trinity never took flesh; still, our human word "spouse" is far too weak to express the reality of the relationship between the Immaculata and the Holy Spirit. It is the Holy Spirit that we love in her; and through her we love the Son.[65]
>
> Just as the second divine Person appears in his Incarnation as the "seed of the woman," so the Holy Spirit manifests his share in the work of the Redemption through the Immaculate Virgin who, although she is a person entirely distinct from him, is so intimately associated with him that our minds cannot understand it. So, while their union is not of the same order of the hypostatic union linking the human and divine natures in Christ, it remains true to say that Mary's action is the very action of the Holy Spirit.[66]

If we can assume the veracity of Kolbe's insight about Mary and apply it to her action at Cana, then it greatly aids the understanding of all that is being revealed about the Triune God here. We know that God is three Persons in one divine nature, that Christ is the Second Person of the Holy Trinity, the Word of the Father (cf. Jn 1:1-5), and that, as the Word of the Father, to have seen Him is to have "seen the Father" (Jn 14:9).

We also know that in order to show us who His Father is, He "emptied himself, taking the form of a servant, being born in the likeness of men" (Phil 2:7). But this emptying of Himself imposes a limitation upon Himself. How does Jesus show us the fullness of the communion of Persons in the Blessed Trinity? How does He depict for us the living image of the Holy Spirit beyond merely speaking

---

[64] cf. Fr. H. M. Manteau-Bonamy, O.P., *Immaculate Conception and the Holy Spirit*, 95.

[65] St. Kolbe, *ibid.*, 50.

[66] *ibid.*, 91

about Him, a person of the Blessed Trinity distinct from Himself and His Father? With some unpacking of what is recorded in the fourth Gospel, we will ourselves be able to "marvel" in wonder at the brilliance and beauty of the communion of the Father, Son and Holy Spirit conveyed here, along with the intimacy of that *communion of hearts* shared by Jesus and His mother.

The Mother of All the Living

The first theme to unpack in our study of John's Gospel is the process of a *re-Creation* alluded to in its beginning paragraphs. The Redemption is a kind of restoration of God's original intention for Creation. This theme depicted in John's Gospel can be juxtaposed with the original Creation story of the first three chapters of Genesis. The very first words of the Bible are "In the beginning ..." (Gn 1:1). The Gospel of John begins, *"In the beginning* was the Word, and the Word was with God, and the Word was God. He was in the beginning with God; all things were made through him, and without him was not anything made that was made" (Jn 1:1-3).

Thus, from the very start we are drawn into a parallel with the original Creation story. The Gospel then goes on to tell of God's intended act of redemption through the "Word":

> In him was life, and the life was the light of men. The light shines in the darkness and the darkness has not overcome it ... The true light that enlightens every man was coming into the world. He was in the world, and the world was made through him, yet the world knew him not. He came to his own home, and his own people received him not. But to all who received him, who believed in his name, he gave power to become children of God; who were born, not of blood nor of the will of the flesh nor of the will of man, but of God.
>
> And the Word became flesh and dwelt among us, full of grace and truth; we have beheld his glory, glory as of the only begotten Son from the Father. (Jn 1:4-5,9-14)

So, at the beginning of John's Gospel we are alerted to this process of the restoration of Creation that is being accomplished through "all who received him, who believed in his name, [and are given] power to become children of God." In the story of the wedding feast at Cana this theme of the restoration of Creation is carried forward because it begins with the words, "On the third day ..." (Jn 2:1). Though this phrase harkens forward to the restoration accomplished by Christ in the Resurrection *on the third day* from His Crucifixion, it also harkens back to the Creation week, for

> The third day is actually the seventh day of Jesus' opening week of ministry. The evangelist hints at this when he delineates the successive days in 1:29, 35, 43 and 2:1, imply-ing that the creation fashioned in seven days (Gn 1:1 – 2:3) is being transformed and renewed through Jesus (2 Cor 5:17; Rv 21:1-5).[67]

So, beginning with John the Baptist's questioning by the Phari-sees in 1:19-28, the next verse reads, *"The next day* he saw Jesus com-ing toward him, and said, 'Behold, the Lamb of God, who takes away the sins of the world." Then, in 1:35 we read, *"The next day* again John was standing with two of his disciples; and he looked at Jesus as he walked, and said, 'Behold, the Lamb of God!'" Then one more time, in 1:43 it states, *"The next day* Jesus decided to go to Galilee. And he found Philip and said to him, 'Follow me.'" After this, we come to the scene at Cana, which is introduced as being, *"On the third day."* So four days plus the three following the call of Philip bring us to the seventh day.

If what is being referenced at Cana is the beginning of a resto-ration of Creation, then the reference to Mary's presence and activi-ty, very fittingly, correlates to her role as the *New Eve* in cooperation with the restoration of Creation being accomplished by her Son. Her own Son, there, referring to her as "woman" helps to reinforce this interpretation:

---

[67] *Ignatius Catholic Study Bible, New Testament, Revised Standard Version,* 2nd Catho-lic ed. (San Francisco: Ignatius Press, 2001), 164.

Genesis 3 is the reverse image of the Cana episode. As Eve prompted Adam to defy the Lord and drag the human family into sin, so Mary prompts Jesus, the new Adam, to initiate his mission of salvation. The description of Mary even alludes to Gen 3:15, where Yahweh speaks of a "woman" whose son will trample the devil underfoot (CCC 489, 494).[68]

The fact, too, that this is a wedding feast draws us back to Genesis, when "the Lord God said, 'It is not good that the man should be alone; I will make him a helper fit for him'" (Gn 2:18). And the man rejoiced at seeing *the woman*, and declared, "This at last is bone of my bones and flesh of my flesh; she shall be called Woman ...'" (Gn 2:23). Though Jesus also calls His mother "woman," Adam gives his wife a name, "*Eve*, because she was the *mother of all living*" (Gn 3:20). At Cana, there is no mention of the bride and groom in the story; the reader is drawn, rather, to focus on the relationship between Jesus and His mother. What we see is that, with the aid of her Son, Mary is able to assume a maternal role for others in need. In *Redemptoris Mater*, St. John Paul II explains that,

> The Cana event outlines what is actually manifested as a new kind of motherhood according to the spirit and not just according to the flesh, that is to say *Mary's solicitude for human beings*, her coming to them in the wide variety of their wants and needs. At Cana in Galilee there is shown only one concrete aspect of human need, apparently a small one of little importance ("They have no wine"). But it has a symbolic value; this coming to the aid of human needs means, at the same time, bringing those needs within the radius of Christ's messianic mission and salvific power. Thus there is a mediation: Mary places herself between her Son and mankind in the reality of their wants, needs and sufferings. *She puts herself "in the middle,"* that is to say *she acts as a mediatrix not as an outsider, but in her position as*

---

[68] ibid.

mother. She knows that as such she can point out to her Son the needs of mankind, and in fact, she "has the right" to do so. Her mediation is thus in the nature of intercession: Mary "intercedes" for mankind. And that is not all. As a mother she also wishes the messianic power of her Son to be manifested, that salvific power of his which is meant to help man in his misfortunes, to free him from the evil which in various forms and degrees weighs heavily upon his life. [69]

This intercessory mediation of the mother of Jesus parallels neatly with what St. Paul describes as the action of the Holy Spirit, interceding through us for the restoration of all creation:

> We know that the whole creation has been groaning with labor pains together until now; and not only the creation, but we ourselves, who have the first fruits of the Spirit, groan inwardly as we wait for adoption as sons, the redemption of our bodies … Likewise the Spirit helps us in our weakness; for we do not know how to pray as we ought, but the Spirit himself intercedes for us with sighs too deep for words. And he who searches the hearts of men knows what is the mind of the Spirit, because the Spirit intercedes for the saints according to the will of God. (Rm 8:22-23, 26-27)

We may say that at Cana the Holy Spirit moved the tender, compassionate, Immaculate Heart of the mother of Jesus to intercede on behalf of a newlywed couple for a "need, apparently a small one of little importance ('They have no wine.'). But [this need is one which] has a symbolic value." [70] Because "creation was subject to futility … in hope" (Rm 8:20), we experience countless needs for ourselves and our loved ones every day. In the frustration and sorrow of the moment, such needs rarely seem "small;" rather, we "groan inward-

---

[69] *RM*, 21.

[70] *ibid.*

ly" (and often outwardly), while "the Spirit himself intercedes for us with sighs too deep for words." The "symbolic value" of Mary's spoken concern, "They have no wine," carries with it an underlying expression of the Spirit's "sighs too deep for words" (Rm 8:26). By articulating this concern to her Son, she brings this particular concern of seemingly "little importance ... within the radius of Christ's messianic mission and salvific power."[71] Jesus' response to her makes reference to a decisive "hour" of His which, He seems to imply, holds some bearing on their relationship and, possibly, the concern she is presenting Him with: "O woman, what have you to do with me. My *hour* has not yet come." This statement of His, along with His mother's statement to the servants, "Do whatever He tells you," helps to qualify the action He is about to take as more than a miracle: It is a "sign," which symbolically prefigures something of what will later be fulfilled in His "hour." The precise way in which Jesus determines to fulfill His mother's request brings her expressed need "within the radius of [His] messianic mission and salvific power."[72]

· · ·

Understanding Jesus' broad usage of the term "hour" in the fourth Gospel is essential to grasping something of what is happening here. The *Ignatius Catholic Study Bible* devotes an entire page to explaining its meaning. It begins by stating,

> Seventeen times the Gospel of John mentions the "hour" of Jesus. In the first half of the book, the "hour" is a highly anticipated moment in the ministry of Jesus that constantly grabs the attention of the reader and drives the narrative forward (Jn 2:4; 4:21; 5:25; 7:30; 8:20). In the second half of the book, readers discover that Jesus comes upon his "hour" only in the final days of his life (Jn 12:23, 27; 13:1; 17:1).[73]

---

[71] ibid.

[72] ibid.

[73] *Ignatius Bible*, 170.

This commentary goes on to explain that Jesus' "hour" has two very broad dimensions, which are integrally linked: the historical event of His Passion, extending from the Last Supper to the Resurrection, and the timeless, immortalized dimension that this event makes possible as the very source of the Church's Sacramental worship in her liturgy.[74] This is referred to now in Catholic doctrine as the "Paschal Mystery" or "Paschal Sacrifice,"[75] and is most especially commemorated in the Eucharistic Liturgy. So, while Jesus is yet gathering His disciples and has not yet begun His public ministry, He already clearly anticipates where all of it is heading, and His mother seems to share in His understanding.

When Jesus refers to His "hour" in the brief exchange with His mother at Cana, He speaks about it as if He knows she is already familiar with what it means. With others, He says "an hour is coming …" (Jn 4:21,23; 5:25,28; 16:32) and then goes on to further explain something about His "hour." But, with Mary, He says simply, "My hour has not yet come," without any additional explanation. Though we can only speculate that they would have discussed Jesus' anticipated public ministry at some point during their 30 long years of private life, such a speculation should not surprise anyone. That she was rapt with interest in the coming mission of her Son we have already seen from Luke's Gospel, which testifies that "Mary kept all these things, pondering them in her heart" (Lk 2:19).

It is the common nature of motherhood to nurture a vocation in a child. In the case of Mary, we have the "fullness of grace" of the Holy Spirit building upon the most perfect of maternal natures. Mary would surely have had many hours a week of deep and meaningful dialogue with the divine and eternal Word of God; one can only imagine the depth of understanding she had of Jesus before He commenced His public teaching ministry.

We know from Luke's Gospel that Mary "was greatly troubled" by the greeting used by the angel Gabriel to her, "Hail, full of grace! The Lord is with you," and that she "considered in her mind what

---

[74] *ibid.*

[75] cf. *CCC* Glossary entry, "Paschal Mystery / Sacrifice."

sort of greeting this might be" (cf. Lk 1:28-29). It does not stretch credulity to suppose that at some point during their hidden years together, Mary would have put the question to Him about this greeting. It is possible that Jesus would have explained it in a way similar to how the Church, through Pope Bl. Pius IX, defined the dogma of the Immaculate Conception, *Ineffabilis Deus* in 1854:

> The first instance of [your] conception, by a singular grace and privilege granted by Almighty God, in view of the merits [that I will gain in *My hour* that is coming], as Savior of the human race, preserved you free from all stain of original sin.[76]

His mother at Cana helps us to recognize the action He took, in compliance with her request, as prefiguring the new maternal dimension she will assume in relation to all who believe in Him, "in view of the merits" He will gain in His anticipated *hour*.

This anticipation is made more plausible by the fact that the next time St. John records Jesus speaking directly to His mother is precisely at the climax of His long anticipated *hour*. There, from the cross, "Jesus saw his mother, and the disciple whom he loved standing near; he said to his mother, 'Woman, behold your son!' Then he said to the disciple, 'Behold, your mother!' And from that *hour* the disciple took her to his own home" (Jn 19:26-27). That He tells "the disciple whom he loved" to "Behold, your mother" appears to confirm the maternal role His mother anticipated at Cana. Christian Tradition was quick to recognize that, from the cross, our Lord was confirming here that His Mother's maternal role was not confined to being the Mother of God, but included the maternal spiritual regeneration of all who would come to believe in Him, His *beloved disciple[s]*.

St. John carries this theme of Mary's universal, maternal role into Chapter 12 of the Apocalypse: The dragon was angry with the

---

[76] English translation of the definition of the Immaculate Conception, issued in the Apostolic Constitution *Ineffabilis Deus*, taken from Papal Encyclicals Online. Accessed July 29, 2015. www.papalencyclicals.net/Pius09/p9ineff.htm.

woman [who had 'brought forth a male child, one who is to rule all the nations with a rod of iron' (Rv 12:5)] and went to make war *on the rest of her offspring, on those who keep the commandments of God and bear testimony to Jesus.* (Rv 12:17)

This description of "the rest of her offspring," as "those who keep the commandments of God and bear testimony to Jesus," parallels very neatly with what Mary asked of the servants at the wedding feast at Cana: "Do whatever he tells you" (Jn 2:5). Revelation 12 also parallels dramatically with the *protoevangelium* of Genesis 3:15, with all that is claimed about "the woman" and "the serpent," because the "the serpent" of the Genesis account is transformed by the last book of the Bible into "the great dragon . . . that ancient serpent, who is called the Devil and Satan, the deceiver of the whole world – he was thrown down to the earth and his angels were thrown down with him" (Rv 12:9). So, in all three Marian sections of John's writings, there can be discerned a clear reference to the involvement of Mary's real spiritual maternity in the lives of all who believe in her Son.

The Blood of the Lamb

There is another very important parallel that runs through the three Marian sections of St. John's writings: the symbol of the "wine" and what it prefigures and sacramentally represents – the "blood of the Lamb." At a particular point in the Book of Revelation, the author describes a vision where he beheld "a great multitude which no man could number ... standing before the throne and before the lamb, clothed in white robes" (Rv 7:9). The author goes on to say that an elder explained to him that, "These are they who have ... washed their robes and made them white in the *blood of the Lamb*" (7:14). Something similar is repeated in Chapter 12, where "the woman" is mentioned: "And they have conquered him ['the accuser of our brethren' (12:10)] by the *blood of the Lamb* and by the word of their testimony" (12:11).

Recalling the scenes of the Creation-restoration week leading to the event at Cana, John the Baptist had directed the attention of his disciples to Jesus, referring to Him as "the Lamb of God, who takes away the sin of the world" (Jn 1:29). This reference to "the Lamb of

God" recalls to the mind of every person familiar with the faith of Judaism their most important annual celebration, the feast of Passover. Chapter 12 of Exodus recalls the historic, miraculous event that the Lord, speaking to Moses and Aaron, commanded to be commemorated each year:

> Tell all the congregation of Israel that on the tenth day of this month they shall take every man a lamb according to their fathers' houses, a lamb for a household ... Your lamb shall be without blemish ... and you shall keep it until the fourteenth day of this month, when the whole assembly of the congregation of Israel shall kill their lambs in the evening. Then they shall take some of the blood, and put it on the two doorposts and the lintel of the houses in which they eat them ... It is the Lord's Passover. For I will pass through the land of Egypt that night, and I will smite all the firstborn in the land of Egypt, both man and beast; and on all the gods of Egypt I will execute judgments: I am the Lord. The blood shall be a sign for you, upon the houses where you are; and when I see the blood, I will pass over you, and no plague shall fall upon you to destroy you, when I smite the land of Egypt ...
>
> And when your children say to you, "What do you mean by this service?" you shall say, "It is the sacrifice of the Lord's Passover ..." (Ex 12:3, 5, 6-7, 11-13, 26-27)

Historically, the "blood of the Lamb" referred to in the Book of Revelation was given, as Jesus implied at Cana, during that same *hour* in which Mary became the mother of "the disciple whom [Jesus] loved," that is, when Jesus was hanging upon the cross. The evangelist then describes what immediately followed the spiritual adoption between Jesus' mother and "the disciple whom he loved" (Jn 19:26-27):

> After this Jesus, knowing that all was now finished, said (to fulfill the Scriptures), "I thirst." A bowl full of vinegar

stood there; so they put a sponge full of the vinegar on hyssop and held it to his mouth. When Jesus had received the vinegar, he said, "It is finished;" and he bowed his head and gave up his spirit. (Jn 19:28-30)

Thus, immediately after Jesus establishes the universal, spiritual maternity of His mother with reference to "the disciple whom he loved," the Gospel claims that Jesus knew "that all was now finished [and so], said (to fulfill the Scriptures), 'I thirst.'" What follows is that Jesus was then given some vinegar – some translations say, "sour wine" or "common wine" – soaked in a sponge and lifted to His mouth by the use of "hyssop." Immediately after Jesus received the "sour wine," He pronounced His final words, 'It is finished;' and he bowed his head and gave up his spirit." These few sentences are packed, and they set the stage for what is next about to happen; but first consider the detail that John includes in mentioning the "hyssop."

In the story of the original Passover in Exodus, hyssop is used to apply the lamb's blood on the doorposts and lintel: "Take a bunch of *hyssop* and dip it in the blood which is in the basin, and touch the lintel and the two doorposts with the blood which is in the basin ..." (Ex 12:22).

This detail also helps to strengthen the parallel connection between the event at Cana and Jesus' *hour,* which is reaching its climactic point. Jesus' cry, "I thirst," parallels the need which Mary articulated at Cana: "They have no wine" (Jn 2:3). Along with the conclusion of His last will and testament in the gift of His mother to the "disciple whom he loved," His words spoken to His mother at Cana, "O woman, what have you to do with me? My hour has not yet come" (Jn 2:4), now find a consummate response to His mother's request in what is about to take place. "The transformation of water into wine anticipates the transubstantiation of wine into blood when Jesus gives himself to the world in the Eucharistic Liturgy (6:53; 1 Cor 10:16)."[77]

What takes place next fulfills the words spoken by the steward of the wedding feast at Cana who, in amazement, said to the bride-

---

[77] *Ignatius Catholic Study Bible*, New Testament, 165.

groom, "Every man serves the good wine first; and when men have drunk freely, then the poor wine; but you have kept the good wine until now" (Jn 2:10). Jesus, as "the Lamb of God, who takes away the sin of the world," was transforming by His divine authority the Judaic rites into "the new covenant in [His] blood" (Lk 22:20). These rites anticipated and prefigured the sacramental rites of the New Covenant. When Jesus glanced around the room at the wedding feast in Cana with the intention of fulfilling the request of His mother and to bring it "within the radius of [His] messianic mission and salvific power,"[78] He recognized that "six stone jars were standing there, for the Jewish rites of purification ..." (Jn 2:6). These Jewish rites of purification along with the Old Covenant Passover are transformed by Jesus' total gift of Himself in the New Covenant. Because St. John wrote his Gospel long after the other three Gospels were already in circulation, he knew it was unnecessary to repeat the details of Jesus' act of instituting the Eucharist at the Last Supper, about which He commanded His Apostles to "Do this in remembrance of me" (Lk 22:19). Rather, as an eyewitness of the Crucifixion, St. John provided invaluable detail about the priceless reality of the true content of "This chalice which is poured out for you ..." (Lk 22:20):

> Since it was the day of Preparation, in order to prevent the bodies from remaining on the cross on the Sabbath (for that Sabbath was a high day), the Jews asked Pilate that their legs might be broken, and that they might be taken away. So the soldiers came and broke the legs of the first, and of the other who had been crucified with him; but when they came to Jesus and saw that he was already dead, they did not break his legs. But *one of the soldiers pierced his side with a spear, and at once there came out blood and water.* He who saw it has borne witness – his testimony is true, and he knows that he tells the truth – that you also may believe. For these things took place that the Scripture might be fulfilled, "Not a bone of him shall be broken."

---

[78] RM, 21.

And again another Scripture says, "They shall look on him whom they have pierced." (Jn 19:28-37)

From the earliest days of the Church, catechumens have been taught that this flow of "blood and water," from the very bosom of the Lord, is the source of the sacramental graces they are preparing to receive. The catechetical commentary on this passage by St. John Chrysostom (347 – 407) can hardly be improved upon:

> *There flowed from his side water and blood.* Beloved, do not pass over this mystery without thought; it has yet another hidden meaning, which I will explain to you. I said that water and blood symbolized baptism and the holy eucharist. From these two sacraments the Church is born: from baptism, *the cleansing water that gives rebirth and renewal through the Holy Spirit,* and from the holy eucharist. Since the symbols of baptism and the eucharist flowed from his side, it was from his side that Christ fashioned the Church, as he had fashioned Eve from the side of Adam. Moses gives a hint of this when he tells the story of the first man and makes him exclaim: *Bone from my bones and flesh from my flesh!* As God then took a rib from Adam's side to fashion a woman, so Christ has given us blood and water from his side to fashion the Church. God took the rib when Adam was in a deep sleep, and in the same way Christ gave us the blood and the water after his own death.[79]

Witnessing this flow of "water and blood" from the side of Jesus upon the cross, along with Jesus' total self-surrender of His spirit in His last breath (cf. Jn 19:30), made a lasting impression upon the beloved disciple (cf. 1 Jn 5:6-8). The actions that St. John recorded occurring immediately before these took place cannot be trivialized. They are all incorporated into a single event, one that has become,

---

[79] St. John Chrysostom, *Catechesis* 3, 13-19, taken from *The Liturgy of the Hours according to the Roman Rite,* Office of Readings for Good Friday (Catholic Book Publishing Co: New York, 1976).

by the grace of the sacramental liturgy, the source of salvation for all who believe.

But there was one there in attendance who was more than simply a witness of the event. By her intercession at Cana she had actively anticipated this event. We have no reason to doubt that she understood where her Son's mission was leading even before He had begun His public ministry.

In Christ's infancy, Mary was forewarned at the Presentation in the Temple that her "child is set for the fall and the rising of many in Israel, and for a sign that is spoken against (and a sword will pierce through your own soul also), that thoughts out of many hearts may be revealed" (Lk 2:34-35).

We can be confident that, like other topics relevant to the fulfillment of Jesus' mission, the meaning of these prophetic words was also likely discussed between them at some point in their hidden years together in Nazareth. Mary had been called upon by God to an action prefigured by the faith of the patriarch, Abraham. As Abraham's trust in God was confirmed by his willingness to obey the command of the Lord to sacrifice his only son, Isaac, so Mary, even more perfectly, radiates a sterling trust in God by her total surrender of self. She willingly endured with her Son, through the compassion of her Immaculate Heart, the unimaginable pain of offering in supplication to the Father the torture of the betrayal, flogging and crucifixion her Son endured, so that His purifying Blood from His sacrificial hour might flow for all who believe.

The reference to the fulfillment of the prophetic statement in Zechariah 12:10, "They shall look on him whom they have pierced" (Jn 19:37), at the end of the Crucifixion account in John's Gospel, further reinforces this point. Jews familiar with the Scriptural reference would have been drawn to further examine its more complete expression. In the scroll of the prophet Zechariah they would have read:

> And I will pour out on the house of David and the inhabitants of Jerusalem a spirit of compassion and supplication,

so that, when they look on him whom they have pierced, *they shall mourn for him, as one mourns for an only child, weep bitterly over him, as one weeps over a first-born* ... On that day there shall be a fountain opened for the house of David and the inhabitants of Jerusalem to cleanse them from sin and uncleanness. (Zec 12:10; 13:1)

The supernatural exchange of total self-giving love between the divine and Sacred Heart of Jesus on the cross and the Immaculate Heart of His mother at the foot of the cross is a mystery beyond telling. Mary did not "mourn for him, [merely] *as one* mourns for an only child, weep bitterly over him, [merely] *as one* weeps over a first-born," for Jesus *was* Mary's "only child" and "first-born." She is, thus, the most perfect model of this "spirit of compassion and supplication." "On that day there [was] a fountain [of Divine Mercy] opened for the [whole world] to cleanse them from sin and uncleanness."

Mary precedes the Church,[80] which was conceived there in the wounded Heart of Jesus and, we can say, in Mary's own sorrowful and Immaculate Heart (cf. Lk 2:35). What we as the Church participate in sacramentally, she engaged in totally, perfectly, purely and in real time. For this reason, she is venerated by all who have come to believe, as one who participated in a universal and maternal manner in the very act of our redemption.

We can also say that her perfect participation in the redemptive actions of our Lord makes her what theologians call a personal, material "collaboratrix" or "cooperatrix" in their accomplishment. Because that event is preserved as a perpetual institution and memorial in the sacred and divine Liturgy of the Eucharist and the other sacraments, her own participation in our Lord's saving action is also perpetually memorialized.[81] She is, thus, joined with her divine Son in a universal, spiritually maternal manner in the personal salvation of everyone, to gain for them the graces needed to be drawn to Him who has been "lifted up from the earth" (Jn 12:32).

---

[80] cf. *CCC*, 773.

[81] cf. John Paul II Encyclical Letter, *Ecclesia De Eucharistia*, *57*.

In this light, we can reasonably ask the question how St. John was able to find the courage to be "standing near" (Jn 19:26) Mary at the foot of the cross, when all the other Apostles were hiding in fear. As Jesus had prophesied, the "shepherd" had been struck "and the sheep of the flock [had been] scattered" (Mt 26:31; cf. Mk 14:27); apart from the mention of certain women at the foot of the cross, no other disciples were present. And John himself would be found later cowering with the others behind locked doors, "for fear of the Jews" (Jn 20:19). Can we suppose that in his association with Mary and the other disciples, Mary had beckoned him; and he, moved by a desire to console the pain of her Immaculate Heart, overcame his present fear and accompanied her to the place of execution? We thus have good reason to speculate that Mary's intervention obtained for us St. John's own eyewitness account in his Gospel. And it is by his inspired testimony that we have infallible confirmation of the images of our Lord's Sacred Heart being pierced with a lance, so fittingly representative of our sins, and the Divine Mercy image of the blood and water gushing forth for our purification and sanctification from that very wound.

Thus, even in Mary's very subtle interventions, we witness the movement of the Holy Spirit, "draw[ing] all men to [Jesus]" who is "lifted up from the earth" (cf. Jn 12:32), so that we all might "look on him whom [we] have pierced" (Jn 19:37; Zec 12:10). And in the depths of the Love that is the Holy Spirit, we come to know something of the true sorrow of the Immaculate Heart of Mary, for we are given "a spirit of compassion and supplication, so that, when [we do] look on him whom [we] have pierced, [we] shall mourn for him, as one mourns for an only child, and weep bitterly over him, as one weeps over a first-born" (Zec 12:10).

A Spirit of Compassion and Supplication

There is yet another dimension to the *blood of the Lamb*, or rather, the symbolic value of the "wine," for which Mary made supplication to God. That dimension is the *spiritual fruit* that can be seen as the effective result of the cleansing from sin; a spiritual fruit for which the cleansing by the *blood of the Lamb* makes room.

St. Paul lists some of the fruits of the Holy Spirit in Galatians 5:22-23: "love, joy, peace, patience, kindness, goodness, faithfulness, gentleness, self-control." The Catechism explains that these "are perfections that the Holy Spirit forms in us as the first fruits of eternal glory."[82] Like the analogy of *the wind* that Jesus made to Nicodemus about the effects of the Spirit, so the Spirit can be discerned from His transforming effects on us interiorly, turning our actions from vice to virtue, and bringing our souls into greater harmony with God's will in a way that is recognizable to ourselves and to others. In Luke's Gospel, Mary drew attention to this spiritual fruit as a testimony to the state of her soul when she proclaimed, "my soul magnifies the Lord, and my spirit *rejoices* in God my Savior" (Lk 1:46-47). On the day of Pentecost, because of their ecstatic exuberance, the disciples were accused by some observers of being "filled with *new wine*" (Acts 2:13), when, in fact, they had just received "the promise of [Jesus'] Father" (Lk 24:49), and thus had become "filled with the Holy Spirit" (Acts 2:4). The prophet Isaiah predicted that the coming of salvation would produce joy within the soul and confidence for evangelization: "With joy you will draw water from the wells of salvation. And you will say in that day: 'Give thanks to the Lord, call upon his name; make known his deeds among the nations, proclaim that his name is exalted …'" (Is 12:3-4). When the Jews returned from the Babylonian exile to Jerusalem and were preparing to rebuild what had been lost, the leaders encouraged them not to "be grieved, for the *joy of the Lord is your strength*" (Neh 8:10). And to show that true sorrow for sin and joy in God are not incompatible, the author of the Letter to the Hebrews encourages us to "lay aside every weight, and sin which clings so closely, and let us run with perseverance the race that is set before us, looking to Jesus the pioneer and perfecter of our faith, who *for the joy that was set before him endured the cross …*" (Heb 12:1-2). We can imagine Mary, recognizing this sustaining quality of her interior joy, wanting to intercede on behalf of others that they, too, might have this interior sustenance. When she expressed her concern for the wedding celebration to her Son, "They have no wine" (Jn 2:3), she could

---

[82] *CCC*, 1832.

well have thought, along with the wisdom Book of Sirach, that "wine is like life to men, if you drink it in moderation. What is life to a man who is without wine? It has been created to make men glad. Wine drunk in season and temperately is *rejoicing of heart and gladness of soul*" (Sir 31:27-29). And the abundance of wine that was produced by the miracle at Cana was a sign of the coming of the messianic age (cf. Is 25:6; Jl 3:18; Am 9:13).[83] But most of all, "the sign of water turned to wine at Cana . . . makes manifest the fulfillment of the wedding feast of the Father's kingdom, where the faithful will drink the new wine that has become the Blood of Christ."[84] So, we can say, we see in this seemingly small symbol, both the means for cleansing our souls from sin and the source of eternal life in God.

It is interesting that shortly following the changing of water into wine at Cana in John's Gospel, Jesus goes to Jerusalem and cleanses the temple by driving out the money-changers there (cf. Jn 2:13-22); and then, shortly after that, Nicodemus comes to Jesus at night and questions Him, "How can a man be born when he is old? Can he enter a second time into his mother's womb and be born?" (Jn 3:4). In a spiritual sense, we can answer Nicodemus' question affirmatively. In the womb of the Church, we enter into a real relationship with Jesus and His Mother where we can truly be "born [sacramentally] of water and the Spirit" (Jn 3:5). And like the beloved disciple, who "from that *hour* ... took [Mary] to his own home" (Jn 19:27), we, too, can obtain the grace needed to make greater room for the Spirit of God in our own hearts and souls by entrusting ourselves to Mary's maternal care. By her supreme example and maternal favor, she predisposes us toward a greater increase of grace and transformation of heart, that we might find ourselves in the company of "the rest of her offspring ... those who keep the commandments of God and bear testimony to Jesus" (Rv 12:17).

---

[83] cf. Ignatius Study Bible, 165.

[84] *CCC*, 1335; cf. Rv 19:7-9.

Further Development of Marian Devotion and Doctrine throughout the Centuries

We have seen thus far that the Apostles likely taught, though in a subtle manner, that the mother of Jesus holds a sovereign and exalted place among all believers. We have viewed this, especially, in the Gospels of St. Luke and St. John and in St. John's Apocalypse. We have seen that St. Luke drew attention to Mary's predisposition to the will of God and to her docility of heart toward the movement of the grace of the Holy Spirit.

In St. John's writings, we have seen how Mary embodied, in a maternal manner, the mission of the Holy Spirit in the work of our Redemption and that she was subsequently confirmed by her Son on the cross in her position as Mother of the Church, represented by the beloved disciple.

If these views about the teachings of the Apostles are correct, then we should be able to find some evidence that very early in the history of the Church the faithful had already recognized Mary's exalted role and were calling upon Mary's intercession for their daily needs and concerns. Before the Edict of Milan (313) was promulgated during the reign of the Roman Emperor Constantine I, which put an end to the series of persecutions suffered by Christians until then, the faithful were extremely cautious about possessing any physical evidence of their faith. Despite this, we still have some archeological evidence that during those very early years the faithful were already expressing strong devotion to Mary. Probably the most significant forms of evidence we have are the numerous and varied images depicting Mary in the Roman catacombs, where the faithful could express their devotion without fear of being exposed to public authorities.

Dr. Mark Miravalle tells us that, "as early as the end of the first century to the first half of the second century, Mary is depicted in frescos in the Roman catacombs both with and without her divine Son."[85] Some of these images depict Mary in certain scenes from the

---

[85] *Introduction to Mary*, 41.

Gospels, like the Annunciation of the angel Gabriel and the adoration of the Magi, while others depict her as a particular model of prayer in the *orans* position, that is, with her arms outstretched in a gesture of openness to receiving grace from heaven.[86] Dr. Miravalle draws attention to one such fresco in particular, located in the catacombs of St. Agnes, where Mary is

> Situated between St. Peter and St. Paul with her arms out-stretched to both. This fresco reflects, in the language of Christian frescoes, the earliest symbol of Mary as "Mother of the Church." Whenever St. Peter and St. Paul are shown together, it is symbolic of the one Church of Christ ... Mary's prominent position between Sts. Peter and Paul illustrates the recognition by the Apostolic Church of the maternal centrality of the Savior's Mother in his young Church.[87]

Dr. Miravalle also highlights that the sheer number of these various images of Mary and the very prominent locations in which they are often found, as on tombs and "large central vaults of the catacombs," testify to the early Church's confidence in her intercession to provide maternal protection against dangers.[88]

This confidence in Mary's maternal protection is also expressed in the oldest written prayer we have on record that is addressed to Mary, the *Sub Tuum Praesidium*. Its English translation reads,

We fly to your patronage
O Holy Mother of God
Despise not our petitions
In our necessities,
But deliver us from all danger,
O ever glorious and blessed Virgin.[89]

---

[86] cf. *ibid.*

[87] *ibid.* 41-42.

[88] cf. *ibid.* 24.

[89] *ibid.* 11.

In 1917, a fragment of papyrus containing this prayer, written beautifully in ancient Greek, was discovered. That fragment of papyrus could not be dated any later than the middle of the third century (250). Until the discovery of this papyrus fragment, it was generally assumed that the origin of this prayer was much later in time because of certain expressions it contained, like *Theotokos* ("Mother of God"), which many historians thought was originally coined by St. Athanasius in the fourth century.[90] This discovery, though, sparked further research that showed Alexandrian Christians were already referring to Mary under this title in the third century[91] and helped to confirm that the Church's official pronouncements are proclaimed in affirmation of the living Tradition with which the Church has been entrusted, and do not represent a reshaping by the Church in any way inconsistent with the Sacred deposit of Faith.[92]

In the case that prompted the convening of the Council of Ephesus, the devotion and tradition of referring to Mary as the *Theotokos*, Greek for "God-bearer," or "Mother of God," was challenged by the newly appointed Patriarch of Constantinople, Nestorius, in sermons he gave in the summer of 429. He claimed that it was legitimate to call Mary *Christotokos*, or "Christ-bearer," but not *Theotokos*. His insistence stirred up a hornet's nest of opposition, which very quickly led to his condemnation and the title's solemn definition at the Council of Ephesus two years later; such was the veneration held by the Christian world for Mary, the Mother of God, already by that time. The primary intention of the council was in defense and preservation of a true understanding of the mystery of the Incarnation of Christ and *hypostatic union* of His human and divine natures. The council fathers recognized that the challenge to calling Mary, "Mother of God," risked challenging the truth that Christ is truly a divine Person

---

[90] Anthony M. Buono, "The Oldest Prayer to Mary," *Catholic Digest*, St. Paul, MN, August, 1984.

[91] *ibid.*

[92] cf. Fr. Luigi Gambero, S.M., *Mariology: A Guide for Priests, Deacons, Seminarians, and Consecrated Persons.* Edited by Dr. Mark Miravalle. (Goleta, CA: Seat of Wisdom Books Queenship Publishing, 2007), 138; and, Dr. Mark Miravalle, *Introduction to Mary*, 45.

who has assumed a human nature, or of obscuring the true unity of the two natures in Christ by exaggerating *their* division and attributing a distinct personality to Christ's human nature.

Here, we can see how true devotion to Mary has lent practical help to preserving faith in the full truth about her Son.[93] To put the action taken by the Church at the Council of Ephesus into its true context and give it proper perspective, it is helpful to include here a rather lengthy (though abbreviated) quote from the great patristic scholar and convert to Catholicism, Bl. John Henry Cardinal Newman. In his *Essay on the Development of Christian Doctrine*, he lists, almost in litany fashion, quotes from the Church Fathers prior to and contemporaneous with the Nestorian controversy:

> In order to do honour to Christ, in order to defend the true doctrine of the Incarnation, in order to secure a right faith in the manhood of the Eternal Son, the Council of Ephesus determined the Blessed Virgin to be the Mother of God. Thus all heresies of that day, though opposite to each other, tended in a most wonderful way to her exaltation …
>
> But the spontaneous or traditional feeling of Christians had in great measure anticipated the formal ecclesiastical decision. Thus the title *Theotokos*, or Mother of God, was familiar to Christians from primitive times, and had been used among other writers, by Origen, Eusebius, St. Alexander, St. Gregory Nazianzen, St. Gregory Nyssen, and St. Nilus. She had been called Ever-Virgin by others, as by St. Epiphanius, St. Jerome, and Didymus … St. Augustine says that all have sinned "except the Holy Virgin Mary, concerning whom, for the honour of the Lord, I wish no question to be raised at all, when we are treating of sins." …
>
> St. Proclus calls her "the unsullied shell which contains the pearl of price," "the sacred shrine of sinlessness,"

---

[93] cf. Fr. Manfred Hauke, *Mariology*, 198.

"the golden altar of holocaust," "the holy oil of anointing," "the costly alabaster box of spikenard," "the ark gilt within and without," "the heifer whose ashes, that is, the Lord's Body taken from her, cleanses those who are defiled by the pollution of sin," "the fair bride of the Canticles,"... "the Church's diadem," "the expression of orthodoxy." These are oratorical expressions; but we use oratory on great subjects, not on small. Elsewhere he calls her "God's only bridge to man;" and elsewhere he breaks forth, "Run through all creation in your thoughts, and see if there be equal to, or greater than, the Holy Virgin Mother of God."
...

Such was the state of sentiment on the subject of the Blessed Virgin, which the Arian, Nestorian, and Mono-physite heresies found in the Church; and on which the doctrinal decisions consequent upon them impressed a form and a consistency which has been handed on in the East and West to this day.[94]

The early councils of the Church dealt with Christological heresies, heresies that confused the full truth about Christ and the mystery of His Incarnation. The Arian heresy taught that Christ was a human person who achieved or was granted divinity; the Mono-physite heresy taught that the human nature of Christ was absorbed to annihilation by Christ's divinity; and the Nestorian heresy con-fused the mystery of the union of the two natures in Christ, giving Christ a split personality. The recognition of Mary as "Mother of God" helped to clarify and settle all these Christological confusions. Dr. Mark Miravalle tells us that, following the Council of Ephesus, "Marian prayers, Marian liturgical feast days, Marian icons, Marian paintings and Marian artwork became ubiquitous throughout the Christian world."[95] Devotion to Mary would remain a universal and integral part of Christian devotion everywhere, until the Protestant

---

[94] *Conscience, Consensus, and the Development of Doctrine*, 156
[95] *Introduction to Mary*, 46.

Reformation more than a thousand years later. Protestantism effectively uprooted the devotion of many from the solid foundation grounded in Sacred Tradition, under the mistaken impression that (capital "T") Tradition is analogous to the build-up of a centuries-old accretion, like barnacles on the hull of a ship, which, over time, has obscured the simplicity and purity of the true faith.

During those thousand years prior to the Protestant Reformation, eastern and western segments of the Church became more isolated from each other due to the political difficulties which emerged from the collapse or shrinking of the Roman - Byzantine Empire. In the East as well as in the West, Mary's total sanctification was held to be a revealed doctrine, but the development of this teaching toward the eventual proclamation of the Dogma of the Immaculate Conception of Mary took place primarily within the West.

Before the fullness of this teaching could be accepted, though, an obstacle had to be overcome: that of comprehending how Mary could call God her "Savior" (Lk 1:47) if she were without even the slightest stain of original sin from her conception, thus seemingly possessing no need for salvation. Many thought that God must have allowed Mary to be conceived in a state of original sin but then, almost instantaneously, purified her soon after the conception in the womb of her mother. This opinion remained the dominant view among Catholic intellectuals until Blessed Duns Scotus (1266-1308) formulated a solution. Since it had already become widely accepted that Mary possessed a purity that was the greatest possible to conceive of, Bl. Scotus argued that a purity such as this could only be brought about by an immaculate conception. Scotus' great contribution was to make it clear that Mary was saved, not by "liberation" from sin, but by a "preservation" in the most perfect way possible: She was preserved from any morally corrupting effect of original sin from the very first moment of her existence, her conception. Thus, being free from any corrupting effect of both original and actual sin, and therefore being free of any obstacle to the free flow of God's grace in her life, the angel Gabriel could call her "full of grace" (Lk

1:28).[96] That Mary was *"preserved immune* from all stain of original sin" were the precise words adopted by Pope Bl. Pius IX in his solemn definition of the Immaculate Conception in 1854. Bl. Scotus' defense of the Immaculate Conception of Mary, which for a few centuries prior even to his time, was already being celebrated as a feast day in various locations of the Church,[97] found ever increasing support and shrinking opposition in the years that followed; so much so that

> By the beginning of the nineteenth century, the Magisterium had settled all principal objections, and petitions began flowing into the Vatican from cardinals, bishops, priests, laity, and various heads of state requesting the papal definition of the Immaculate Conception. After consulting with the bishops of the world and establishing a theological commission to study the question, Bl. Pius IX decided to proclaim the doctrine as a solemn dogma on December 8, 1854.[98]

Just a few decades after this solemn definition, Lucia dos Santos would record the prophetic words spoken to her by the very one so immaculately conceived: "God wishes to establish in the world devotion to my Immaculate Heart."[99] To those who think that exercising such an exalted devotion toward the Mother of God has the practical effect of diverting attention away from her divine Son, Bl. John Henry Cardinal Newman, who lived and wrote contemporaneously with Bl. Pius IX's act of solemnly defining the Immaculate Conception on December 8, 1854, responds:

> If we take a survey at least of Europe, we shall find that it is not those religious communions which are characterized by devotion towards the Blessed Virgin that have ceased to adore her Eternal Son, but those very bodies ... which

---

[96] cf. *ibid.,* 258.

[97] cf. *ibid.,* 256.

[98] Dr. Mark Miravalle, *Introduction to Mary,* 69.

[99] July 13, 1917 Apparition, *Fourth Memoir, Documents,* 440.

have renounced devotion to her. The regard for His glory, which was professed in that keen jealousy of her exaltation, has not been supported by the event. They who were accused of worshipping a creature in His stead, still worship Him; their accusers, who hoped to worship Him so purely, they, wherever obstacles to the development of their principles have been removed, have ceased to worship Him altogether.[100]

True and authentic worship of God is, precisely, the goal and effect of true devotion to the Immaculate Heart of Mary in the heart of everyone who practices this devotion. To recognize and appreciate the universal mediation of Mary's compassion acting between Christ, her Son and the rest of humanity does not in any way denigrate the role of mediation Christ assumes between God the Father and all of humanity, including His mother. Understanding her position is a continuous reminder that her Son is more than a prophet, more than a teacher, more than an exemplar of virtuous living. She is a constant reminder that our shared nature continuously pines for nothing less than total communion with God through her Son's Sacred Humanity and Person.

As St. Augustine famously prayed so long ago, "You have made us for Yourself, Oh God, and our hearts are restless until they rest in You."[101] It is especially Mary's desire and effective activity to dispense the many and varied graces of the Holy Spirit in such a manner as to foster such a communion between the Sacred Heart of her Son and the individual hearts of the rest of humanity. This understanding also helps preserve her devotees from the spiritual pride that can result from thinking that God's blessings are in any way an entitlement. If we find ourselves drawing near to the ideal of Christ, it is not because there is anything special about us, apart from the grace of God, without which we could not even utter a single syllable of prayer in supplication for God's mercy upon us. We are reminded that, before we

---

[100] *An Essay on the Development of Christian Doctrine*, (London: Basil Montagu Pickering), 424.

[101] Augustine of Hippo, *Confessions*, 1,1.

obtained any level of maturity, we were in need of being born again from above and nurtured through a spiritual childhood. All this will become abundantly clearer as we examine the nature of this devotion in the following chapters.

Conclusion

We set forth in this chapter to examine the sources that support the teaching on devotion to the Immaculate Heart of Mary. We found that the Gospels of St. Luke and St. John and the Book of Revelation, along with Sacred Tradition, all combine to establish a solid foundation for the doctrinal development of the teaching about Mary and the Church's corresponding devotion to her. We saw, too, that Mary is not only recognized as a supreme model of discipleship, but that she helps to mediate the blessings of her Son in a spiritually maternal and universal way. She works in union with the Holy Spirit to draw people to the foot of the cross and ever more intimately into sacramental communion with the wounded Heart of her Son.

All elements examined in this chapter will continue to be referred to and expounded upon as we examine more closely what has been privately shown to and recorded by Sister Lucia. As we know, so-called "private revelation" is not Revelation in the strict sense of the word, as are Sacred Scripture and Sacred Tradition. What has been shown to Sister Lucia, though meant for the whole world to ponder and make fruitful, is intended primarily to recall to our minds certain aspects of what has already been revealed by our Lord through His Apostles, preserved and expounded upon by His Church. In this sense, the Blessed Virgin Mary is acting in complete accord with her Spouse, the Holy Spirit, whom, Christ promised, will "bring to your remembrance all that I have said to you" (Jn 14:26), and "will guide you into all the truth, for he will not speak on his own authority, but whatever he hears he will speak, and he will declare to you the things that are to come" (Jn 16:13).

The promised *triumph of the Immaculate Heart* is a triumph that does not terminate in itself. Rather, it accomplishes a victory of the grace of the Holy Spirit over sin in the human heart, thereby "guid[ing] our feet into the way of peace" (Lk 1:79) and to the foot of the cross of Him who is there, "lifted up from the earth" (Jn 12:32), so that we might come to Him, and, "through him, and with him, and in him,"[102] "worship the Father in spirit and truth, for such the Father seeks to worship him" (Jn 4:23).

---

[102] *Liturgy of the Eucharist,* English - Latin Rite.

CHAPTER II

MATTER OF THE HEART

In the first chapter, we examined the sources of Revelation – Sacred Scripture and Sacred Tradition – in reference to the Church's teachings about Mary, in order to better understand the devotion to her Immaculate Heart, as requested at Fatima. We will now examine more closely the content of the Church's developed teaching about Mary and its implications in the light of the words and imagery presented to us at Fatima.

The role of Mary in God's plan of Salvation is not widely understood, even among those who maintain a regular devotion to her. As we will see, the words, actions and imagery utilized by Mary at Fatima can be a tremendous tool for helping us to understand Mary's role in salvation history. In fact, Fatima may provide the simplest of all means for gaining this understanding.

St. Maximilian Kolbe once wrote in a letter,

> Our imagination leads us to think of God the Father, of Jesus, of the Immaculata, as the objects of "devotions" which are more or less similar. Instead, we should think of them as links in a single chain, as elements all leading to a single goal: God, who is One in his Trinity.[103]

In this statement, St. Maximilian faults "our imagination" for obscuring the distinctions among the various persons or "objects" of our devotion, toward which we are rightly called in faith to direct our attention. It can be argued that the ambiguity, which results from this lack of clarity, contributes no small part to the view that devotion to Mary in some manner diminishes or detracts from devotion to her Son. If there is a tendency to view the various persons toward which

---

[103] *Immaculate Conception and the Holy Spirit*, 33

we are called to direct our devotion as "more or less similar," then it becomes possible to imagine that they are, in a sense, *competing* for our attention; time directed toward one, it may be argued, is time spent ignoring the others. Or, as I have often heard, "Why should I pray to Mary when I can go directly to Jesus?"

Of course, the reality is that these persons are in such profound communion with one another that it is only by gaining an understanding of their relationships that we are best able to understand each individually.[104] St. Maximilian's suggestion for remedying this distortion is to supply some suitable *matter* for our imaginations to consider, thereby allowing Revelation to better influence our imaginations. The "matter" for the imagination that he suggested is an image of a "chain." "We should think of them [the various persons to whom we direct our devotion] as links in a single chain, as elements all leading to a single goal: God, who is One in his Trinity."

With this understanding in mind, let us consider a vision given to Sister Lucia in 1929 (12 years after the Fatima apparitions), at the Dorothean convent in Tuy, Spain. We will examine the vision with the intention of supplying our imaginations with an image like St. Maximilian's analogy of "links in a single chain." It should be understood that there is no evidence to suggest that St. Maximilian Kolbe ever heard about the events of Fatima during his lifetime, which was cut short by martyrdom at Auschwitz on August 14, 1941. Before the end of World War II (1945), news about Fatima barely reached beyond the borders of Portugal. It is likely he would have been very intrigued with the events of Fatima and in particular this vision (especially considering the great interest he had in previous Marian events) and the way in which this vision provides an image of the relationships that link the various persons of our devotion. Sister Lucia described her vision this way:

> Suddenly a supernatural light illuminated the whole chapel and on the altar appeared a cross of light which reached to the ceiling. In a brighter light could be seen,

---

[104] cf. *CCC*, 255.

on the upper part of the cross, the face of a man and his body to the waist, with a dove of light on his breast and, nailed to the cross, the body of another man. A little below the waist, suspended in the air, was to be seen a Chalice and a big Host on which fell some drops of blood from the face of the crucified and from a wound in his breast. These drops ran down over the Host and fell into the Chalice. Under the right arm of the cross was Our Lady (Our Lady of Fatima with Her Immaculate Heart, without sword or roses, but with a crown of thorns and flames), with Her Immaculate Heart in Her hand: ... Under the left arm, some big letters, as it were of crystal-clear water running down over the altar, formed the words: "Grace and Mercy."

I understood that it was the mystery of the Most Holy Trinity which was shown to me and I received lights about this mystery which I am not permitted to reveal.[105]

---

[105] From a compilation of writings of Lucia and notes of her confessor, Fr. Jose Bernado Gonzalves, S.J., *Documents*, 394.

Joe DeVito

If it is true, as the colloquial proverb states, that "a picture is worth a thousand words," then the value of a symbolic vision, like the one described here by Sister Lucia, must hold a worth exponentially greater than that of any ordinary picture. We see in this vision something akin to what St. John the Evangelist was attempting to convey in the inclusion of various details of the Crucifixion in his Gospel. We see the blood from Jesus' Passion falling into the Chalice, which sacramentally serves for our purification, redemption and sanctification. Included are the words, "Grace and Mercy," flowing down like "crystal-clear water" from the wound in Jesus' left hand. We also see Mary at the foot of the Cross in a kind of mediation, facing toward the visionary (and us), seeming to appeal for our compassion and greater self-donation in a more complete and perfect worship of her Son. In other words, she appeals to us "to look on him whom [we] have pierced" (Jn 19:37) with something of the sense of the pain of her own Immaculate Heart, which she displays for us in her hand.

Recall the event of the Presentation in the Temple, and Simeon's prophecy to Mary about her Son and her share in the sorrow of her Son's act of Redemption, bearing the fruit of exposing the thoughts and hearts: "Behold, this child is set for the fall and rising of many in Israel, and for a sign that is spoken against (*and a sword will pierce through your own soul also*), *that thoughts out of many hearts may be revealed*" (emphasis added, Lk 2:34-35).

The position of Our Lady "beneath the *right arm* of the cross" and the words "Grace and Mercy" coming down from "under the *left arm* of the cross" convey a symbolic meaning significant in the language of Sacred Scripture. In Scripture, the "right" and the "left" can hold opposing meanings. This is the case in Christ's parable of the "sheep and the goats," where at the final judgment the sheep are assembled at the right and the goats to the left (cf. Mt 24:31ff). According to the *New International Dictionary of New Testament Theology*, "The right hand symbolizes power, success, good fortune, loyalty,"[106] and the left "folly and ill fortune."[107] Keeping in mind the symbolic nature of the vision, the meaning of our Lady's position in the vision would indicate her highly exalted status of influence before the majesty of God and her recognizable appeal to all her children in an effort to gain from them a similar sense of compassion.

By the power of the intercession welling up from the depths of her Immaculate Heart, being extended to us in her hand for our consideration, she obtains "Grace and Mercy" for all of us who, though not deserving, stand in need. She appeals to the depths of human hearts, to consciences, to draw out, "with human chords" (cf. Hos 11:4), compassion from us, so as to draw us ever nearer to the fount of that Mercy – the pierced wound in the side of Jesus, made ever more accessible to all in the Church's sacraments and liturgy. Once there, endowed with some semblance of the sentiments of her own

---

[106] Colin Brown, *The New International Dictionary of New Testament Theology*, Vol. 2. (Grand Rapids, MI: Zondervan Publishing House, 1976), 146.
[107] *ibid.*, 148.

Immaculate Heart, we are better equipped to join in union with her to make intercession and reparation for the sake of others.

It is very interesting that the words "Grace and Mercy" come, not from the wound in the side of Jesus, or our Lord's breast, or the host and chalice to where His Precious Blood is flowing, but from the left hand or arm of Jesus. Less than two years after Sister Lucia received this vision, St. Faustina saw the vision of our Lord as depicted in the now famous image of the Divine Mercy (February 22, 1931), with rays of red and white emanating from the breast of Jesus that she was asked to have painted. Both are images which depict God's mercy, but why is there this discrepancy between the two images, both of which the recipients claim to be of supernatural origin? Both visions clearly show Jesus as the immediate source of Divine Mercy, but there are significant differences.

The Divine Mercy image of St. Faustina, it has been said, reflects the miraculous post-Resurrection appearance of our Lord to the Apostles and disciples, who were gathered together, but hiding behind locked doors. The image is integrally bound to the Divine Mercy Sunday celebration, the Second Sunday of the Octave of Easter. The Gospel Reading for that Sunday describes that scene of which the image is said to initially depict:

> On the evening of that day, the first day of the week, the doors being shut where the disciples were, for fear of the Jews, Jesus came and stood among them and said to them, "Peace be with you." When he had said this, he showed them his hands and his side. Then the disciples were glad when they saw the Lord. Jesus said to them again, "Peace be with you. As the Father has sent me, even so I send you." And when he had said this, he breathed on them, and said to them, "Receive the Holy Spirit. If you forgive the sins of any, they are forgiven; if you retain the sins of any, they are retained."
>
> Now Thomas, one of the twelve, called the Twin, was not with them when Jesus came. So the other disciples

told him, "We have seen the Lord." But he said to them, "Unless I see in his hands the print of the nails, and place my finger in the mark of the nails, and place my hand in his side, I will not believe."

Eight days later, his disciples were again in the house, and Thomas was with them. The doors were shut, but Jesus came and stood among them, and said, "Peace be with you." Then he said to Thomas, "Put your finger here, and see my hands; and put out your hand, and place it in my side; do not be faithless, but believing." Thomas answered him, "My Lord and my God!" Jesus said to him, "Have you believed because you have seen me? Blessed are those who have not seen and yet believe." (Jn 20:19-29)

Though the Divine Mercy Devotion as revealed to St. Faustina draws much attention to what is referred to as "the hour of great mercy" (the three o'clock hour when our Lord died upon the Cross), the Divine Mercy image seems to only refer to this moment indirectly through our Lord's wounds. It is rather the vision of Sister Lucia at Tuy, Spain, which more directly appears to depict that "hour of great mercy." Our Lord told St. Faustina,

> At three o'clock, implore My mercy, especially for sinners; and, if only for a brief moment, immerse yourself in My Passion, particularly in My abandonment at the moment of agony. This is the hour of great mercy for the whole world. I will allow you to enter into My mortal sorrow. In this hour, I will refuse nothing to the soul that makes a request of Me in virtue of My Passion. [108]

Our Lord's words here are striking: "… immerse yourself in My Passion, particularly in My abandonment at the moment of agony." It seems from these words our Lord is saying that what pained Him most of all "at the moment of agony" was being deserted precisely by the ones who had already become His Apostles and disciples. Our Lord prophesied their abandonment of him after the Last Supper as they went out to the Mount of Olives. "You will all fall away because of me this night. … But after I am raised up, I will go before you to Galilee" (Mt 26:30-32; cf. Mk 14:26-28).

The image of Divine Mercy shown to St. Faustina depicts our Lord's appearance to many of the very ones who were guilty of abandoning Him "at the moment of agony." Our Lord later confided to St. Faustina that, "The great sins of the world are superficial wounds on My Heart, but the sins of a chosen soul pierce My Heart through and through."[109]

Our Lord's appearance to the Apostles and disciples after the Resurrection reads like an absolution of their shared guilt in their

---

[108] *Divine Mercy in My Soul: Diary.* (Stockbridge, MA: Marian Press, 1987), entry 1320.

[109] *ibid.,* entry 1702.

abandonment of Him at the crucial *hour of great mercy*. While appearing to them He, thus, transmits the *grace and mercy* He gained for them from His Heavenly Father precisely in that timeless hour. Is this why Sister Lucia's vision at Tuy depicts "Grace and Mercy" flowing from the left hand of Jesus rather than directly from the Host and chalice or our Lord's wounded side? Though they had all promised Him their courageous loyalty (cf. Mt 26:35; Mk14:31), they were guilty of the moral cowardice involved in abandoning Him at His arrest and trials, and they stood in need of Christ's forgiveness, absolution and grace. After the Resurrection, our Lord sought them out behind locked doors to convince them all of the overflowing abundance of God's Mercy.

The word *grace* is a very broad term that encompasses many particular categories. Two such categories are *sanctifying grace* and *actual graces*. *Sanctifying grace* is precisely the life of God within us and is what the Church refers to when speaking of a person being in the *state of grace*. On the other hand, *actual graces* are mediated influences or Divine interventions upon an individual, and come to us in a countless number of ways. St. Joan of Arc was famously asked during her long trial if she was in the state of grace. She wisely responded, "If I am not, I pray that God place me there; if I am, I pray that God keep me there."

Well, how does God do that? By dispensing His *actual graces*, which "refer to God's interventions, whether at the beginning of conversion or in the course of the work of sanctification."[110] *The Catechism* explains that these *graces* are distinguished from "sanctifying grace," which is "an habitual gift, a stable and supernatural disposition that perfects the soul itself to enable it to live with God, to act by his love."[111]

Sanctifying grace is "a participation in the life of God"[112] Himself. We can say that sanctifying grace is the goal and actual graces are the means to that end. Actual graces are the many, innumerable and

---

[110] *Ibid.*, 2000.

[111] *ibid.*

[112] *CCC*, 1997.

varied ways in which the Holy Spirit can influence the soul to act in ways oriented toward sharing God's Life and Spirit for one's self and for others. If we are in God's sanctifying grace, it was by His mercy granted to us in His actual graces that we were brought there and are able to abide there (cf. Jn 6:65; 15:16). Sanctifying grace is what we would expect to receive (in addition to other graces) from the Host and the Blood in the chalice, as our Lord said, "Unless you eat my flesh and drink my blood, you have no *life* in you" (Jn 6:53). It is also why, when our Lord was speaking about the coming of the Holy Spirit to His Apostles, He makes a distinction when He tells them that they already "know him, for he dwells *with* you, [but, when He comes, He] will be *in* you" (Jn 14:17). It is the plea of the Immaculate Heart of Mary that all people should be so endowed, the ultimate fulfillment of her request at the wedding feast at Cana, "they have no wine" (Jn 2:3). According to one theologian,

> Mary at the foot of the cross is not merely the Mother of the Church. ... At this moment Mary's heart is, in a very special way, the heart of the Church. When almost all the other members are unfaithful to the Head, the heart remains more vitally united to Him then ever in the name of the entire Body. ... In the Church she is the heart watching in faith while many sleep the sleep of unbelief. She is the heart that causes the blood, that is, charity, to flow throughout the body. ... She personifies the Church participating in its own salvation, as she, at the same time, efficiently causes this participation.[113]

St. Maximilian Kolbe seemed to have an intimate understanding of all this. In the very first sentence of his formula of total consecration to Mary, Kolbe writes, "O Immaculata, Queen of heaven and earth, refuge of sinners and our most loving Mother, God has willed

---

[113] Rev. Bertrand de Margerie, *Heart of Mary, Heart of the Church*, (Washington, NJ: AMI Press, 1991), 30-31.

to entrust the entire order of mercy to you."[114] This is a bold statement, but notice that Kolbe does not claim that Mary is *the source* of mercy; the source is God in her Son. But, our Lord's Sacrifice upon the cross is not merely an act of mercy but also a judgement, calling us to come to Him in repentance. Mary stands at the foot of the cross, interceding on our behalf and beckoning to us, that we might respond with gratitude to His great act of mercy toward us.

St. Maximilian Kolbe and His Marian Insight

As was mentioned in the previous chapter, St. Maximilian Kolbe provides a keen insight into the relationship of Mary with the Holy Spirit, which is helpful for explaining why devotion to her is so essential and powerful. To go more deeply into the mystery that is being highlighted to us in Sister Lucia's vision, we need now give greater attention to that unique insight provided by St. Maximilian. Though, as we already mentioned, St. Maximilian probably never heard of the events of Fatima, his life, thoughts and apostolic pursuits anticipate and echo the message of Fatima so closely that it seems unmistakably clear that the events of Fatima and the witness borne by St. Maximilian are providentially linked.

Within the same week that the great miracle of the sun took place in Fatima on October 13, 1917, St. Maximilian, while yet a seminarian studying in Rome, founded an ecclesial movement with a mission statement remarkably similar to God's desired intention for humanity, as expressed by Mary at Fatima and recorded by Sister Lucia. Recall that at Fatima, Mary told Lucia that in order "to save them [sinners], God wishes to establish in the world devotion to my Immaculate Heart." St. Maximilian Kolbe's biographer, Br. J. Mlodozeniec, OFM Conv., explains the scenario which prompted St. Maximilian to found the Militia of the Immaculata:

> When Freemasons were celebrating the 200th anniversary of their founding, they held their major festivities in Rome. There through the streets marched the Masonic

---

114 "Act of Consecration." St. Maximilian Kolbe. Accessed February 25, 2019. https://saintmaximiliankolbe.com/consecration/.

groups with black banners bearing the image of Lucifer trampling down St. Michael the Archangel. Against such insults, the noble sentiments of Maximilian's knightly soul rose up in revolt, and he determined then and there to take up the challenge in a spiritual battle in the name of the one to whom he felt bound and who, already in paradise, will one day crush the serpent's head.

Along with six colleagues, Maximilian, with the permission of the superiors, organized a new association called the MILITIA OF THE IMMACULATE, on **October 17, 1917.** As initiator of the association, he prescribed for it his Maximilian goal: ***To win the souls of the whole world for the Sacred Heart of Jesus through the Immaculate Mother.*** (emphasis added)[115]

The unplanned, but almost simultaneous, concurrence of this event and the miracle of the sun at Fatima, along with the mission to pursue the same devotional ideal as expressed by Mary at Fatima, manifests the wonder and power of God's providence and the hidden power of the consecration to Mary that St. Maximilian practiced throughout his life. There was, here, no clever *conspiring* of individuals, only the brilliant yet hidden activity of the Holy Spirit, *inspiring* individuals willing to respond. These were not enormous newsworthy events at the time, as were the developments of World War I and, to a lesser extent, the turmoil and revolution taking place in Russia. Like our Lord's conception and birth, these ecclesial events moved under the radar of the awareness of almost everyone living outside their local reach. As already mentioned, before World War II, the events of Fatima were hardly known outside of Portugal. It was the prophetic fulfillment of some of the predictions at Fatima – the coming of "another even worse war" and the growing and spreading threat from "Russia" – that helped to awaken greater interest in the events and message of Fatima.

---

[115] Br. J. Mlodozeniec, OFM Conv., *I Knew Saint Maximilian*, (Washington, NJ, AMI Press, 1979), 8, 9

In the years that followed between the wars, Fr. Kolbe's movement helped to fulfill our Lord's expressed wish of Fatima, to strengthen devotion to Mary, especially within his own native country of Poland. In 1927, Fr. Kolbe founded a Franciscan community near Warsaw, which he called *Niepokalanow*, Polish for "Marytown," which, within a short time, "became one of the largest friaries in the world, numbering 609 brothers, 13 priests, 18 clerics, and 122 seminarians."[116] This friary conducted a major evangelizing apostolate that published a magazine called *Knight of the Immaculate*, devoted to spreading devotion to Mary, and reached a distribution of almost a million copies.[117] Providentially, Poland would later play a key role in the demise of the communist Soviet Russian Empire, especially following the election of Cardinal Karol Wojtyla, the Archbishop of Krakow, Poland, to the papacy on October 16, 1978. Upon ascending to the chair of St. Peter, Pope St. John Paul II took *"Totus Tuus"* as his papal motto – a Latin phrase meaning, "I am totally yours" – signifying his total, personal and papal consecration to Mary. Of course, we know that halfway through John Paul II's papacy, the world witnessed the great miracle of the collapse of the Soviet Empire.

Knowing that Fr. Kolbe accomplished his work in Poland in those years before his martyrdom on August 14, 1941, without perhaps ever knowing anything about the events at Fatima should give us pause. Recall how Sister Lucia characterized her own mission to the world, given to her by God, as "not that of a prophet, but rather that of a voice in the desert where only God hears."[118] In that "desert," where it seemed that "only God hears," God was listening to her prayer and the anguish of her heart, and He responded providentially. While men were conspiring in their plots and relishing their sense of inevitable triumph, God was allowing His own plan to unfold in relative obscurity. St. Faustina – who, like Sister Lucia bore the weight of bringing a message from God to the world – was told by our Lord:

---

[116] *ibid.,* 16.

[117] cf. *ibid.*

[118] Letter written by Sr. Lucia from Tuy, Spain on 12/16/1940 to her confessor, Fr. Aparicio, *Documents,* 387.

I know what you can do. I myself will give you many
orders directly, but I will delay the possibility of their
being carried out and make it depend on others. But what
the superiors will not manage to do, I Myself will accomplish directly in your soul. And in the most hidden depths
of your soul, a perfect holocaust will be carried out, not
just for a while, but know, My daughter, that this offering
will last until your death.[119]

Although the circumstances of these two chosen souls are different, the way in which our Lord operated interiorly with St. Faustina
is comparable to that of Sister Lucia. She, too, was entrusted with
a message to be conveyed to superiors, laden with duties that required their cooperation in order to be carried out. What Sister Lucia
confides about herself being "a voice in the desert where only God
hears," sounds very close to what our Lord was telling St. Faustina,
that "in the most hidden depths of your soul, a perfect holocaust will
be carried out."

Even more remarkable, our Lord tells St. Faustina that He, Himself, "will accomplish directly ... what the superiors will not manage
to do." Praying and making sacrifices for the salvation of souls in
order to obtain *graces and mercy* for them and for the whole world, is
a central ingredient of both the Fatima and Divine Mercy messages.
Though God utilized both of these extraordinary women to convey
messages to strengthen the faith of believers, He did it in a way that
transformed them both into human channels of His *graces and mercy*.
Our Lord's graces are never frustrated. If superiors or members of
the Church hierarchy were slow to respond to heaven's directives, all
was not lost. Our Lord's words to St. Faustina confirm this: "I want
to give myself to souls and to fill them with My love, but few there
are who want to accept all the graces My love has intended for them.
**My grace is not lost; if the soul for whom it was intended does not
accept it, another soul takes it.**"[120] We have every reason to assume

[119] *Divine Mercy in My Soul: Diary.* (Stockbridge, MA: Marian Press, 1987), entry
923.
[120] *ibid.,* entry 1017.

that one person who was open and ready to receive much of the graces God was intending to pour out on His Church during those years between the wars was St. Maximilian Kolbe.

A look at the life of St. Maximilian helps us to place the events and message of Fatima more neatly into their rightful context within the greater purview of salvation history. St. Maximilian Kolbe is most widely known for taking the place of a fellow prisoner who had been condemned to death at Auschwitz. In doing so, he was later canonized by St. John Paul II as a "martyr of brotherly love," in remembrance of our Lord's words: "Greater love has no man than this, that a man lay down his life for his friends" (Jn 15:13). That one deed, which displayed a most supreme degree of heroic virtue, was preceded by a lifetime of total self-donation to the will of God, through a personal consecration to His Immaculate Mother. Though his life was cut short at the age of 47, without the witness of his martyrdom, it might have happened that what this great saint had to teach us about devotion to Mary may have become quickly forgotten. By his martyrdom, however, our Lord's words have proven true, that "unless a grain of wheat falls into the earth and dies, it remains alone; but if it dies, it bears much fruit" (Jn 12:24).

As a Franciscan priest, Maximilian studied in the same tradition that Bl. Duns Scotus helped to illumine more than six centuries earlier. We have already seen in the previous chapter how the Franciscan, Scotus, most brilliantly and tenaciously defended the teaching of the Immaculate Conception during the Middle Ages. As a student, St. Maximilian diligently pursued his studies with great success, earning doctoral degrees in both theology and philosophy.[121] He was also very intrigued with the renowned Marian apparitions to St. Catherine Labouré in Paris, France, in 1830; to Alphonse Ratisbonne in 1842; and to St. Bernadette in Lourdes, France, in 1858, all of which confirmed the doctrine of the Immaculate Conception. He recognized in these events God's providential response to the growing loss of faith in the world and the way God was pointing to spiritually combat the influence of certain groups, like the Freemasons, which have inten-

---

[121] cf. *I Knew Saint Maximilian*, 8.

tionally worked to undermine faith in the world. Thus, we can see how St. Maximilian became so keenly prepared to anticipate God's initiative "to establish in the world the devotion to [Mary's] Immaculate Heart." He recognized that the Immaculate Conception was not merely a special privilege granted to Mary, like some ornament to be displayed in isolation from God's greater plan for all humankind, but was granted, rather, in view of her providential role in God's glorious design for the redemption of humanity.[122]

There was one thought and meditation that preoccupied the mind of St. Maximilian beyond all others – the name that Mary applied to herself in response to St. Bernadette's request at Lourdes. During the early appearances of Mary at Lourdes, Bernadette did not know who it was that was appearing to her and would thus just call her the "beautiful lady." Bernadette's pastor told her that she needed to ask the lady who she was. Bernadette attempted several times in subsequent appearances to get the lady to reveal her name, without success. Finally, her perseverance paid off on the vigil of the feast of the Annunciation, March 24, 1858. St. Bernadette recorded the story this way:

> She was there. I asked her to forgive me for coming late. Always kind and gracious, she made a sign to me with her head to tell me that I need not make excuses. Then I spoke to her of all my love, all my reverence and the happiness I had in seeing her again. After having poured out my heart to her, I took up my rosary. Whilst I was praying, the thought of asking her name came before my mind with such persistence that I could think of nothing else. I feared to be presumptuous in repeating a question she had always refused to answer and yet something compelled me to speak.
>
> At last, under an irresistible impulse, the words fell from my mouth, and I begged the Lady to tell me who she was. The Lady did as she had always done before; she

---

[122] cf. *Immaculate Conception and the Holy Spirit*, p. xxv.

bowed her head and smiled but she did not reply. I cannot say why, but I felt bolder and asked her again to be so kind as to tell me her name; however, she only bowed and smiled as before, still keeping silence. Then once more, for the third time, clasping my hands and acknowledging myself unworthy of the favor I was seeking of her, I again made my request.

The Lady was standing above the rose-tree, in a position very similar to that shown in the miraculous medal. At my third request her face became very serious and she seemed to bow down in an attitude of humility. Then she joined her hands and raised them to her breast ... She looked up to heaven ... then slowly opening her hands and leaning forward towards me, she said to me in a voice vibrating with emotion, 'I Am The Immaculate Conception (Que Soy Era Immaculate Councepcion).'

Immediately Our Lady vanished.

I repeated the words all the way home, in order not to forget them, and hurried to relay the message to Fr. Peyramalle [her pastor].[123]

Without the full text of St. Bernadette's retelling of the story, it is difficult to convey the true sense of the momentous weight in Our Lady's response. It is readily apparent that Mary remains fully aware that "he who is mighty has done great things for [her], and holy is his name" (Lk 1:49). This response of Mary to St. Bernadette, calling herself "the Immaculate Conception," was for St. Maximilian Kolbe a great mystery to come to grips with. In one letter he wrote:

In her apparition at Lourdes she does not say: "I was conceived immaculately"; but "I am the Immaculate Conception." This points up not only the fact that she was conceived without sin, but also the manner in which this

---

123 Breen, Stephen, "Lourdes and Bernadette," Recent Apparitions of the Blessed Virgin Mary, (The Scapular Press, 1952), taken from EWTN Online Library. Accessed August 2, 2015. http://www.ewtn.com/library/mary/lourbern.htm.

privilege belongs to her. It is not something accidental; it is something that belongs to her very nature. For she is Immaculate Conception in person.[124]

Fr. Manteau-Bonamy, O.P., characterizes the nature of St. Maximilian's fascination with her response by highlighting the audaciousness of Mary's claim:

> In the fact that at Lourdes [Mary] called herself "Immaculate Conception," we find the manner of expressing the mystery of her immaculate conception which, at first sight, does not seem to follow from the dogmatic definition. This name that the Virgin attributes to herself, as though defining who she is, seems to go beyond her, to divinize her so to speak. Here we find ourselves in the very heart of the problem that Father Kolbe sought, all through his life, to unravel.[125]

Ironically, but providentially, only hours before he was arrested and sent to Auschwitz, on February 17, 1941, Fr. Kolbe sat down and penned out his most complete answer to this nagging question, in what Fr. Manteau-Bonamy has called, Fr. Kolbe's "spiritual testament."[126] Here we will read the full text of what he wrote on that fateful day, knowing that the insight gained by this highly intelligent and holy philosopher and theologian, into the question and meaning of Mary's identity as "the Immaculate Conception" can help to shed light on Sister Lucia's vision at Tuy, of the Father, Son and Holy Spirit in the Paschal Mystery, along with Mary holding her Immaculate Heart out to us. Recall that, after describing what she saw, Lucia said, "I understood that it was the mystery of the Most Holy Trinity that was shown to me and I received lights about this mystery which I am not permitted to reveal."[127] Here is St. Maximilian's *spiritual testament*

---

[124] *Immaculate Conception and the Holy Spirit*, 7.

[125] *ibid.*, 8.

[126] *ibid.*, 1.

[127] Notes gathered by Fr. Gonzalves at Tuy, Spain 4/24/1941, *Documents*, 394.

(I have numbered the paragraphs for referencing purposes):

1. IMMACULATE CONCEPTION. These words fell from the lips of the Immaculata herself. Hence, they must tell in the most precise and essential manner who she really is.

2. Since human words are incapable of expressing divine realities, it follows that these words: "Immaculate" and "Conception" must be understood in a much more profound, much more beautiful and sublime meaning than usual: a meaning beyond that which human reason at its most penetrating, commonly gives to them.

3. St. Paul wrote, quoting the prophet Isaiah: "'Things that the eye has seen, that the ear has heard, that the heart of man has not imagined' (Is 64:4), such are the good things that God has prepared for those who love him" (1 Cor 2:9). Here, these words apply fully.

4. However, we can and should reverently inquire into the mystery of the Immaculata and to express it with words provided by our intelligence using its own proper powers.

5. Who then are you, O Immaculate Conception?

6. Not God, of course, because he has no beginning. Not an angel, created directly out of nothing. Not Adam, formed out of the dust of the earth (Gen 2:7). Not Eve, molded from Adam's rib (Gen 2:21). Not the Incarnate Word, who exists before all ages, and of whom we should use the word "conceived" rather than "conception." Humans do not exist before their conception, so we might call them created "conceptions." But you, O Mary, are different from all other children of Eve. They are conceptions stained by original sin; whereas you are the unique, Immaculate Conception.

7. Everything which exists, outside of God himself, since it is from God and depends on him in every way, bears within

itself some semblance to its Creator; there is nothing in any creature which does not betray this resemblance, because every created thing is an effect of the Primal Cause.

8. It is true that the words we use to speak of created realities express the divine perfections only in a halting, limited and analogical manner. They are only a more or less distant echo – as are the created realities that they signify – of the properties of God himself.

9. Would not "conception" be an exception to this rule? No; there is never any such exception.

10. The Father begets the Son; the Spirit proceeds from Father and Son. These few words sum up the mystery of the life of the Most Blessed Trinity and of all the perfections in creatures which are nothing else but echoes, a hymn of praise, a many-hued tableau, of this primary and most wondrous of all mysteries.

11. We must perforce use our customary vocabulary, since it is all we have; but we must never forget that our vocabulary is very inadequate.

12. Who is the Father? What is his personal life like? It consists in begetting, eternally; because he begets his Son from the beginning, and forever.

13. Who is the Son? He is the Begotten-One, because from the beginning and for all eternity he is begotten by the Father.

14. And who is the Holy Spirit? The flowering of the love of the Father and the Son. If the fruit of created love is a created conception, then the fruit of divine Love, that prototype of all created love, is necessarily a divine "conception." The Holy Spirit is, therefore, the "uncreated, eternal conception," the prototype of all the conceptions that multiply life throughout the whole universe.

15. The Father begets; the Son is begotten; the Spirit is the "conception" that springs from their love; there we have the intimate life of the three Persons by which they can be distinguished one from another. But they are united in the oneness of their Nature, of their divine existence.

16. The Spirit is, then, this thrice holy "conception," this infinitely holy, Immaculate Conception.

17. Everywhere in this world we notice action, and the reaction which is equal but contrary to it; departure and return; going away and coming back; separation and reunion. The separation always looks forward to union, which is creative. All this is simply an image of the Blessed Trinity in the activity of creatures. Union means love, creative love. Divine activity, outside the Trinity itself, follows the same pattern. First, God creates the universe; that is something like a separation. Creatures, by following the natural law implanted in them by God, reach their perfection, become like him, and go back to him. Intelligent creatures love him in a conscious manner; through this love they unite themselves more and more closely with him, and so find their way back to him. The creature most completely filled with this love, filled with God himself, was the Immaculata, who never contracted the slightest stain of sin, who never departed in the least from God's will. United to the Holy Spirit as his spouse, she is one with God in an incomparably more perfect way than can be predicated of any other creature.

18. What sort of union is this? It is above all an interior union, a union of her essence with the "essence" of the Holy Spirit. The Holy Spirit dwells in her, lives in her. This was true from the first instant of her existence. It was always true; it will always be true.

19. In what does this life of the Spirit in Mary consist? He himself is uncreated Love in her; the Love by which God loves himself, the very love of the Most Holy Trinity. He is a fruitful Love, a "Conception." Among creatures made in God's image the union brought about by married love is the most intimate of all (cf. Mt 19:6). In a much more precise, more interior, more essential manner, the Holy Spirit lives in the soul of the Immaculata, in the depths of her very being. He makes her fruitful, from the very first instant of her existence, all during her life, and for all eternity.

20. This eternal "Immaculate Conception" (which is the Holy Spirit) produces in an immaculate manner divine life itself in the womb (or depths) of Mary's soul, making her the Immaculate Conception, the human Immaculate Conception. And the virginal womb of Mary's body is kept sacred for him; there he conceives in time – because everything that is material occurs in time – the human life of the Man-God.

21. And so the return to God (which is love), that is to say the equal and contrary reaction, follows a different path from that found in creation. The path of creation goes from the Father through the Son and by the Holy Spirit; this return trail goes from the Spirit through the Son back to the Father; in other words, by the Spirit the Son becomes incarnate in the womb of the Immaculata; and through this Son love returns to the Father.

22. And she (the Immaculata), grafted into the Love of the Blessed Trinity, becomes from the first moment of her existence and forever thereafter the "complement of the Blessed Trinity."

23. In the Holy Spirit's union with Mary we observe more than the love of two beings; in one there is all the love of

the Blessed Trinity; in the other, all of creation's love. So it is that in this union heaven and earth are joined; all of heaven with all the earth, the totality of eternal love with the totality of created love. It is truly the summit of love.

24. At Lourdes, the Immaculata did not say of herself that she had been conceived immaculately, but, as St. Bernadette repeated it, "Que soy era immaculada councepciou": "I am the Immaculate Conception."

25. If among human beings the wife takes the name of her husband because she belongs to him, is one with him, becomes equal to him and is, with him, the source of new life, with how much greater reason should the name of the Holy Spirit, who is the divine Immaculate Conception, be used as the name of her in whom he lives as uncreated Love, the principle of life in the whole supernatural order of grace?[128]

An Analysis of St. Maximilian Kolbe's Spiritual Testament

Though what St. Maximilian Kolbe wrote in his *spiritual testament* above may sound very new and overly technical to many people, much of what is written, especially about "the central mystery of Christian faith and life,"[129] the mystery of the Most Holy Trinity, does not wander beyond the range of traditional Christian theology. St. Maximilian's effort to ground his meditation about the mystery of the "Immaculate Conception" solidly within the mystery of the Holy Trinity testifies to the sobriety of his thought and faithfulness to the Church's theological Tradition. *The Catechism* asserts that,

The Fathers of the Church distinguish between theology (*theologia*) and economy (*oikonomia*). "Theology" refers to the mystery of God's inmost life within the Blessed Trinity and "economy" to all the works by which God

---

[128] *Immaculate Conception and the Holy Spirit*, 2-5.
[129] CCC, 234.

reveals himself and communicates his life. Through the *oikonomia* the *theologia* is revealed to us; but conversely, the *theologia* illuminates the whole *oikonomia*. God's works reveal who he is in himself; the mystery of his inmost being enlightens our understanding of all his works. So it is, analogously, among human persons. A person discloses himself in his actions, and the better we know a person, the better we understand his actions.[130]

Though St. Maximilian was probably the first person in the history of the Church to call the Holy Spirit the "eternal 'Immaculate Conception'" (paragraph 20), his claim that the Holy Spirit is the "flowering of the love of the Father and the Son" (paragraph 14) is not something novel. This identification of the Holy Spirit as the "love" of the Father and the Son is often made, especially in efforts to give some explanation of the dynamic relationships among the three Persons of the Holy Trinity. St. John Paul II wrote in his Encyclical, *Dominum et Vivificantem, On the Holy Spirit in the Life of the Church and the World,*

> In his intimate life, God "is love" (cf. 1 Jn 4:8, 16), the essential love shared by the three divine Persons: personal love is the Holy Spirit as the Spirit of the Father and the Son … It can be said that in the Holy Spirit the intimate life of the Triune God becomes totally gift, an exchange of mutual love between the divine Persons, and that through the Holy Spirit God exists in the mode of gift. It is the Holy Spirit who is *the personal expression* of this self-giving, of this being-love.[131]

In the philosophical personalism employed by St. John Paul II in this encyclical, the gift of self is the defining expression of the Love of God. The Father gave of Himself, totally, by giving us His

---

[130] *CCC*, 236.

[131] *Dominum et Vivificantem (D et V), On the Holy Spirit in the Life of the Church and the World,* (Boston, MA: St. Paul Books and Media, 1986), 10.

only Son; the Son gave of Himself, totally, to His Father and to us by giving up His life in atonement for our sin and for our nourishment of eternal life; the Holy Spirit is the Spirit that animates and moves this expression of their overflowing, self-giving Love. St. Maximilian roots the thought of his meditation deeply within this "central mystery of Christian faith and life."

St. Maximilian's *spiritual testament* follows a meticulously logical train of thought. He begins by referencing the words by which Mary identified herself at Lourdes and attempts to move his readers toward a properly exalted contemplation of these words as reflective of "divine mysteries." In paragraph 6, he contrasts and eliminates any possible contenders for this identity in divine Revelation by drawing attention to some obvious distinctions between them and Mary, helping to illuminate something of the precision of clarity that her chosen terms are intended to convey. Then, in paragraph 7, he shifts his emphasis from speaking of the inner life of the Triune God toward explaining the dependency of form that all the created works of God hold in reference to their Creator:

> Everything which exists, outside of God himself, since it is from God and depends on him in every way, bears within itself some semblance to its Creator; there is nothing in any creature which does not betray this resemblance, because every created thing is an effect of the Primal Cause.

Understanding this connection between God and His Creation is essential to understanding the logical development of St. Maximilian's argument, for Mary, as a creature of God, possesses a "semblance to [her] Creator," shaped by a union with God, "in an incomparably more perfect way than can be predicated of any other creature" (paragraph 17).

In paragraphs 8 thru 16, St. Maximilian demonstrates that the idea of "conception" expresses a meaning most helpful for conveying the understanding of the dynamic, creative love that is shared and exchanged between the Father and the Son in the Person of the Holy Spirit. The reasoning, which St. Maximilian applies in concluding that the word "conception" can be used in reference to the Holy Spirit, can be summed up in a syllogism extracted from paragraph 14:

> If the Holy Spirit is "the flowering of the love of the Father and the Son,"
>
> And, "If the fruit of created love is a created conception,"
>
> Then the fruit of divine Love, that prototype of all created love, is necessarily a divine 'conception.' The Holy Spirit is, therefore, the 'uncreated, eternal conception,' the prototype of all the conceptions that multiply life throughout the whole universe."

St. Maximilian is so confident of this conclusion that he certifies it as "necessarily" true. If the premises are true (which all Catholics must accept), "[t]hen the fruit of divine Love [the Holy Spirit], that prototype of all created love, is *necessarily* a divine 'conception.'" Since God is the Creator of everything in the Universe, and everything He has created is "very good" (cf. Gn 1:31), for it was all made "through" and "with" His "Word" (cf. Jn 1:3), and since we observe "conception" as a procreative act of these creatures God has created, accomplished by various forms and degrees of "[u]nion [which] means love" (paragraph 17), "[t]hen the fruit of divine Love, that prototype of all created love, is necessarily a divine 'conception.'"

This idea of "conception" as "the flowering" of the dynamic and creative "love of the Father and the Son" in the divine Person of the Holy Spirit fits remarkably well with the specific command spoken by God given to particular creatures at the moment of their Creation, as related in the Book of Genesis. To all the living animals that God creates, He gives the command: "Be fruitful and multiply" (Gn 1:22, 28). This command we all recognize as an inclination sown within the very natural makeup of God's bodily creatures. This command takes on a significance endowed with moral responsibility in regard to human beings, since they are called to reflect God's perfections, most completely, as sharers of His image and likeness:[132]

---

[132] cf. *CCC*, 2331.

Then God said, "Let us make man in our image, after
our likeness; and let them have dominion over the fish of
the sea, and over the birds of the air, and over the cattle,
and over all the earth, and over every creeping thing that
creeps upon the earth." So God created man in his own
image, in the image of God he created him; male and
female he created them. And God blessed them, and God
said to them, "Be fruitful and multiply, and fill the earth
and subdue it; and have dominion over the fish of the sea
and over the birds of the air and over every living thing
that moves upon the earth." (Gn 1:26-28)

Thus, the procreative activity of God's creatures, especially that
of human beings, is reflective of the creative Love of God in the dynamic activity of the Blessed Trinity. In human beings, this procreative capacity is a bestowal of divine authority, a "dominion" granted
to human beings, an authority charged with moral responsibility. We
can say that this procreative activity among God's creatures is the
most physically obvious pattern of the Trinity within God's Creation,
the most readily apparent to the perception of our senses. But, the
wonder of the pattern of God's divine activity among His creatures
is present at many levels, most of which need to be understood in a
more abstract, philosophical manner.

In paragraph 17, St. Maximilian attempts to move his readers
from the more obvious to the more abstract:

Everywhere in this world we notice action and the reaction
which is equal but contrary to it; departure and return;
going away and coming back; separation and reunion. The
separation always looks forward to union, which is creative. All this is simply an image of the Blessed Trinity in
the activity of creatures. Union means love, creative love.
Divine activity, outside the Trinity itself, follows the same
pattern. First, God creates the universe; that is something
like a separation. Creatures, by following the natural law
implanted in them by God, reach their perfection, become

like him, and go back to him. Intelligent creatures love him in a conscious manner; through this love they unite themselves more and more closely with him, and so find their way back to him. The creature most completely filled with this love, filled with God himself, was the Immaculata, who never contracted the slightest stain of sin, who never departed in the least from God's will. United to the Holy Spirit as his spouse, she is one with God in an incomparably more perfect way than can be predicated of any other creature.

The first few sentences of this paragraph draw attention to that level that we most easily observe in creation, the procreative activity of creatures. Then, St. Maximilian moves our attention to an abstract meaning of what the union sought by creatures in their procreative activity represents – "Union means love, creative love" – and he goes on to speak about the determination towards a given perfection, which living creatures follow in their maturation and development. Philosophers of science apply the term, *teleology*, when referring to the observation that organisms mature in a fashion directed toward an end goal set by their given natures. If the conditions are right, the creature can mature naturally toward its perfection.

In this manner, St. Maximilian states that Creation, in all its forms, at its beginning stages, "is something like a separation." Creation implies a beginning. Though God is eternal, He creates in time. Living creatures begin their existences as seeds and conceptions, bursting with unimaginable potential; then as seedlings and embryos, multiplying cells, bustling with activity of incomprehensible wonder, they further develop according to the mysterious designs encoded within the genetic and epigenetic "blueprints" of their given natures. As they mature, they grow upward, toward that perfection implanted within them by their Creator. This growth in maturity leads to something like a "union" in perfection, and unintelligent creatures are moved toward this instinctively and biologically in a way that is analogical to "love." But, "intelligent creatures love him in a conscious manner;

through this love they unite themselves more and more closely with him, and so find their way back to him."

The primary way in which we, as human beings, share in God's "image" is in our spiritual capacity for rational thought and in the potential we possess, linked to our rationality, to freely choose what we rationally recognize as true and good, the "natural moral law."[133] This capacity allows for the possibility of a real communion of love with God, a covenant. This intellectual capacity and freedom is also reflective of the interactive relationships among the Persons of the Blessed Trinity.

Recall that in the prologue of St. John's Gospel, Christ is referred to as "the Word", "the Logos," (cf. Jn 1:1-18) of God. We can say that He is the Father's eternal expression of thought. God's thought is so completely conveyed and expressed in His Word that there is nothing left wanting. Therefore, God's Word itself is God (cf. Jn 1:1). The same can be said of the Holy Spirit. The love between the Father and the Son, the Word, is so totally and completely communicated that nothing is left wanting. Therefore, this Love, which always chooses that which is true and good, as expressed in the Word and as spoken, or "begotten," by the Father (cf. Jn 14:26; 16:13-14), is also God. So, in God's nature, His divinity, these three relating Persons are One; but in their dynamic, intimate life, they are Three.

The human moral capacity reflects the Trinitarian order of procession. The Word that is spoken eternally by the Father is what is loved by the Father, and the Father who speaks this Word is, in turn, loved by the Word: Thus, among the Father, His Word, and their Love, the Holy Spirit, there is a dynamically flowing current of Truth and Love. In like manner, we, as created beings of God, are not free to determine what is true and good for ourselves (cf. Gn 2:17). Our rational natures possess a capacity that we call "conscience," a capacity to recognize and identify, in given situations, that which is true and good, which we call the "natural moral law." Though our wills are free to choose evil, our consciences allow us to recognize the choice that our intellects confess to us in truth to be good. The integral uni-

---

[133] cf. CCC, 195.

ty of the mind does not allow for, what some psychologists refer to as, unresolved *cognitive dissidence*. If we deliberately choose folly, we sense our guilt (though there are limitations to this brought on by our present fallen condition).[134] We are then faced with the choice of either repenting of our sin or of further abusing our capacity for reason and conscience by "rationalizing" our previous choice[s]. If we choose the latter, we then find ourselves in the unenviable position of those "who call evil good and good evil" (Is 5:20). The true love of God aids us to choose and carry out the will of God, as recognized in the natural moral law. We should be able to recognize the Trinitarian image here, in the reflection of God's Word in the natural law and His Love reflective and evidenced in our willingness to abide by the Word as conveyed through our consciences.

The biblical story of Creation draws attention to this moral capacity bestowed upon human beings: Adam was given the intellectual capacity to name the various creatures of Creation (cf. Gn 2:19), and even the moral authority to rule over Creation (cf. Gn 1:28–31). But man was warned not to eat "of the tree of the knowledge of good and evil" (Gn 2:17), an action that implies a kind of experimental or experiential testing of moral truth, a testing that expresses a distrust in the goodness and truthfulness of God (cf. Gn 3:5). When the serpent tempted our first parents, he did so with a lie proposed to cast the good intentions and truthfulness of God under a cloud of suspicion: "You will not die. For God knows that when you eat of it your eyes will be opened, and you will be like God, knowing good and evil" (Gn 3:4-5). With the fall that resulted from original sin, the human capacity to easily recognize the truth and follow it became impaired, though not completely destroyed.[135] At the root of this impairment is the inherited cloud of suspicion of God's goodness and the goodness of His moral order for human beings, infecting both the clarity of their intellects and the inclination of their wills.[136] This resulting fog of mind and ambivalence of heart hampers the witness

---

[134] cf. *CCC*, 1960.

[135] cf. *CCC*, 405.

[136] cf. *D et V*, 37.

that ought to be borne by every human being to the truth, goodness and beauty of God.

There is one human creature, though, who expresses God's "image" and "likeness" to a supreme degree of perfection, whose "soul magnifies the Lord" (Lk 1:46). St. Maximilian concludes in paragraph 17 that, "United to the Holy Spirit as His spouse, she is one with God in an incomparably more perfect way than can be predicated of any other creature." In fact, with Mary, we are no longer speaking merely about a human "image" or "likeness" to God based on *moral* capacity, for she is more like a perfectly transparent, "Immaculate," window unto the Love of God, His Holy Spirit: For "if you are led by the Spirit you are not under the law" (Gal 5:18). In Mary, there is no question of her obedience to God's moral law. She reflects and participates in the fruitful love of God in an infinitely more perfect way than that expressed through moral conformity: "Can a woman forget her suckling child, that she should have no compassion on the son of her womb?" (Is 49:15). She is completely moved by compassion for her divine Son, a living expression of the Spirit of God that fills her soul without measure, that bears the fruit of the Incarnation in her womb. Therefore, St. Maximilian shows throughout the remainder of his *spiritual testament* that Mary, in her role as "spouse" of the Holy Spirit, spouse of "the principle of life in the whole supernatural order of grace" (paragraph 25), stands in an intermediary position between God and His creation, in a capacity of ineffable union with the divine mission of the Holy Spirit, together with whom she has become "the source of new life" (*ibid.*). Just as the intermediary role exercised by the Holy Spirit depends upon, rather than detracts from, Christ as the "one mediator between God and men" (1 Tm 2:5; also, cf. Jn 6:44), so also does the Love of the Immaculate Heart of Mary.

The intimacy of life and love shared by Mary and the Holy Spirit draws her, without any restraint, into the very intimate life of God in the Mystery of His Blessed Trinity. Her acts of procreation and love do not merely "image" the intimate life of God in His Trinity, rather she participates in a universally maternal manner in the expression of the Holy Trinity's action in the *oikonomia*, that is, God's works in

Creation. St. Maximilian states in paragraphs 19-20 that,

> Among creatures made in God's image the union brought about by married love is the most intimate of all (cf. Mt 19:6). In a much more precise, more interior, more essential manner, the Holy Spirit lives in the soul of the Immaculata, in the depths of her being. He makes her fruitful from the very first instant of her existence, all during her life, and for all eternity.
>
> This eternal "Immaculate Conception" (which is the Holy Spirit) produces in an immaculate manner divine life itself in the womb (or depths) of Mary's soul, making her the Immaculate Conception, the human Immaculate Conception. And the virginal womb of Mary's body is kept sacred for him; there he conceives in time – because everything that is material occurs in time – the human life of the Man-God.

In the Franciscan school of thought, of which St. Maximilian was an exemplary student, the *mystery of the Incarnation* (the next mystery in importance in the Christian faith, after that of the Blessed Trinity) is not merely an incredible work of God accomplished in order to affect the *Redemption* of the world, as though it were merely an afterthought of God, intended solely to *remedy* the problem of evil and sin following the fall of Creation. Even before the fall and original sin, the Father had already intended that the Incarnation of the Second Person of the Blessed Trinity, the Word of God, be accomplished in time, as a means of more completely revealing to His Creation the fullness of truth about Himself, "that they may have life, and have it abundantly" (Jn 10:10). According to the speculation arrived at in the Franciscan school, when this plan of God about the mystery of the Incarnation became known to the angels, it triggered an envious reaction from some of them about God's intended condescension toward human beings, and particularly toward the predestined Virgin Mary, destined to become the mother of the Incarnate Son of God, and, thus, to be raised above them all in glory. The Letter to the Hebrews confirms the remarkable condescension that God made towards human beings, despite the fact that the angels more closely share His spiritual nature:

> It was not to angels that God subjected the world to come, of which we are speaking. It has been testified somewhere, "What is man that you are mindful of him, or the son of man, that you care for Him? You made him for a little while lower than the angels, you have crowned him with glory and honor, putting everything in subjection under his feet." (Heb 2:5-8)

The Book of Wisdom testifies that, although from the beginning of Creation "God created man for incorruption, and made him in the image of his own eternity ... *through the devil's envy* death entered the world" (Ws 2:24). The Book of Revelation provides some enlightening imagery of this envious rebellion initiated by some of the angels. St. John witnessed in a vision that "the great dragon ... that ancient serpent, who is the Devil and Satan, the deceiver of the whole world ... was thrown down to the earth, and his angels were thrown down with him" (Rv 12:9), and that "his tail swept down a third of the stars of heaven, and cast them to the earth" (Rv 12:4). As we examined in the previous chapter, this rebellion took place immediately after "God's temple in heaven was opened, and the ark of his covenant was seen within the temple ... And a great sign appeared in heaven, a woman clothed with the sun, with the moon under her feet, and on her head a crown of twelve stars" (Rv 11:19, 12:1). Thus, it can be argued that the rebellion of certain angels in heaven was prompted by the appearance of "a woman clothed with the sun ... who was about to bear a child ... who is to rule all the nations with a rod of iron ..." (Rv 12:1,4,5). Since the angels, God's messengers, would have been to some degree privy to God's plan before He carried it out, this rebellion could have happened very early at the dawn of Creation, as indicated by the Book of Genesis.

Satan brought death into the world by deceiving our first parents. He exploited a *weakness* he saw in human nature. Unlike the angels, human beings do not have direct knowledge of God but must gain knowledge through the medium of their senses. We must trust in God's Revelation, both in the beauty of His Creation and in His Word, and we must discern His goodness through His providential works. No matter what Satan's motivation may have been, by his actions he became the very antithesis of what he was called to be: the title "angel" means "messenger," and the name "Lucifer" means "light-bearer." In his scheme of deception, Lucifer became, in an instant, "the father of lies" (Jn 8:44). The deception of the devil sowed distrust into the hearts of human beings by placing God's intentions under suspicion. In the Franciscan school of thought, God had always intended to supply for this *limitation* in human nature through the gift of the Mystery of the *Incarnation*, in which He had always intended for the predestined Mother of God to play an integral role. By the *Incarnation*, God is most capable of raising human beings ever more near to His divine perfection, through the most perfect human expression of communion as conveyed by the lives of Jesus and Mary.

This train of thought helps to make sense of God's targeted wording in the *protoevangelium* of Genesis 3:14, 15: "The Lord God said to the serpent, 'Because you have done this ... I will put enmity between you and the woman, and between your seed and her seed; he shall bruise your head, and you shall bruise his heel." God, knowing the envy that motivated "the serpent," refers directly to the object of Satan's envy, "the woman," and "her seed."

This "enmity" that God would establish between Satan and "the woman" implied that God would set a strict limit on the process of corruption, which Satan had just set in motion with his deception. Though the menacing result of that corruption would "bruise" "the woman ... and her seed" with pain and suffering, it would not infect them with its contamination. Here the ancient symbol of the serpent biting its own tail proves to be cogently applicable. God was not fooled by the devil's treason. He did not have to scrap one plan and begin another. God was not sent reeling by the fall to come up with some clever means, within the parameters He had already set into His Creation, in which to bring about its reformation. From the evil set into motion by Satan, God draws out His greatest good: The redemption of all Creation. Satan provided God with the opportunity to supremely display, in time, to all of Creation, the infinite immensity of His love, compassion and mercy. The creative and fruitful love of God, as would be expressed through the mystery of His Incarnation, was now able to assume an expression of a greater depth and dimension. Through the mystery of the Incarnation, the Father's only begotten Son, for love of His Father and all of us, would willingly take on a redemptive/salvific mission, for which we can all rejoice, with the words of the *Exsultet*, sung during the Easter Vigil in the Latin Rite, "O happy fault! O necessary sin of Adam, which gained for us so great a Redeemer!"

The Incarnation brings the divine activity of creative love to its point of return to the Father. In the Incarnate Word's act of total self-surrender to the will of the Father, Christ, in His human nature, *repaired* the original offense given to God at the beginning of Creation, and opened the way for the full participation of all of Creation in the intimacy of God's own Life. The consideration of "the woman" in the *economy* of God's plan is not an afterthought, a merely incidental placement of a character in the performance of a divine drama. Rather, her consideration in the *economy* is integral to all that follows in the providential unfolding of God's plan from its very beginning, second only to the consideration of the great mystery of the Incarnation of the divine Word, her Son.

Though she was created later in close anticipation of "the fullness of time" (Gal 4:4) in which the Incarnation of her Son took place within her, she was not an afterthought in God's plan. In God's *wisdom*, which "was set up, at the first, before the beginning of the earth" (Prv 8:23), and "was beside [God], like a master workman" (Prv 8:30), she is His masterpiece. Where all other creatures express to a limited degree the divine activity in their created forms, in accord with the eternal wisdom of God's plan, the Mother of God participates in the total and ultimate fulfillment of the continually unfolding economy of Creation/Incarnation/Redemption:

And so the return to God (which is love), that is to say the equal and contrary reaction, follows a different path from that found in creation. The path of creation goes from the Father through the Son and by the Holy Spirit; this return trail goes from the Spirit through the Son back to the Father; in other words, by the Spirit the Son becomes incarnate in the womb of the Immaculata; and through this Son love returns to the Father. (paragraph 21)

And she (the Immaculata), grafted into the Love of the Blessed Trinity, becomes from the first moment of her existence and forever thereafter the "complement of the Blessed Trinity." (paragraph 22)

Insight into Sister Lucia's Vision at Tuy

In the light of St. Maximilian's insight into the Blessed Virgin Mary's self-identification at Lourdes as the "Immaculate Conception" and what those words imply, Sister Lucia's vision at Tuy, can assume in our minds a new dimension. Let us look again at this symbolic vision, recalling that Sister Lucia said, "I understood that it was the mystery of the Most Holy Trinity which was shown to me and I received lights about this mystery which I am not permitted to reveal."[137]

We do not know whether some of the "lights" Sister Lucia received regarding the mystery of the Holy Trinity align with the insight provided by St. Maximilian. But, if she would have attempted to explain something about the mystery of the Most Holy Trinity in a way that was at all similar to what St. Maximilian explained, it would likely have cast a very critical cloud over the entire message of Fatima, or, at least, over Sister Lucia's competence as a messenger.

From personal conversations I have had with devout individuals who have studied St. Maximilian's writings, individuals I have met during my travels with the International Pilgrim Statue of Fatima, even St. Maximilian, with all his grasp of philosophy and Catholic theology, and his heroic witness to his faith, is considered by many to be *too extreme* in his devotion to Mary and in his teaching on her

---

[137] Notes of Fr. Gonzales, *Documents*, 394.

role in our redemption and sanctification. It seems to me, though, that the position and intellectual light that St. Maximilian provides is a providential aid for integrally drawing together and better understanding all that the Church already proclaims about Mary. The position held by St. Maximilian is carefully thought out and fits well with all that has been revealed. Whereas, the contrary opinions I've heard were mere reactions to the sheer magnitude of the place he held for Mary in his theology and devotion.

The question that one must ask in regard to Mary is whether God willingly created His mother in such a fashion so as to make her capable of assuming the spiritual maternity of "the rest of her offspring" (Rv 12:17). Since God is omnipotent, we cannot say that He is incapable of doing this. As we have seen, Sacred Scripture and the Church already teach this about Mary; it is the duty of theologians to show how this is so, according to the *economy* of Salvation. If we are all called to "become partakers of the divine nature" (2 Pt 1:4), then we should not be surprised that God has called His own mother to partake in His own nature in "an incomparably more perfect way than can be predicated of any other creature."[138] Knowing that God commands us to "Honor your father and mother," (Dt 5:16), we should expect that God honors, without measure, the one He predestined from all eternity to bear Him into the world.

It seems to me the reactionary position is based upon a fear that exalting the Mother of God *too much* somehow lessens the praise rightfully directed only toward her Son, when in fact the opposite is true. As we have already seen, true devotion to Mary is very efficient at dispelling "errors" of every kind, and a right understanding of Mary guides us into a right understanding of and relationship with her Son.

As Jesus promised about the Holy Spirit, so we can likewise extend to Mary, that she will "bring to your remembrance all that I have said to you" (Jn 14:26) and "will guide you into all the truth" (Jn 16:13). St. Maximilian, in particular, seemed to have understood this. The insight he has provided shows that, since the mystery of the

---

[138] *Testament*, paragraph 16.

Incarnation of the Word is of central and primary consideration in the *economy* of grace, God's chosen instrument in the achievement of this supreme divine project within Creation is similarly of central importance and integral to understanding well everything that devolves outward from this center. It is in this light that the insight provided by St. Maximilian becomes invaluable for examining Sister Lucia's vision at Tuy in all its rich symbolism.

The vision presents to us the *economy* of the Most Blessed Trinity at and above the Sacramental dimension of the work of our Salvation, a dimension that St. Maximilian's *spiritual testament* does not cover, but one, we can be confident, he does not overlook. His linking of the role of Mary to the work of the Blessed Trinity within Creation directly with the mystery of the Incarnation is foundational to understanding her relationship to all other matters that proceed from this in the *economy* of God's works in creation.

St. Maximilian's argument shows that Mary's relationship to the Blessed Trinity transcends and is prior to the mediation that Christ provides by the gift of Himself through His sacraments to the rest of humanity, which, we have discerned from St. John's Gospel, was something for which Mary particularly interceded. The sacraments are a merciful extension of the life of Christ to us. Her life, however, was and is defined by His total and unmediated manifestation and presence to her "in an incomparably more perfect way than can be predicated of any other creature."[139] The holiness she was granted was not mediated through the sacraments; rather, it was bestowed directly by her Son and her divine spouse, the Holy Spirit. She herself was the physical, instrumental cause of His *Sacred Humanity*, which, in turn, is the physical, instrumental cause of the grace of the sacraments. Fr. Garrigou-Lagrange, O.P., in his book, *The Mother of the Savior and Our Interior Life*, stated that,

> According to the teaching of St. Thomas [Aquinas] and many other theologians, the Sacred Humanity is a physical instrumental cause of grace, an instrument always united

---

[139] *Testament*, paragraph 16.

to the divinity and higher than the sacraments, which are instruments separated from the divinity.

St. Thomas has treated of this question in many places in so far as it refers to Christ, the Head of the Church (IIIa, q. 8, a. 2, ad I; q. 13, a. 2; q. 48, a. 6; q. 49, a. I; q. 50, a. 6; q. 62, a. I, and *De Potentia*, q. 6, a. 4.). It is but reasonable to ask if something similar to what he says about the Head may be affirmed of her who is, according to the teaching of Tradition, as it were the neck of the Mystical Body which unites the Head to the members and transmits the vital impulse to them.[140]

Lucia's vision shows that Mary, in her *extraordinary* position and capacity, assumes an essential role in mediating sacramental grace – the *ordinary means* by which God has chosen to confer grace on the rest of humanity. In God's plan, God has assumed His Sacred Humanity from Mary by her *fiat* and retains it for all eternity as a means for communicating His grace of divinity. We see in the vision the connection between the Sacred Humanity of Christ and His sacraments, and Mary's total unity of intention with her Son. The vision shows the essential link of the sacraments with the Passion of Christ, and how all graces are bestowed "by virtue of the merits of Jesus Christ, Savior of the human race,"[141] as especially merited in superabundance in His Passion and Death on the cross.[142] The graces bestowed by instrumentality of the sacraments are imaged in the Blood flowing down upon the Eucharist and into the chalice. But we also see a superabundant overflowing of the benevolence of God as expressed in Christ's Passion – a merciful extension of the merits of Christ's Passion and further reach of Mary's intercession and mediation – in the *grace and mercy* that flow out from the left hand of our Lord. Christ exercises His office of priesthood by offering Himself to the Father. He is both priest and victim. The possibility of participating with Him in

---

[140] (Tan Books and Publishers, Inc., Rockford, Il. 1993), 202-203

[141] Pius IX, *Ineffabilis Deus*.

[142] cf. *CCC*, 1076.

this priestly act of self-offering is extended to all people sacramentally in Baptism.[143] With His mother, however, this participation was lived out perfectly throughout her life from the first moment of her conception, in tandem with the Holy Spirit and in union with her Son's self-offering, prior to and apart from the sacramental dispensation, a dispensation that she cooperates in bringing about by the total gift of herself, as represented in the offering of her Heart.

If we apply here an analogy of the movement of God's grace to that of the physical movement of electricity in nature, we know that a material conductor and a completed circuit are required in order for electricity to flow. Both at the Annunciation and at the foot of the cross (and presumably everywhere in between), Mary supplied the personal conductivity and completed circuitry for the movement of the Love of the Holy Spirit, not only to return to the Father through the Son, but also to help further extend God's *grace and mercy* to the rest of humanity through the *economy* of her Immaculate Heart.

Although this analogy has its limitations (a material conductor is not *personally* moved by the flow of electricity), like the analogy of "a single chain" referred to by St. Maximilian, it can help us to imagine the role assumed by Mary in the communication of the graces of the Holy Spirit. It was "by the Holy Spirit" that our Lord "was incarnate of the Virgin Mary, and became man"[144] and, thus, given a body by which He could further extend His tangible presence through His sacraments. Just as our Lord told His Apostles at the Last Supper, "it is to your advantage that I go away, for if I do not go away, the Counselor [the Holy Spirit] will not come to you; but if I go, I will send him to you" (Jn 16:7); so, also, at the beginning of His public life He told His mother, "O woman, what have you to do with me? My hour has not yet come" (Jn 2:4). His hour is the painful moment of His departure, the moment that opened up the new dispensation of the sanctifying grace of the Holy Spirit through the sacraments, completing a circuit of self-offering love between God and His creation in the union of His most Sacred Heart and that of the Immaculate

[143] cf. *CCC*, 1141.
[144] *Nicene Creed*

Heart of His mother. This is the furnace of love in which the rest of humanity is sacramentally enabled to participate, and overflows in an abundance of *grace and mercy*. The movement of the Holy Spirit in connection with the Paschal mystery, in which our Lord forged the repair for the sin of Adam and of all mankind, bears with it the fruit of Himself, the fruit of the *tree of life*, to allow, through the sacraments, that conductivity and circuitry to be perpetuated and extended throughout His redeemed creation. As God's *grace and mercy* is extended in the conductivity forged by the participation of Mary in His Passion, so can be expected a further extension of His *grace and mercy* with the further responses of the rest of her offspring who participate sacramentally, in a worthy manner, in the Paschal sacrifice of her Son.

It is the combined role of the Holy Spirit and of Mary, in dispensing the graces of the Holy Spirit, to draw human hearts ever closer to the Heart of Christ by their repenting of deeply rooted habits of sin and willingly uniting with Christ's own priestly self-offering to His Father. Mary, displaying her Immaculate Heart to us in her hand, shows us a heart opened to the fullness of the truth of her Son, in all its painful consequences.

Recall that, during the presentation of her Son in the temple, the holy Simeon prophesied directly to Mary, saying, "this child is set for the fall and rising of many in Israel, and for a sign that is spoken against (and a sword will pierce through your own soul also), that thoughts out of many hearts may be revealed" (Lk 2:34-35). That last phrase, "that thoughts out of many hearts may be revealed," seems to reveal something very central to God's intended effect of the grace of His Holy Spirit within the human heart.

In St. John Paul II's encyclical, *Dominum et Vivificantem, On the Holy Spirit in the Life of the Church and the World*, he centers primarily on the theme of a particular point of Christ's prophetic description of the mission of the Holy Spirit, as recorded in St. John's Gospel: "And when he comes, he will convince the world concerning sin ... because they do not believe in me" (Jn 16:8, 9). In the Gospel, it is precisely the rejection and condemnation of Christ that is the *evidence* that the Holy Spirit draws upon in order to "convince the world concerning sin" in man.[145] The fact that God in the flesh is rejected by man, of course, says more about man than it does about God. This action of the Holy Spirit to "convince the world concerning sin" sets into motion the reversal of sin at its roots, in the original disobedience at the tree of the knowledge of good and evil, because "at the root of sin is the lie which is a radical *rejection of the truth* contained in the Word of the Father."[146] The image of Mary standing at the foot of the cross holding out her Immaculate Heart to us in a compassionate plea for our consideration of the various degrees of our separation from her divine Son, extends the reach of the Holy Spirit in His effort to "convince the world concerning sin."

Sentiments common to the human heart find it difficult to remain indifferent in the face of the suffering of Christ, especially when it witnesses that suffering shared by the tender sorrow of the Immaculate Heart of His own mother. I myself was struck by the potency of this imagery while watching Mel Gibson's famous cinematic representation of *The Passion of the Christ* and listening to the reactions of others who also watched the film. Despite the very raw depictions representing the sufferings Christ endured for our salvation, everyone seemed to be in agreement that the most emotionally moving parts of the film were those where the sorrowful reactions of Christ's mother were depicted. The human heart is made in the image and likeness of the Triune God. Scripture confirms this natural correspondence of *tender compassion,* which ought to reign within every human heart, when it warns, "Today, when you hear His voice, do not harden your hearts" (Heb 4:7; cf. also 3:7-9, 15; Ps 95:7-11, 81:13; Dt 15:7; etc.).

Despite our fallen condition, we are most naturally disposed to the appeal of the tenderness of God's love as expressed through the familial relationship between the Son of God and His most holy Mother. We know that in the Old Testament, the Holy Spirit had already drawn an analogy of His love from that of a mother for her

---

[145] cf. *D et V.* 27, 31.

[146] *ibid.,* 33.

child. Speaking through the prophet Isaiah about His compassion, the Holy Spirit asked, "Can a woman forget her suckling child, that she should have no compassion on the son of her womb?" (Is 49:15). And again, the prophecy of Zechariah is most applicable:

> And I will pour out on the house of David and the inhabitants of Jerusalem a spirit of compassion and supplication, so that, when they look on him whom they have pierced, they shall mourn for him, as one mourns for an only child, and weep bitterly over him, as one weeps over a first-born....
>
> On that day there shall be a fountain opened for the house of David and the inhabitants of Jerusalem to cleanse them from sin and uncleanness. (12:10, 13:1)

The Spirit of God bears witness to the Word of God (especially as it is displayed to us in the Paschal Mystery), that "the word of God is living and active, sharper than any two-edged sword, piercing to the division of soul and spirit, of joints and marrow, and discerning the thoughts and intentions of the heart" (Heb 4:12). So, as St. John Paul II explains in his encyclical, "Conversion *requires convincing of sin*; it includes the interior judgment of the conscience, and this, being a proof of the action of the Spirit of truth in man's inmost being, becomes at the same time a new beginning of the bestowal of grace and love."[147] We see in the vision given to Sister Lucia at Tuy, an image of the joint mission of the Holy Spirit and Mary; she whose "own soul also" was "pierced" "that thoughts out of many hearts may be revealed" (Lk 2:35). She aids the Holy Spirit in obtaining for these "many hearts" the predisposition necessary for the fruitful participation in the sacraments of her Son.

After the fall of Adam and Eve in the Garden of Eden, God barred the way to the garden, by placing a "cherubim [with] a flaming sword, which turned every way, to guard the way to the tree of life" (Gn 3:24), in order that man might not "put forth his hand and take also of the tree of life, and eat, and live forever" (Gn 3:22). The

---

[147] *D et V*, 31.

way to the "tree of life" has been reopened for human beings by the Passion, Death and Resurrection of Jesus Christ, and its fruit is to be found in the sacraments of the Church, especially the Eucharist. This is not to say, however, that we are now free to simply "put forth [our] hand and take" of the sacraments without first making an appropriate examination of the thoughts of our hearts.[148] The Paschal Mystery and the Sacred Liturgy are patterned, in such a way, as to elicit the conversion of our hearts and to allow them to be shaped according to the sacrificial self-offering of Christ. By the initiating sacrament of Baptism, every believer in Christ is indelibly marked by the priesthood of Christ's own self-offering to the Father. The hope for a *triumph* of grace in the world hinges upon the correspondence of our hearts with the self-offering of Christ. Joined with the Immaculate Heart of Mary at the foot of the cross (as is made sacramentally real at every Eucharistic Liturgy), every believer is called to further the extension and reach of God's *grace and mercy*, "and in [their own] flesh … complete what is lacking in Christ's afflictions for the sake of his body, that is, the Church" (Col 1:24). This is something that Mary did in a total and universal manner through her role in the Paschal mystery.

As we will see in the following chapter, this element of allowing Mary and the grace of the Holy Spirit to convert our hearts to the fullness of Christ, especially as He is given to us in the sacraments and the liturgy, is of central importance to understanding the message given by Mary at Fatima, and the key to obtaining the triumph of the Immaculate Heart of Mary and a new outpouring of the grace of the Holy Spirit throughout the world.

---

[148] cf. *CCC* 1385; also, 1 Cor 11:27-29.

CHAPTER III

HEART OF THE MATTER

Up to this point, we have been closely examining the solid ground upon which to base an insightful interpretation of the message given by Mary at Fatima that devotion to her Immaculate Heart be established. We have seen how the particular vision given to Sister Lucia in her convent at Tuy, Spain, is very helpful for depicting Mary's intimate relationship with the Holy Trinity and her role in maternally mediating the grace of God, as obtained from her divine Son in His Passion. Having given adequate attention to the foundation and development of the revealed truths upon which the message of Fatima securely rests, we are now prepared to focus more exclusively on the particular message itself, so latent with the potency for bringing peace to the world by reconciling human hearts more completely with the Heart of God in Christ. We will begin by focusing more closely on another symbolic vision that Sister Lucia had and described in detail, the very last part of the message of Fatima made known to the public, the so-called *third secret* of Fatima.

After great deliberation, St. John Paul II released the *third secret* to the public on June 26 during the Great Jubilee of the year 2000, along with a suitable commentary provided by the Prefect of the Congregation for the Doctrine of the Faith, Joseph Cardinal Ratzinger, the future Pope Benedict XVI. Although the commentary is well-suited for the purposes it was intended to serve, neither the pope nor the prefect intended for that commentary to be an exhaustive exposition of the *third secret*, precluding any further examination and interpretation. The commentary is about five pages in length and only half of that falls under the heading, *"An attempt to interpret the 'secret' of Fatima,"* in which the prefect examines its "single images." The first half of the commentary outlines the guidelines that should govern any Catholic who intends to examine any vision of private revelation.

Like the vision given at Tuy, Spain, this vision is also rich in symbolic meaning, where the only words spoken are not by Mary, but by "an Angel with a flaming sword" who "cried out in a loud voice: 'Penance, Penance, Penance!'" Understanding the meaning of what this vision is alluding to, thus, depends primarily upon gaining an accurate interpretation of the symbolism it utilizes. Nothing of what follows below in any way contradicts what was highlighted by the prefect in his commentary, but in some instances I do attempt to further develop his insights.

We will notice that the vision of the *third secret* is capable of neatly knitting together the many and varied elements of the Fatima message into an integrated whole. The vision provides a framework, or paradigm, that our minds can more easily *see, grasp* and *digest*. By meaningfully arranging the various elements of the message into this framework, we will then be better able to understand the message as a whole and how those various elements relate to each other, to the Gospel and to our current situation in salvation history. With this understanding, we will then be better equipped to implement into our own lives the devotions that Our Lady said would hasten the triumph of her Immaculate Heart in the world.

The Secret of Fatima

The vision of the *third secret* was shown to the three children of Fatima during the July 13, 1917 apparition. It followed the other two parts of the secret: the vision of hell, and the warning of the possibility of another "worse" war to come and a new menace in the world coming from "Russia." Although Mary did not speak at all in the third part of the *secret*, the second part provides some verbal context for the vision. Sister Lucia herself affirmed this connection when she wrote to St. John Paul II in a letter on May 12, 1982:

> The third part of the 'secret' refers to Our Lady's words:
> 'If not, [Russia] will spread her errors throughout the

world, causing wars and persecutions of the Church. The good will be martyred; the Holy Father will have much to suffer; various nations will be annihilated."[149]

The message with its "secrets" is the pivotal part of the overall message given at Fatima. Everything hinges on the veracity of what Mary prophetically communicated at that noon hour. Even the secular local government leaders became obsessed with knowing the secret. The children were arrested immediately prior to the scheduled time of the August apparition and threatened with torturous death if they refused to disclose the secret. The children's unanimity in fidelity to Mary's request that they confidentially retain its secrecy, even while isolated from one another during their frightful interrogations, lends further credence to the veracity of the whole message.

Further, it was at the beginning of the July apparition when, in response to Lucia's pleading, Our Lady told Lucia, "In October I will tell you who I am and what I wish, and *I will perform a miracle that everyone will see in order to make them believe.*" Ultimately, though, the accurate unfolding of the historic events prophesied in the secret would become its own best confirmation. These were passed on to legitimate Church authorities within the time frame by which Sister Lucia was inspired to do so, with remarkable precision in anticipation of their dreaded developments. Still, this part of the Fatima message can only be fully understood within the greater context of the whole message of Fatima and of what is revealed in Sacred Scripture and Tradition. For this reason, we will read the text of the *third secret* within the context of the message that preceded it. Then, we will proceed from there to assemble its whole structure, based on the foundation that has already been laid down in the previous chapters. What follows is Sister Lucia's description of that pivotal event of July 13, 1917, recorded in her *Fourth Memoir*, along with the third part of the secret that was made known to the public on June 26, 2000:

---

[149] Cardinal Ratzinger, *Commentary on the Third Secret*, taken from *Fatima for Today: The Urgent Marian Message of Hope* (San Francisco: Ignatius Press, 2010), 281.

Some moments after we arrived at Cova da Iria, near the holm oak amongst a big crowd of people, when we were praying the Rosary, we saw the radiance of light and afterwards our Lady over the holm oak.

"What do you want of me?" I asked.

"I want you to come here on the thirteenth day of the coming month, and to continue to say the Rosary every day in honor of our Lady of the Rosary to obtain the peace of the world and the end of the war. For she alone will be able to help."

[Lucia] "I wish to ask you to tell us who you are and to perform a miracle so that everyone will believe that you appear to us!"

"Continue to come here every month. In October I will tell you who I am and what I wish, and I will perform a miracle that everyone will see in order to make them believe."

Here I made some requests that I don't remember exactly. What I remember is that our Lady said it was necessary to say the Rosary to obtain graces during the year. And she went on, "Sacrifice yourselves for sinners and say many times, especially when you make some sacrifice: 'Jesus it is for Your love, for the conversion of sinners and in reparation for the sins committed against the Immaculate Heart of Mary.'"

The First Part of the Secret

When the Lady spoke these last words, she opened her hands as she had in the two months before. The radiance seemed to penetrate the ground and we saw something like a sea of fire. Plunged in this fire were the demons and the souls, as if they floated about in the conflagration, borne by the flames which issued from it with clouds of smoke falling on all sides as sparks fell in great conflagrations without weight or equilibrium, among shrieks and groans of sorrow and despair that horrify and cause people to shudder with fear. It must have been when I saw this sight that I cried out, "Alas!" which people say they heard.

The devils were distinguished by horrible and loathsome forms of animals, frightful and unknown, but transparent like black coals that have turned red hot. Frightened, and as if we were appealing for help, we raised our eyes to our Lady who said with tenderness and sadness:

"You saw hell, where the souls of poor sinners go. To save them God wishes to establish in the world the devotion to my Immaculate Heart. If they do what I will tell you, many souls will be saved, and there will be peace.

The Second Part of the Secret

"The war is going to end. But if they do not stop offending God, another even worse war will begin in the reign of Pius XI.

"When you see a night illuminated by an unknown light, know that it is the great sign that God gives you that He is going to punish the world for its crimes by means of war, hunger, and persecutions of the Church and of the Holy Father [the Pope].

"To prevent this I will come to ask for the consecration of Russia to my Immaculate Heart and the Communion of reparation on the first Saturdays. If they listen to my requests, Russia will be converted and there will be peace. If not, she will spread her errors throughout the world, provoking wars and persecutions of the Church. The good will be martyred, the Holy Father will have much to suffer, and various nations will be annihilated. In the end my Immaculate Heart will triumph. The Holy Father will consecrate Russia to me, and it will be converted and a certain period of peace will be granted to the world. In Portugal the dogma of Faith will always be kept ..."[150]

[150] July 13, 1917 Apparition, *Fourth Memoir, Documents,* 439-440.

The Text of Sister Lucia's letter to the Pope describing the Third Part of the Secret

I write in obedience to you, my God, who command me to do so through his Excellency the Bishop of Leiria and through your Most Holy Mother and mine.

After the two parts which I have already explained, at the left of Our Lady and a little above, we saw an Angel with a flaming sword in his left hand; flashing, it gave out flames that looked as though they would set the world on fire; but they died out in contact with the splendor that Our Lady radiated towards him from her right hand: pointing to the earth with his right hand, the Angel cried out in a loud voice: "Penance, Penance, Penance!" And we saw in an immense light that is God: 'something similar to how people appear in a mirror when they pass in front of it' a Bishop dressed in White 'we had the impression that it was the Holy Father.' Other Bishops, Priests, men and women Religious going up a steep mountain, at the top of which there was a big Cross of rough-hewn trunks as of a cork-tree with the bark; before reaching there the Holy Father passed through a big city half in ruins and half trembling with halting step, afflicted with pain and sorrow, he prayed for the souls of the corpses he met on his way; having reached the top of the mountain, on his knees at the foot of the big Cross he was killed by a group of soldiers who fired bullets and arrows at him, and in the same way there died one after another the other Bishops, Priests, men and women Religious, and various lay people of different ranks and positions. Beneath the two arms of the Cross there were two Angels each with a crystal aspersorium in his hand, in which they gathered up the blood of the Martyrs and with it sprinkled the souls that were making their way to God.[151]

---

[151] Third Part of the Secret vision as described in a written letter by Sr. Lucia, dated 3/1/1944, Documents, 505-506.

Conclusion of the July 13 Apparition

"Tell this to no one. Francisco, yes, you may tell him. When you say the Rosary, say after each mystery, 'O my Jesus, pardon us and deliver us from the fire of hell. Draw all souls to heaven, especially those in most need.'"

After a short period of silence, I asked, "Do you want nothing more of me?"

"No, today I want nothing more of you."

And as usual, she began to arise towards the east and disappeared in the immense distance of the firmament.[152]

An Angel with a Flaming Sword

The third part of the secret begins with an image of "an Angel with a flaming sword in his left hand," which,

> flashing, it gave out flames that looked as though they would set the world on fire; but they died out in contact with the splendor that Our Lady radiated towards him from her right hand: pointing to the earth with his right hand, the Angel cried out in a loud voice: 'Penance, Penance, Penance!'

In our examination into the meaning of what is being symbolized here, let us begin by looking at Cardinal Ratzinger's own comments on these words:

> The angel with the flaming sword on the left of the Mother of God recalls similar images in the Book of Revelation. This represents the threat of judgment which looms over the world. Today the prospect that the world might be reduced to ashes by a sea of fire no longer seems pure fantasy: man himself, with his inventions, has forged the flaming sword. The vision then shows the power which stands opposed to the force of destruction–the splendor of

---

[152] July 13, 1917 Apparition, *Fourth Memoir, Documents*, 439-440.

the Mother of God and, stemming from this in a certain way, the summons to penance ..."[153]

Before the release of the third secret, there was much speculation about its contents. One of those speculative opinions wondered if it referred to the threat of a nuclear war, which has especially become a weight upon the human psyche since the "Enola Gay" dropped its explosive cargo on Hiroshima, Japan, on August 6, 1945. This speculation is confirmed by Cardinal Ratzinger's commentary, at least in reference to the "flaming sword." Some Fatima experts, like the late John Haffert, were convinced that part of the meaning of the great miracle of the sun was itself intended as a warning of the coming threat of nuclear devastation. Haffert, who wrote a book specifically about the miracle, commented that,

> To write a book about the "sun miracle" of 1917, as said before, I interrogated dozens upon dozens of living witnesses to recreate *what actually happened*. This event, unprecedented in the history of the world, was at once so awesome and terrible that it is virtually impossible for anyone who was not there to *realize* how terrifying it was. A *fireball*, which the crowd thought was actually the sun, plunged towards the earth over the mountain of Fatima. It was objectively real. It was not something created in the imaginations of those tens of thousands of witnesses. *Everyone* saw it! Furthermore, it was seen over a radius of 32 miles. *Everyone* who saw it, at least within a six mile radius, *thought it was the end of the world ... and they felt the heat.*[154]

In light of this description of the miracle of the sun, it is not a stretch of the imagination to draw a connection to the danger that emerged in the world with the advent of nuclear weapons. This part of the miracle of the sun took place at its conclusion. It was preceded by approximately twelve minutes of a delightfully wonderful

---

[153] *Fatima For Today*, 279-280.

[154] *Her Own Words to the Nuclear Age*, (Asbury, NJ: The 101 Foundation, 1993), 9-10.

spectacle, where the sun was capable of being observed by the na-
ked eye. During these twelve minutes, the sun appeared as a glowing
disk (some described it like a Host) that seemed to move and spin,
giving off a kaleidoscope of colors that settled upon everything in
sight. If the last part of this miraculous phenomenon is connected
with what Cardinal Ratzinger called, "the threat of judgment that
looms over the world," then the crime that most bears the guilt for
this "threat" can best be understood in direct relation to the abuse of
the very remedy that our Lord has prescribed for the spiritual health
of humankind.

In the context of the whole message, it seems plausible that
the meaning of the twelve minutes of wonder, which preceded this
"threat of judgment," symbolizes the graces that Christ has always
intended for humanity through the gift of Himself in the sacrament
of the Eucharist. The "threat of judgment" which follows is, particularly, a warning to us of what could be expected if His prescription
for humanity's healing is ignored or, even worse, abused. This interpretation seems quite applicable. If this Eucharistic connection is
made, then those who have speculated before its release that the *third
secret* is a reference to the growing crisis of faith that has beleaguered
the Church over the past decades are also in part correct. The crisis
of faith in the Real Presence of Christ in the Eucharist and, through
it, Christ's essential sacramental connection to all the faithful and the
rest of humanity and all Creation, is integrally central to any evalua-
tion of a crisis of faith within the Church and the world.

This Eucharistic connection fits very neatly with other elements
of the Fatima message. This becomes more apparent when we apply
another biblical reference to the image of the "Angel with a flaming
sword," after the fall in Paradise,

> The Lord God said, "Behold, the man has become like one
> of us, knowing good and evil; and now, *lest he put forth his
> hand and take also of the tree of life, and eat, and live for ever"*
> – therefore the Lord God sent him forth from the garden
> of Eden, to till the ground from which he was taken. He

drove out the man; and at the east of the garden of Eden *he placed the cherubim* [very high-ranking angels], *and a flaming sword which turned every way, to guard the way to the tree of life.* (Gn 3:22-24)

The Church has long affirmed that "... the Cross of Christ stands revealed as the [new] tree of life."[155] If Christ's Passion, Death and Resurrection reopened for human beings access to the "tree of life" in the sacraments, and if it has become a common practice for people to receive the sacraments, especially the Eucharist, without having properly prepared themselves – to unreflectively "*put forth* [their] *hand and take*" – then the image of the angel with a flaming sword assumes a fairly well-defined significance. In the greater context of the message, this definition is well-grounded.

Recall that the three children were visited three times by an angel during the year prior to the apparitions of Mary in 1917. Though Lucia did not know the specific dates of these visits, she recalled the first visit was in the spring, the second in the summer and the third in the fall. As the angel in the *third secret* vision cried out the word "Penance" three times, so in these three consecutive appearances of 1916, the angel first encouraged the children to pray a prayer of reparation, then to pray and make sacrifices, then to make Eucharistic reparation. In her *Second Memoir*, Sister Lucia recalls these appearances of the angel. In the first one, she describes how she and her cousins were approached by a "figure ... of great beauty... whiter than snow that the sun had rendered transparent as if it were made of crystal," who said to them,

> "Do not be afraid, I am the Angel of Peace. Pray with me." Kneeling on the ground, he prostrated himself until his forehead touched it and made us repeat three times, "My God, I believe, I adore, I hope [or, 'trust'] and I love You. I beg pardon of You for those who do not believe, do not adore, do not hope, and do not love You." Then arising, he

---

[155] From the antiphon for the 1st psalm, Office of Readings, week 1.

said, "Pray thus. The hearts of Jesus and Mary are attentive to the voice of your supplications."[156]

On the second occasion, the children were playing in the back-
yard of Lucia's home, and suddenly the angel appeared to them and
said,

> "What are you doing? Pray! Pray a great deal! The most
> holy hearts of Jesus and of Mary have merciful designs for
> you. Offer prayers and sacrifices constantly to the Most
> High."
> "How are we to make sacrifices?" I asked. The Angel
> replied, "In everything you can, offer a sacrifice as an act
> of reparation for sins by which He is offended, and of sup-
> plication for the conversion of sinners. Thus draw peace
> upon your country. I am its Guardian Angel, the Angel
> of Portugal. *Above all accept and endure with submission the
> suffering which the Lord will send you.*"[157]

In the final appearance of the angel, we come to the most perti-
nent part of his messages of the three angel appearances in regard to
the crisis of faith. It reveals the angel's incremental manner of edu-
cating the children in prayer and self-sacrifice so that their hearts cor-
responded more fully to the depths of the Faith. The angel appeared
to them while they were saying the prayer he had taught them in his
first appearance. The incident happened while they were pasturing
their sheep. Here is Lucia's description of the event:

> After lunch we decided to pray in the cave on the opposite
> side of the mount, so we made a turn through the ascent and
> we had to climb over some stones on the top of Pregueira.
> The sheep reached the place, but with difficulty. As soon
> as we arrived there, we fell to our knees and prostrated
> with our foreheads on the ground, repeated the Angel's
> prayer, "My God, I believe, I adore, I hope and I love you."

[156] *Second Memoir, Documents,* 339.
[157] *Ibid.*

I don't remember how many times we had repeated this prayer when we saw an unknown light glittering over our heads. We got up to see what was going on and we saw the Angel with a chalice in his left hand and suspended over it, a Host, from which drops of blood fell into the chalice.

Then, leaving the chalice suspended in the air, the angel knelt beside us and made us repeat three times:

"Most Holy Trinity, Father, Son and Holy Spirit, I offer You the most precious Body and Blood, Soul and Divinity of Jesus Christ present in all the tabernacles of the world, in reparation for the outrages, sacrileges and indifference with which He Himself is offended. And through the infinite merits of His Most Sacred Heart and of the Immaculate Heart of Mary, I beg the conversion of poor sinners."

Then rising, he took the Chalice and the Host in his hands. He gave the Holy Host to me and divided the Blood of the Chalice between Jacinta and Francisco, while he said, "Take and drink the Body and the Blood of Jesus Christ, horribly insulted by ungrateful men. Make reparation for their crimes and console your God." Prostrating anew on the ground, he repeated again with us the same prayer, "Most Holy Trinity, etc." and disappeared. We remained in the same position and repeated the same words without stopping. When we got up we saw it was evening and time to go home.[158]

We see here in this angelic intercession an attempt by the angel to repair for some offensive treatment of the *Bread of Life*, "the Body and Blood of Jesus Christ, horribly insulted by ungrateful men." The congruence of this angelic action, with the one in Genesis posting guard at the east of Eden, and the one crying for "Penance" in the *third secret*, appears too refined to be accidental. The Angel of Peace calls upon these innocent children to make atonement for the "out-

---

[158] *Ibid.*, 339-340.

rages, sacrileges, and indifference" of "ungrateful men," who offend
the sacred dignity of Christ's vulnerable presence in the Holy Eucharist, the sacrament specifically intended to communicate and cultivate the *Eternal Life* of God in human beings. In the Genesis account,
the guardian "cherubim" of the "tree of life" were posted with their
"flaming sword" precisely to protect against any prohibited advance
toward the *fruit* of the "tree of life." Thus, in consideration of the
image of the "Angel with the flaming sword" in the *third secret,* which
bears a "threat of judgment," it is not a stretch to conclude that this
corresponds rightly to the ignorant, careless or deliberate mistreat-
ment of the very remedy that God supplied for the healing of the
wounds of sin in the world – the Eucharist and other sacraments.

The seamless transition from the last appearance of the angel
in the fall of 1916 to the first appearance of Mary on May 13, 1917,
fits the order of Mary's intervention, as depicted in the *third secret.*
Recall that the flaming sword held by the angel in the beginning of
the *third secret* "gave out flames that looked as though they would
set the world on fire; but they died out in contact with the splendor
that Our Lady radiated toward him from her right hand." Thus, from
the angel to Our Lady, a transition from a threat of judgment to an
intervention of mercy occurs. In comparing and contrasting the interventions of the angel with those of Our Lady in the pages ahead,
we will see that Our Lady possesses a particular capacity for drawing
her children to fulfill the command of the angel for "Penance," and
for making Eucharistic reparation in a manner that affects a greater
interior correspondence of the human heart with the expressed will
of God. Mary's intervention, though preventing the threat of judgment, does so by inspiring a more consonant interior response to the
angel's call for reparation. Let us now look with greater depth at that
"splendor that Our Lady radiated" and come to understand better
what it most likely represents.

The Splendor that Our Lady Radiated

Sister Lucia's descriptions of the Fatima apparitions portray
Mary's active interventions as accomplished in the radiation of a su-

pernatural "light," which she directs and mediates by mere gestures of her hands, as we have already seen in the vision of the *third secret*. Sister Lucia's description of Mary's first apparition on May 13 is a perfect example:

> On May 13, 1917, while I was playing with Jacinta and Francisco on the top of the ascent of Cova da Iria, building a little wall of stones around a thicket, suddenly we saw a flash like lightning. "We should go home," I told my cousins. "That was lightning. It is possible it will thunder."
>
> "Yes," they replied.
>
> And we began to go down the ascent, driving the sheep in the direction of the road. When we were more or less at the middle of the ascent near a big ilex tree, we noticed more lightning and as soon as we went a little farther, we saw ahead of us, over a holm oak, a Lady dressed all in white. She was more brilliant than the sun, and radiated a light more clear and intense than a crystal glass filled with sparling water, when the rays of the burning sun shine through it. We stopped, surprised by the apparition. *We were so close that we stood within the radiance which surrounded her* and reached a distance of perhaps five feet.
>
> Then our Lady said, "Do not be afraid, I won't hurt you!"
>
> "Where does your Excellency come from?" I asked.
>
> "I am from Heaven."
>
> "And what is it you want of me?"
>
> "I have come to ask you to come here for six months in succession, on the thirteenth day at this same hour. Then I will tell you who I am and what I want. Afterwards, I will return here a seventh time.
>
> "And shall I go to Heaven, too?"
>
> "Yes, you will."
>
> "And Jacinta?"
>
> "Also."

"And Francisco?"

"Also, but he will have to say many Rosaries!"

Then I remembered to ask about two girls who had died recently. They were friends of mine and used to go to my house to learn weaving from my oldest sister.

"Is Maria das Neves now in Heaven?" I asked.

"Yes, she is."

I think she was about 16 years old.

"And Amelia?"

"She will be in purgatory until the end of the world."

I think she was about 18 or 20 years old when she died.

[Then Mary asked Lucia a question which went right to the heart of the matter, and Lucia's affirmative response to that question allowed *the splendor that Our Lady radiated* to affect the beginnings of a real transformation within their own hearts.]

"Do you wish to offer yourselves to God, to endure all the sufferings that He may be pleased to send you, as an act of reparation for the sins by which He is offended, and to ask for the conversion of sinners?"

"Yes, we do."

"Then you will have much to suffer, but the grace of God will be your comfort."

As she spoke these last words (the grace of God, etc.) she opened her hands for the first time, and from the palms came two streams of light so intense that they penetrated our breasts and reached the most intimate parts of our souls, making us see ourselves in God, who is that light, more clearly than in the best of mirrors. Then, forced by an interior impulse, we went down on our knees and we repeated intimately, "O most Holy Trinity, I adore You! My God, my God, I love You in the Most Blessed Sacrament."

Some moments later our Lady added, "Say the Rosary every day to obtain peace for the world and an end of the war."

Immediately after this, she began to rise, serenely going up towards the east until she disappeared in the immensity of the distance. The light which surrounded her was going ahead of her as though it was in charge of making way through the massive stars. This is why sometimes we said we had seen the Heavens open.[159]

What is truly remarkable is that Our Lady accomplishes, by the appearance of a supernatural "light" communicated directly into the interior of the children's innocent souls, an outcome far surpassing anything the angel could accomplish by his example and instruction to the children in the previous year. The grace that she communicates in the light, which Lucia equates with God "who is that light," provides valuable insight into the imagery of the *third secret* where that splendor that radiated from Mary is similarly represented. Although Mary's appearance to the children is considered in mystical theology to be an *extraordinary* grace (a grace not given in the ordinary course of purification and sanctification to which every person is called), the interior grace that Mary communicates to them, that "light" and love that she radiates and infuses into the depths of their souls, is considered to be an *ordinary* grace which God gives to souls for their purification and sanctification.[160] This grace is ordinary, not in the sense of being common, but in the sense that it is the usual way in which God operates in bringing souls to holiness. This is not to say that the *dramatic way* in which it was delivered to the children and received by them is in any way *ordinary*; rather, what Sister Lucia describes as happening within the depths of their souls, ought to be viewed as how God – gently and gradually – leads all people who are docile to His grace. What she describes is precisely Mary's mediation of God's purifying and sanctifying grace, which Lucia described as having, "penetrated our breasts and reached the most intimate parts of our souls ..." What

[159] May 13, 1917 Apparition, *Fourth Memoir, Documents*, 437-438.

[160] cf. *Fire Within*: Fr. Thomas Dubay, S.M., devotes the entirety of Chapter Eleven of this book to the subject of "infused contemplation" as the universal means by which God purifies and sanctifies souls.

happened in a very sensational and sudden manner to the children, we can all expect to happen in a more subtle, gentle and incremental way by Mary's intercession and mediation of the Holy Spirit, if we, also, trustingly surrender our lives to the will of God.

Now, recall in the vision of the *third secret*, the flames that flashed from the angel "died out in contact with the splendor that Our Lady radiated towards him from her right hand." Subsequently, Lucia describes seeing "an immense light that is God: 'something similar to how people appear in a mirror when they pass in front of it.'" Though Lucia doesn't make an explicit connection here between "the splendor that Our Lady radiated" and the "immense light that is God," she had already made this connection in her description of what happened in the two previous apparitions in May and June. What Lucia describes as having subjectively experienced on those previous occasions, now in this vision she describes as an objective observer, while using the same analogies and metaphors. Both include a vision of the splendor that Our Lady radiated and the "immense light" that is God. In the *third secret*, the children saw "something similar to how people appear in a mirror when they pass in front of it," while in the May apparition, the light penetrated the depths of their souls, "making us see ourselves in God ... more clearly than in the best of mirrors."

Thus, she uses the image of a *mirror*, to describe the vision of the *third secret*, and also as a metaphor to describe the spiritual effect which that "light" had on her own soul. Might she have described for us here that grace spoken of by Simeon to Mary in the temple: "and a sword will pierce through your own soul also, that thoughts out of many hearts may be revealed" (Lk 2:35)? We have Lucia's description of her own experience of being radiated by that light that is God, and how it moved her interiorly. We also have her observation of the *heroic virtue* portrayed by those in the *third secret* whom she then saw "going up a steep mountain, at the top of which there was a big Cross of rough-hewn trunks." When the Church examines the life of an individual to consider that person for sainthood, one of the most important considerations she examines is whether that person lived a life of *heroic virtue*. Those depicted ascending the "steep mountain" display their holiness by their willingness to deny their own natural inclinations to self-preservation and bear the burden of the Gospel in the face of great opposition. Their heroic witness bears testimony to the grace of God that sustains them and is, therefore, evidence that they share in that same grace of interior correspondence to the will of God that Sister Lucia testified to sensing in the May 13 apparition.

The intensity and effect of this grace, as Sister Lucia described, is truly remarkable. The children seemed to become oblivious to the incredible beauty of the very vision of the Mother of God before them and instead were transfixed by the transcendent source of that beauty – the all-consuming light, which she communicated directly to the interior of their souls. Lucia explained that in that light, *"forced by an interior impulse*, we went down on our knees and we repeated intimately, 'O most Holy Trinity, I adore You! My God, My God, I love you in the Most Blessed Sacrament.'"* The light moved them interiorly to pray, without any instruction (like that which they received from the Angel), a prayer which acknowledges God in the most profound mysteries He has revealed to us, through Jesus, and handed down to us in His Church, and with an expression of the deepest affection of love and reverence towards Him. The "splendor," which Our Lady radiates, directs and dispenses, is nothing less than the very Spirit of God, the Spirit of Life, Love and Truth, the Holy Spirit, her Spouse.

The deepest and most direct communication of God's grace to a soul is called *infused contemplation*. In mystical theology, the grace of *infused contemplation* is often described as being almost imperceptible, like the "still small voice" that the prophet Elijah recognized on Mount Horeb (1 Kgs 19:12). This grace is known primarily by its effects, as our Lord's analogy about the effects of "the wind" in His conversation with Nicodemus: "You hear the sound of it, but you do not know where it comes from or where it goes" (Jn 3:8). The term "infused" indicates that it is an effect of the presence of the Spirit of God (or at least an effect of His activity) within the deepest recesses of the soul of the person, as Sister Lucia has dramatically described.

In mystical theology, a distinction is commonly made between *meditation* and *contemplation*. By *meditation* is usually meant a prayerful pondering upon specific words or actions or themes or events, etc., each of which can serve as a metaphorical "window," which opens up to inexhaustible, infinite and eternal mysteries. When a person meditates on such things, the Holy Spirit might draw that person more deeply into the mystery there alluded to, allowing for the possibility that they come to rest in a kind of faithful and trusting surrender to the mystery itself, whether it be that of God or of the things of God. Once brought to this state, that person can be said to abide in a form of prayerful *contemplation* of "what no eye has seen, nor ear heard, nor the heart of man conceived" (1 Cor 2:9; cf. Is 55:9; 64:4 and Eph 3:19). These transcendent moments are accomplished interiorly by the presence of the Holy Spirit and can experientially accumulate to have a transformative effect upon the life of a person, both purifying and sanctifying him or her over time.

It is interesting to note that Sister Lucia, at one point, specifically contrasted the physiological effects that the children experienced in the apparitions of the angel with those they experienced in the apparitions of Mary. In her *Fourth Memoir*, Lucia quotes Francisco describing the peculiar effect of the angel, "I would like very much to see the Angel [again], but the worst of it is that afterwards we can't do anything. I couldn't even walk. I don't know what was the matter with me."[161] In contrast, they felt no such weakness during the apparitions of Mary, but, instead, felt a lightness of being and joy. Lucia confides that, "The apparition of Our Lady drove us again to concentrate on the supernatural, but in a more gentle way. Instead of that annihilation in God's presence that prostrated us even physically, it produced peace and effusive gladness."[162]

Maybe what the children were feeling in the supernatural aura of the angel was something similar to the weight of the "threat of judgment," represented in the "flaming sword" of the angel of the *third secret*, which Cardinal Ratzinger spoke about. In Mary's presence, on the other hand, we see communicated, instead, the Spirit which animated the ecstatic utterance of Mary's canticle of praise recorded in

---

[161] *Documents*, 415.
[162] *ibid.*, 416.

St. Luke's Gospel, "My soul magnifies the Lord, and my spirit *rejoices* in God my Savior" (Lk 1:46-47). Remember, "joy" and "rejoicing" are the other dimension represented by the "wine" for which she interceded at the wedding feast in Cana (cf. Ps 4:7, Sir 31:27-28, Neh 8:10), that is, the interior disposition that can be expected as a result of the purification of conscience, born of the Spirit, through the Blood of the Lamb. "Love, joy, peace ..." are the first of the fruits of the Holy Spirit listed by St. Paul in his Letter to the Galatians (5:22).

St. Francisco's Unique Observation

Because Francisco was unable to hear Mary speak, Lucia and Jacinta would relay to him what Mary said. It is often presumed that because of this, Francisco must have been less worthy of Mary's apparitions than his sister and cousin. However, God may have had an ulterior motive. Because Francisco was only able to *see* the visions but not *hear*, he seemed to be more keenly focused upon the appearance of that *"light* which is God" and more particularly intrigued with its subjective impact than were Jacinta and Lucia. Like a deaf person who becomes more reliant upon the signals afforded by the senses he retains, St. Francisco was more alert to what was seen and felt. Sister Lucia reflected on some of Francisco's unique insights in her *Fourth Memoir,* where she details their discussions. She wrote,

> In the third apparition [of Mary], it seemed to be Francisco who was less affected by the vision of hell, even though this had caused very strong feelings in him, too. [He was not able to hear what Lucia described as the "shrieks and groans of sorrow and despair that horrify and cause people to shudder with fear."].
>
> What most impressed or captivated him was God, the Most Holy Trinity, in that immense light that penetrated to the most intimate parts of our souls.
>
> Afterwards he said, "We were *burning* in that light which is God and we didn't parch. How wonderful God

is!!! ... But what a pity. He is so sad! If I could only console Him!!!"[163] (Comments in brackets added).

This comment of St. Francisco is a keenly sensitive description of the physiological effect of that light, which penetrated their being. When Our Lady unveiled to the children the vision of hell in the July apparition: "she opened her hands as she had in the two months before. The radiance [which emanated from her hands] seemed to penetrate the ground and we saw something like a sea of fire."[164] Francisco felt the strong sensation of *"burning"* while coming away from it amazed that they didn't "parch." He was probably wondering how they were preserved from the effect the "burning" was having on the figures they had witnessed in hell. His statement seems to imply that this "light which is God" is not only the source of the purification of conscience and the source of blessing, but, for the unrepentant, it may be the source of eternal anguish. Though the experience of St. Francisco is very intriguing to ponder and can strengthen all in their conviction to pray for souls and make reparation to God, it is not in itself a novel insight. The Letter to the Hebrews proclaims, "Our God is a consuming fire" (Heb 12:28); and the prophet Isaiah asks, "Who among us can dwell with the devouring fire? Who among us can dwell with everlasting burnings?" (Is 33:14).

The "burnings" that St. Francisco speaks of are not unrelated to the other feeling that he has coming from the light — that "[God] is so sad!"

"As I live, says the Lord God, I have no pleasure in the death of the wicked, but that the wicked turn from his way and live" (Ez 33:11). Though God eminently transcends all He has created, it is a mistake to think that He is so far beyond and removed from the vexing vicissitudes of our ordinary human lives that He does not feel the sting of the offense of our immoral actions and rejection of His call upon us. Though it is true that God cannot be harmed by His creation and that He did not create us in order to increase His own happiness, but was

---

[163] *Ibid.*, 419
[164] *Documents*, 439.

motivated solely out of Love and a desire to share His own beatitude with His creatures, in creating us conscious and conscientious, intelligent and morally free persons, He opened Himself to the possible moral rejection of His own rational creatures. Though He does not suffer the feelings brought on by the anxieties common to human existence, God is not aloof to these sufferings in us; He is not a stoic. Rather, we know that God is "attentive to [our] supplications," as the angel told the children at Fatima. Further, God the Son assumed a human nature so that He might reveal to us the true sensitivity and love of His own Sacred Heart, a Heart that He showed to St. Margaret Mary Alacoque in June of 1675, and exclaimed,

> Behold this Heart which has loved men so much, that It has spared nothing even to exhausting and consuming Itself in order to testify to them Its love; and in return I receive from the greater number nothing but ingratitude by reason of their irreverence and sacrileges, and by the coldness and contempt they show me in this Sacrament of Love.[165]

It is not difficult to recognize that the words spoken above by our Lord to St. Margaret Mary two and a half centuries prior to 1916 and 1917 are very similar to what the angel and Mary spoke to the children at Fatima. The "Sacrament of [Christ's] Love" is "the new covenant in [His] blood" (Lk 22:20; also cf. 1 Cor 11:25), the Eucharist. Marriage is called a "covenant" because it is an agreement between a man and a woman, where the two profess lifelong fidelity to one another, each making a vow to give himself / herself totally to the other. In the Paschal mystery, Christ has already "poured [Himself] out for you [in] the new covenant of [His] blood" (Lk 22:20). He calls upon us to reciprocate His Love. We have seen that Mary asked the children if they were willing "to offer yourselves to God, to endure all the sufferings that He may be pleased to send you, as an act of

---

[165] *Enthronement of the Sacred Heart*, (Boston, MA: Daughters of St. Paul, 1978), 31.

reparation for the sins by which He is offended, and to ask for the conversion of sinners?"[166]

This proposal that Mary makes to the children is one toward which no one feels a *natural* inclination to comply. Its fulfillment in the lives of anyone depends upon a *supernatural* grace capable of overcoming all the trepidation that naturally arises in the face of suffering or fear of death. Mary does not shield the children from the truth that their "yes" to God makes them targets for the divine application of needed atonement in the world. In response to their "yes," she says, "Then you will have much to suffer, but," she adds, "the grace of God will be your comfort."[167] It was while articulating this last phrase, "the grace of God will be your comfort," that she opened her hands and dispensed to them that grace that moved them interiorly to forget themselves completely in adoration of God in His most profound mysteries. It is here that we arrive at the heart of the matter, *the essence of the triumph of the Immaculate Heart of Mary.*

The Essence of the Triumph of the Immaculate Heart

The "splendor that Our Lady radiated towards [the angel] from her right hand" in the *third secret* is the very Light and Life and Love of God that penetrated the souls of the children of Fatima, and everyone else represented in the image of the *third secret* who were ascending the mountain to the cross at the top. The essence of the triumph of the Immaculate Heart is the essence of Mary's *fiat,* her affirmative response given to the will of God, conveyed to her by the angel Gabriel at the Annunciation: "Behold, I am the handmaid of the Lord; let it be to me according to your word" (Lk 1:38).

In the Heart of Mary, the gulf that separates the natural inclinations of the human heart from the sacrificial, priestly Heart of Christ, by which Christ entered the world (cf. Heb 10:5-7), is bridged by the Spirit of God, with which Mary is perfectly wedded and filled. That part of Christ's Priesthood, which is open to the participation of the faithful and granted in the sacrament of Baptism, is perfectly and

---

[166] First Apparition, *Fourth Memoir, Documents,* 437.

[167] *ibid.*

suitably assumed, modeled and communicated by the Immaculate Heart of Mary.

Christ is the "one mediator between God and men" (1 Tm 2:5), but He has not excluded believers from exercising a participation in His unique mediation.[168] His unique mediation was most fully expressed and accomplished by His sacrifice on the cross. Participation in this priestly sacrifice of Christ has been extended to all in the sacraments of the Church. Since Christ is Head of His Body, the Church (cf. Col 1:18), there is a portion of Christ's priesthood that is proper only to Christ's Headship and another portion that is proper to all the members of His Body, the Church. When Christ instituted the sacraments, He ordained the Twelve Apostles to a ministerial priesthood over those sacraments, to act *in persona Christi Capitis,*[169] which is Latin for "in the person of Christ the Head." This is the form we commonly think of when thinking of "the priesthood," but it is not the *common, royal priesthood* in which He wants to act in every person. It was God's intention from the beginning to form "a kingdom of priests and a holy nation" (Ex 19:6; cf. Is 61:6). All the baptized are consecrated into this common priesthood.[170] In isolation, the actions of the ministerial priesthood are sterile exercises:

> The ministerial or hierarchical priesthood of bishops and priests, and the common priesthood of all the faithful participate, "each in its own proper way, in the one priesthood of Christ" (*LG* 10.2) ... the ministerial priesthood is at the service of the common priesthood ... directed at the unfolding of the baptismal grace of all Christians.[171]

We can say that the essential character of the form of Christ's priesthood is that — as modeled by the Immaculate Heart of Mary — which is bestowed at baptism and is, therefore, *common* to all the baptized. It is the call to *offer oneself* to God. The ministerial priest-

---

[168] cf. *CCC*, 1545-1547.
[169] cf. *CCC*, 1548; *LG*, 10, 28; *SC*, 33; *CD*, 11; *PO*, 2; 6.
[170] cf. 1268
[171] *CCC*, 1547.

hood, of course, provides the necessary functions that perpetuate the memory of Christ's self-offering in the sacraments, the *ordinary means* of the grace for our own self-offering. The sacraments are vital connections to Christ, which help each member of the common priesthood (every baptized individual, including members of the clergy) to habitually conform their lives to Christ's self-offering. In Christ, there is but one priesthood in which He allows the whole Church to participate:

> The Church which is the Body of Christ participates in the offering of her Head. With him, she herself is offered whole and entire. She unites herself to his intercession with the Father for all men. In the Eucharist the sacrifice of Christ becomes also the sacrifice of the members of his Body. The lives of the faithful, their praise, sufferings, prayers, and work, are united with those of Christ and with his total offering, and so acquire a new value. Christ's sacrifice present on the altar makes it possible for all generations of Christians to be united with his offering.[172]

It is not an arbitrary association that the Church makes in referring to herself with the personal feminine pronoun of "she." Mary is a model of the Church in her faith and charity and in her role as mother.[173] What Mary shows us is a life that participates, totally, in the sacrificial self-offering of her Son's priesthood. She does not in any way usurp His authority as Head of the Body or compete for His position as the "one mediator between God and man." Rather, she shows all humanity how to enter into her Son's Priesthood as members of His Body, the Church.

But she doesn't just give an *example* of this self-offering; she *communicates its Spirit*, which animates her Immaculate Heart, as a mother nurtures and nourishes her children. She confronts us with the *memory of her Son*, which her Heart treasures and ponders unceasingly; a condition of heart that our Lord specifically requested His

---

[172] *CCC*, 1368.
[173] cf. *CCC*, 967-969.

faithful be endowed with when commemorating His Eucharistic sacrifice (cf. Lk 22:19, 1 Cor 11:24). In that memory, we grow in the love which she possesses and radiates, and which dispels any fear (cf. 1 Jn 4:18) that might in any way hamper the exercise of this priesthood.

Reciprocity of self-donation between God and His people has always been a foundational principle of Christian spirituality. This is the essence of *covenant*: "I will take you for my people, and I will be your God" (Ex 6:7; cf. Lv 26:12; Jer 31:33; Ez 37:26-27; Rv 21:3).

The great doctor of the Church in matters concerning spirituality, St. Teresa of Avila, expressed the spiritual nature of this reciprocity of self-donation in a spiritual axiom: "This King doesn't give Himself but to those who give themselves entirely to Him."[174] This axiom is given a particularly sacramental dimension and clarified further by the very practical insight provided by Bl. Don Marmion, abbot of the Benedictine Abbey of Maredsous, Belgium, from 1909 – 1923, in his work, *Christ the Life of the Soul*:

> In the offering of the Holy Mass, Jesus Christ associates us in His state of High Priest. In Communion He causes us to participate in His condition of Victim. The Holy Sacrifice presupposes that inward and entire oblation that our Lord made to the Will of His Father when entering into the world, an oblation that He often renewed during His life and completed by His death on Calvary ... Jesus Christ gives Himself to us as food, but after having been first offered as Victim. Victim and food are, in the Eucharist, sacrifice and sacrament – two inseparable characters. And that is why this *habitual disposition* of giving oneself totally is so important. Jesus gives himself to us in the measure we give ourselves to him, to his Father, to our brethren who are the members of his Mystical Body. This *essential disposition* makes us one with Christ, but with Christ as victim. It establishes sympathy between the two terms of the union.

[174] *The Way of Perfection*, Ch. 16, KR, no. 4. Taken from *The Collected Works of St. Teresa of Avila, Volume II*. Translated by Kieran Kavanaugh and Otilio Rodriguez, (Washington, DC: ICS Publications, 1980), 95.

When our Lord finds a soul thus disposed, given up entirely and unreservedly to his action, he acts in it with his divine virtue which works marvels of holiness because it meets with no obstacle. The absence of this self-offering also explains why some advance so little in perfection despite frequent Communions. Christ does not find in these souls the supernatural alacrity which would permit him to act freely in them. Their vanity, self-love, touchiness, selfishness, jealousy and sensuality prevent the union between them and Jesus being made with that intensity, that fullness by which the transformation of the soul is effected and completed. [175]

This area of preparing the faithful to form the needed "habitual disposition," as Bl. Marmion calls it, "of giving oneself totally" in openness to Christ's vital presence in the sacraments seems to be a specially chosen domain granted by God to the Immaculate Heart of Mary. Fr. Garrigou-Lagrange wrote that,

Mary's influence seems to be exercised especially on our sensibility – which is sometimes so rebellious or so distracted – to calm it, to subordinate it to our higher faculties, and to make it easy for these latter to submit to the movement of the Head when He transmits us the divine life. (In this we see the application of St. Thomas's principle that the instrument disposes in preparation for the action of the principal agent.)[176]

Mary's presence at the foot of the cross was not an accident of history but an arrangement specifically willed by the heavenly Father through His Spirit. The Eucharist and the Eucharistic Liturgy, by bringing us potentially into vital contact with Jesus and His sacrificial self-offering upon the cross, do not accomplish this end in isolation

---

[175] Don Marmion, *Christ the Life of the Soul* (Leominster, UK, Gracewing Publishing, 2005), 272 – 273.

[176] *The Mother of the Savior and our Interior Life*, 208.

from the current of love that flows in the Holy Spirit through the Immaculate Heart of Mary. This is the kind of influence Mary had on the children of Fatima and, by extension, on all those pictured ascending the hill in the vision of the *third secret*. All these, by their sufferings, "complete what is lacking in Christ's afflictions for the sake of his body, that is, the Church" (Col 1:24), and thereby fulfill the required need for "Penance, Penance, Penance!," which the angel in righteous indignation, shouted out while pointing to the earth.

.　　.　　.

Recall that the angel appeared to the children in 1916 and asked them to pray an act of "reparation for all the *outrages, sacrileges,* and *indifference*" that offend "the most precious Body, Blood, Soul, and Divinity of Jesus Christ, present in all the tabernacles of the world."[177] It is likely that outrages, sacrileges and indifference represent three degrees of offense that our Lord in His Eucharistic presence often endures; "outrages" being the most severe, and "indifference" being an offense of lesser degree. The *Catholic Encyclopedia* provides a definition of "sacrilege" as:

> The violation or injurious treatment of a sacred object ... This can happen first of all by the administration or reception of the sacraments (or in the case of the Holy Eucharist by celebration) in the state of mortal sin, as also by advertently doing any of those things invalidly. Indeed deliberate and notable irreverence towards the Holy Eucharist is reputed the worst of all sacrileges."[178]

If we count as "outrages" what this definition calls "the worst of all sacrileges," then we can say that "outrages" are "deliberate and notable irreverence towards the Holy Eucharist." The *Catholic Encyclopedia* doesn't have an entry for "indifference," but in St. Faustina's *Diary,* the saint recorded some intriguing words of complaint that our Lord

---

[177] cf. *Second Memoir, Documents,* 340.

[178] Joseph F. Delany, "Sacrilege," in *Catholic Encyclopedia,* 1913 ed.

spoke to her, which may help to shed some light on what the angel may have been referring to by this term in relation to the Eucharist:

> My daughter, write that it pains me very much when religious souls receive the Sacrament of Love *merely out of habit*, as if they did not distinguish this food. I find neither faith nor love in their hearts. I go to such souls with great reluctance. It would be better if they did not receive Me.[179]
>
> Know, My daughter, that when I come to a human heart in Holy Communion, My hands are full of all kinds of graces which I want to give to the soul. But souls do not even pay any attention to Me; they leave me to myself and busy themselves with other things. Oh, how sad I am that souls do not recognize Love! They treat me as a dead object.[180]
>
> You see, although there appears to be no trace of life in Me, in reality it is present in its fullness in each and every Host. But for Me to be able to act upon a soul, the soul must have faith. O how pleasing to me is living faith.[181]

Though incidents of outrage are offenses horrible to imagine, it is far more likely that the more general variety of sacrilege and indifference are a much more common problem. Surveys of Catholics indicate that there often exists a significant disparity between what individual Catholics believe and what the Church teaches, particularly in matters of faith in Jesus' Real Presence in the Eucharist, the Sacrifice of the Mass, and implications of their sacramental encounter with our Lord.[182] We know that St. Paul, even in his day, was concerned about this problem of indifference and sacrilege. He wrote in his *First Letter to the Corinthians*,

---

[179] *Diary*, 1288.

[180] *ibid.*, 1385.

[181] *ibid.*, 1420.

[182] cf. *Sacraments Today: Belief and Practice among U.S. Catholics* – Center for Applied Research in the Apostolate (CARA). Accessed July 31, 2015. www.cara.georgetown. edu/sacraments.html.

Whoever, therefore, eats the bread or drinks the cup of the Lord in an unworthy manner will be guilty of profaning the body and blood of the Lord. Let a man examine himself, and so eat the bread and drink of the cup. For anyone who eats and drinks without discerning the body eats and drinks judgment upon himself. (1 Cor 11:27-29)

St. Paul's first sentence, very likely refers to sacrileges that involve receiving our Lord without having subjected oneself to the moral demands of Christ and His gospel, since he next asks that "a man examine himself" before he "eat the bread and drink of the cup." But the last sentence likely refers more precisely to his concern about an attitude of *indifference*, since he speaks about "discerning the body" within the context of our Lord's physical presence. Though the person may not be guilty of neglecting any one of the negative moral precepts in the Ten Commandments, *indifference* is more a neglect of the very first and greatest Commandment: "You shall love the Lord your God with all your heart, and with all your soul, and with all your mind, and with all your strength" (Mk 12:29; cf. Mt 22:37-38; Lk 10:27; Dt 6:4). In this regard, we can probably apply our Lord's warning in the *Book of Revelation* to those who are "lukewarm." Our Lord said, "I know your works: you are neither cold nor hot. Would that you were cold or hot! So, because you are lukewarm, and neither cold nor hot, I will spew you out of my mouth" (3:15-16).

There is an interesting entry in St. Faustina's *Diary* that we may be able to connect to these offenses against Christ's presence in the Eucharist mentioned by the angel at Fatima:

I saw the Lord Jesus nailed to the cross. When He had hung on it for a while, I saw a multitude of souls crucified like Him. Then I saw a second multitude of souls, and a third. The second multitude were not nailed to [their] crosses, but were holding them firmly in their hands. The third were neither nailed to [their] crosses nor holding them firmly in their hands, but were dragging [their] crosses behind them and were discontent. Jesus then said to me, "Do you see these souls? Those who are like Me in the pain and contempt they suffer will be like Me also in glory. And those who resemble Me less in pain and contempt will also bear less resemblance to Me in glory." (#446 *Diary of St. Faustina*)

If we combine these three with the *offenses, sacrileges and indifference* spoken of by the angel, we can see a full array of individual responses to our Lord's presence in His Eucharistic Sacrifice. Often under normal conditions, when a spectrum of possibilities are plotted like points on a graph that has polar extremes at both ends, the vast majority of outcomes fall somewhere near the middle, with fewer toward the extreme ends. When graphed, these points together form a "bell curve," which humps high in the middle. It is probably fair to suppose that most people's responses to Christ's presence in the Eucharistic Sacrifice fall somewhere in the middle of this full spectrum. This would indicate that a vast majority of people fall somewhere in the general categories of "indifference" or "discontent." We will look at evidence in the next chapter that indicates the general situation might be even worse than that, though. In any case, there exists a great need for all of us to open our hearts more widely to our Lord's presence in the Eucharist and His Sacrifice and to seek to console His Heart, which is so heavily burdened with indifference to His goodness.

Considering that the word "Eucharist" in Greek means, "to give thanks," there is obviously a need for more catechesis in this crucial area of doctrine, to improve the general predispositions of Catholics in their preparation for their encounter with Christ in Holy Communion. Of course, scrupulosity in this regard should also be avoided, since momentary distractions are a common problem of the spiritual life. But one should have a sense that the Sacrifice of the Mass and Holy Communion are the high point of one's week (or day, for daily communicants), the "source and summit of the Christian life." [183] It is the "source" from which all spiritual vitality is drawn and the "summit," or goal, toward which all our activity ultimately ought to

---

[183] *LG*, 11; *CCC* 1324.

gravitate. This recognition of the wondrous gift of our Lord in the Eucharist and His Sacrifice is the ideal toward which the Immaculate Heart of Mary desires to lead us.

Christ reveals to us the Heart of God, but, as we have already seen, it seems to be Mary's special domain, in conjunction with her spouse, the Holy Spirit, to draw us ever closer to this summit of His Heart by drawing us into that current of love within her own heart, forever flowing toward the Heart of her Son. This love of the Holy Spirit, which she possessed even prior to that *hour* when our Lord instituted the sacraments and offered His Paschal Sacrifice to His Father, is a gift for which she actively participated in obtaining for the rest of humanity at the foot of the cross. She helped acquire that source of divine life, that current of love that leads us to the Heart of her Son.

At Fatima, her words and actions indicate that she continues to fulfill this role. We remember her words in the first apparition, after she elicited the children's *fiat* to the will of God, "Then you will have much to suffer, but the grace of God will be your comfort." In her second apparition she made a similar comment, which, in conjunction with the first, seems to allude to this special domain of influence that she shares with the Holy Spirit. In this conversation, Lucia expressed deep concern that she will be left alone when Jacinta and Francisco are taken to heaven soon and she must remain for some time – "I am to stay here alone?" Mary responded, "No, daughter. Do you suffer a great deal? Don't be discouraged, I will never forsake you. *My Immaculate Heart will be your refuge and the road that will lead you to God.*"

We see in this statement that the Immaculate Heart of Mary gives dimensional support, accommodating that previously promised "comfort" which "the grace of God," the Holy Spirit, would provide during times of suffering. The "road that will lead [us] to God," as imaged in the vision of the *third secret* certainly depicts trials of suffering, difficulty and dejection. This confirms our Lord's own words in the Gospel that "the way is hard, that leads to life ..." (Mt 7:14), and that "If any man would come after me, let him deny himself and take up his cross and follow me" (Mt 16:24; see also, Mk 8:34 and Lk 9:23). It is the desire of Mary's Heart to draw us to the foot of the cross of her Son by giving us a share in her love for Him and for all the intentions of His Heart. In this difficult sojourn, Our Lady has promised that "the grace of God will be [our] comfort," and that her "Immaculate Heart will be [our] refuge, and the way that will lead [us] to God."

Though the vision of the *third secret* does not conclude with an image of a final *triumph*, as is promised by Mary in the second part of the secret, we see, instead, an unremitting procession of souls that make their way to God and are comforted and strengthened by Mary along the way and further blessed with the blood of the martyrs, which is gathered up by the angels and sprinkled on them as they proceed to the foot of the Cross.[184]

Two Angels with a Crystal Aspersorium

The vision of the *third secret* begins with an image of "an Angel with a flaming sword" and ends with an image of "two Angels each with a crystal aspersorium in his hand." In between these two images stands the vision of Our Lady "with the splendor that [she] radiated," along with the consequent image seen in that "immense light that is God." The entire final sentence of the *third secret* reads: "Beneath the two arms of the Cross there were two Angels each with a crystal aspersorium in his hand, in which they gathered up the blood of the Martyrs and with it sprinkled the souls that were making their way to God."[185]

An "aspersorium" is the Latin name for a device used by priests for sprinkling holy water in the act of blessing objects or people. The image thus provides a graphic representation of the blessing, or conveying of grace, extended by those who make an offering of themselves to the will of God for the salvation of others. It depicts the *oikonomia* of the communication and distribution of grace in the Father's plan for the salvation of the world. The first angel with the flaming sword was expressly concerned about the severe scarcity of penitential acts needed (as we have concluded) to atone for the abus-

---

[184] *Lucia's Letter describing the Third Part of the Secret, Documents,* 505-506.
[185] *ibid.,* 506.

es and neglect of Christ's gift of Himself in the Eucharist, and for the preservation of peace in the world and the salvation of souls. The long-term effective result of the intervention of "the splendor which Our Lady radiated" is depicted by the actions of the two angels gathering the blood of the martyrs (the image of the "blood of the Martyrs" represents the grace that is drawn from a Christian's total self-offering, as Tertullian famously proclaimed in the second century, "the blood of martyrs is the seed of the Church") and sprinkling the souls making their way to God (symbolizing the extended communication of God's *grace and mercy,* which we saw coming from the left hand of our Lord in Lucia's vision at Tuy, Spain).

We can assume that, within the greater context of the message given at Fatima, this image is not restricted to graces conveyed exclusively by martyrdom. Those who are willing "to offer [themselves] to God, to endure all the sufferings that He may be pleased to send you, as an act of reparation for the sins by which He is offended, and in supplication for the conversion of sinners"[186] are included in this vision, representing spiritual martyrdom. That the splendor which Our Lady radiated is capable of eliciting this penitential offering from faithful believers in Christ is substantiated by St. John Paul II's Apostolic Letter, *On the Christian Meaning of Human Suffering,* where he confirms that,

> The divine Redeemer wishes to penetrate the soul of every sufferer through the heart of His holy Mother, the first and the most exalted of all the redeemed. As though by a *continuation* of that motherhood, which by the power of the Holy Spirit had given Him life, the dying Christ conferred upon the ever-Virgin Mary a *new kind of motherhood* – spiritual and universal – towards all human beings, so that every individual, during the pilgrimage of faith, might remain, together with her, closely united to Him unto the cross, and so that every form of suffering, given

---

[186] First Apparition, *Fourth Memoir, Documents,* 437).

fresh life by the power of this cross, should become no longer the weakness of man but the power of God.[187]

John Paul II explains in the letter that the mystery of human suffering is closely akin to the mystery of evil,[188] since suffering and disorder in creation are consequences of the original disobedience and rebellion against the just authority of God.[189] Christ accomplished the Redemption of the world by an action completely contrary to sin, rightly called *reparation*:

> Jesus Christ, who, though he was in the form of God, did not count equality with God a thing to be grasped, but emptied himself, taking the form of a servant, being born in the likeness of men. And being found in human form he humbled himself and became obedient unto death, even death on a cross. (Ph 2:8)

The original act of disobedience and every subsequent sin is an indulgent abuse of the divine gift of human freedom, a gift associated with our intellectual capacity to distinguish good from evil. Because of this moral capacity, human beings experience suffering at a much more profound level than do our furry friends in the animal kingdom. As John Paul II explains,

> We could say that man suffers *because of a good* in which he does not share, from which in a certain sense he is cut off, or of which he has deprived himself. He particularly suffers when he "ought" – in the normal order of things – to have a share in this good, and does not have it.[190]

The experienced sense of deprivation, thus, often presents human beings with a moral challenge, a temptation toward covetousness. In its disordered form, covetousness in the heart is at the root

---

[187] *Salvifici Doloris* (SD), 26.

[188] *ibid.*, 7.

[189] cf. Gen 3:16-19; CCC, 1521.

[190] SD, 7.

of every transgression of the Law of God.[191] Such covetousness can enslave a person (cf. Jn 8:34). *Resignation* to the cross of Jesus, on the other hand, grants an individual a reprieve in a *paradoxical freedom*, borne of the eternal purpose and meaning Christ has communicated by the word of His cross: "Now I rejoice in my sufferings for your sake ..." (Col 1:24). Archbishop Fulton J. Sheen considered the distortion which Communism makes concerning the religious teaching of *resignation* to the cross, to be one of the fundamental "errors" that "Russia [has] spread ... throughout the world." In a book entitled, *Liberty, Equality, Fraternity*, he wrote,

> The resignation which religion preaches is not passive submission to economic injustices, as Communism contends. Resignation means accepting our lot, while working to better conditions by an intelligent understanding of the nature of things ...
>
> Religion is resigned to the nature of the world and the nature of man. It knows very well that man is prone to evil, that some selfishness will remain under any economic system, and that no paradise can be built here below. But because religion is resigned to these practical limitations, religion does not refuse to better conditions by infusing virtue into the hearts and souls of men, to the end of making a world where the good can live among the bad, where the rich can live without exploiting the poor and the poor can live without being violently destructive of all wealth, and where the majority can live in a state this side of heroism and martyrdom. Communism, however, refuses to accept the nature of things and thinks it can change them by violence and confiscation. ... In fact it is just as foolish to try to build a perfect Paradise here below by revolution, as it is to try to dynamite triangles into four-sided figures. There are certain things to which we must be resigned and the nature of man is one. It is

---

[191] cf. *CCC*, 2534.

simply because Russia has refused to take account of this one fact that it has failed. All its failures are failures incident to human nature. Since it failed to be resigned to that, it must be resigned to failure.[192]

The *paradoxical freedom* provided by the Cross of Jesus Christ, by resignation to the will of the Father, possesses the supernatural hope for a truly peaceful and just world: "For the creation was subjected to futility, not of its own will but by the will of him who subjected it in hope; because the creation itself will be set free from its bondage to decay and obtain the *glorious liberty of the children of God*" (Rm 8:20-21).

At its foundation, reparation for sin is accomplished through a trusting surrender to the providential will and plan of God. That plan of God has been revealed to us most clearly and eloquently by Jesus, the Word of the Father, in His Sacrifice upon the cross. The mystery of suffering and of evil is not merely an intellectual problem, which can be satisfactorily resolved in the mind by logic. It is something that reaches down into the heart of each man as a moral trial to confront him and challenge his personal understanding of his own human existence.[193] In *Salvifici Doloris*, John Paul II has attempted to describe the Heart-to-heart exchange that often takes place between an individual and the grace of God in God's effort to lead each individual to the summit of the cross. He explains that,

> People react to suffering in different ways. But in general it can be said that almost always the individual enters suffering with a *typically human protest* and *with the question "why."* He asks the meaning of his suffering and seeks an answer to this question on the human level. Certainly he often puts this question to God, and to Christ. Furthermore, he cannot help noticing that the One to whom he puts the question is Himself suffering and wishes *to answer him* from the cross, *from the heart of His own suffering.*

---

[192] Excerpt quote from *The Philosophy of Communism*, (New York: Benzinger Brothers, Inc. 1963), 252-253.

[193] SD, 2.

Nevertheless, it often takes time, even a long time, for this answer to begin to be interiorly perceived. For Christ does not answer directly and He does not answer in the abstract this human questioning about the meaning of suffering. Man hears Christ's saving answer as he himself gradually becomes a sharer in the sufferings of Christ.

The answer which comes through this sharing, by way of the interior encounter with the Master, is in itself *something more than the mere abstract answer* to the question about the meaning of suffering. For it is above all a call. It is a vocation. Christ does not explain in the abstract the reasons for suffering, but before all else He says: "Follow me!" Come! Take part through your suffering in this work of saving the world, a salvation achieved through my suffering! Through my cross! Gradually, *as the individual takes up his cross*, spiritually uniting himself to the cross of Christ, the salvific meaning of suffering is revealed before him. He does not discover this meaning at his own human level, but at the level of the suffering of Christ. At the same time, however, from this level of Christ the salvific meaning of suffering *descends to man's level* and becomes, in a sense, the individual's personal response. It is then that man finds in his suffering interior peace and even spiritual joy.[194]

As we noted before, *peace* and *joy* are fruits of the Holy Spirit (cf. Gal 5:22-23). Immediately before St. Paul speaks about completing "what is lacking in Christ's afflictions," he says, "I rejoice in my sufferings for your sake" (Col 1:24). Christ Himself proclaims those "blessed" who suffer for His sake, and says they should "rejoice and be glad for your reward is great in heaven" (cf. Mt 5:11). In like manner, St. Paul affirms "that the sufferings of this present time are not worth comparing with the glory that is to be revealed to us" (Rm 8:18). Those who can find interior peace and even spiritual joy in their

---

[194] *SD,* 26.

sufferings cannot be overcome by the world, but rather, they themselves conquer the world (cf. 1 Jn 5:4-5).

We, thus, see something here of the *triumph of the cross*, which overcomes and conquers the world (cf. Jn 16:33). This *triumph of the cross*, as John Paul II has confirmed, is a fruit of that *"new kind of motherhood"* which "the dying Christ conferred upon the ever Virgin Mary."[195] In that *triumph* is witnessed the essential conviction that "the word of the cross is not folly ... but ... the power of God" (1 Cor 1:18) – that the apparent weakness displayed there transcends all the limitations common to man and revels in joy at "the power of God," in whom "all things are possible" (Mt 19:26; cf. *Magnificat*, Lk 1:46-55, 1 Cor 1:18-25). Thus, the *triumph of the cross* is coextensive with any true understanding of the *triumph of the Immaculate Heart*.

. . .

This "power of God" was prominently on display in the early Church, as shown in the *Acts of the Apostles*, and, particularly, in the well-known conversion and apostolic life of St. Paul. In his various letters, he expounds upon the teaching of redemptive suffering, which is explained and developed in his theology about "the body of Christ ... the Church" (Col 1:24). It is not inconsequential that we first become acquainted with St. Paul in the *Book of Acts* in the section about the martyrdom of St. Stephen. That section of Scripture explains that

> They cast him out of the city and stoned him; and the witnesses laid down their garments at the feet of a young man named Saul. And as they were stoning Stephen, he prayed, "Lord Jesus receive my spirit." And he knelt down and cried with a loud voice, "Lord, do not hold this sin against them." And when he had said this, he fell asleep. And Saul was consenting to his death. (Acts 7:58 - 8:1)

St. Paul is first introduced as "Saul," his Hebrew name prior to his dramatic conversion. What is important to note is how St.

---

[195] *ibid.*

Stephen prayed, specifically, for the conversion of those who were putting him to death, while making a total surrender of himself to the will of God. St. Luke, the author of *Acts*, intentionally highlights the prominent presence of Saul at Stephen's martyrdom so that later, when we witness the *power of God* in the radical conversion of St. Paul, we will draw the spiritual connection to St. Stephen's prayer and self-offering – the blood of his martyrdom.

From an exclusively human point of view, the conversion of Saul from an overly zealous persecutor of the Church, "breathing threats and murder against the disciples of the Lord" (Acts 9:1), to that of becoming the great Christian "Apostle to the Gentiles," is inexplicable. He was completely unmoved by any pity for those who faced the harsh treatment that he helped to unleash upon the nascent Church. The only way to make sense of his abrupt conversion is in trusting the veracity of his own testimony of his dramatic encounter with the risen Christ while on the road to Damascus. It is almost impossible to imagine a life more radically impacted, redirected and reshaped by God's intervention through extraordinary *graces and mercy* than that of St. Paul. His encounter with Christ and the rapid events that followed, became a profound source for all that he would subsequently ponder as he struggled to reconcile his original religious convictions with the meaning of that encounter, which so abruptly frustrated his plans: "Saul, Saul, why do you persecute me?" "Who are you, Lord?" "I am Jesus whom you are persecuting." (cf. Acts 9:4-5). Our Lord's unqualified, personal identification with the individual targets of Saul's "murderous threats" must have made the physical blindness, which Saul contracted during this moment of blinding enlightenment, feel almost comforting in comparison with the weight of horror that must have subsequently crushed down upon his conscience. Such a supernatural encounter must have been not just unforgettable, but so deeply seared into his conscience and memory as to remain an ever-present backdrop to his every thought thereafter. How could he ever again look upon another baptized believer in Jesus as anything less than a member of Christ's own Body, the Church? Scripture scholars testify that,

Of all the inspired writers of the New Testament, St. Paul is the one who speaks most often about the Church, the one who has gone deepest into its mystery and best explained it. His insight into the mystery of the Church began at the very moment of his conversion, when he heard Jesus identify Himself with Christians. [196]

When Jesus personally identifies Himself with Christians, He particularly identifies with those who are being persecuted, those who are suffering for the sake of the kingdom of God. St. John Paul II explains, at some length, St. Paul's seemingly audacious personal claim that, "in my flesh I complete what is lacking in Christ's afflictions for the sake of his body, that is, the Church" (Col 1:24):

In the Paschal Mystery Christ began *the union with men in the community of the Church.* The mystery of the Church is expressed in this: that already in the act of Baptism, which brings about a configuration with Christ, and then through His sacrifice – sacramentally through the Eucharist – the Church is continually being built up spiritually as the Body of Christ. In this Body, Christ wishes to be united with those who suffer ... The sufferings of Christ created the good of the world's Redemption. This good in itself is inexhaustible and infinite. No man can add anything to it. But at the same time, in the mystery of the Church as His Body, Christ has in a sense opened His own redemptive suffering to all human suffering. Insofar as man becomes a sharer in Christ's sufferings – in any part of the world and at any time in history – to that extent *he in his own way completes* the suffering through which Christ accomplished the Redemption of the world.[197]

---

[196] *Navarre Bible, Romans and Galatians: Texts and Commentaries,* (Dublin, Ireland: Four Courts Press, 1990), 43.

[197] *SD,* 24.

The Paschal Mystery is more than an historical event. As an action of Christ, it was accomplished once for all with His Passion, Death, Resurrection and Ascension. But, as His definitive act of redeeming the world, it is a mystery which impacts all time and every person of every generation, from the foundation of the world to its consummation. As such a mystery, then, it affects every person more profoundly than anyone can ever fully comprehend. It matters how we react to *it,* and how we treat every person created in His image and likeness and redeemed at the price of His own Blood: "Truly, I say to you, as you did it to one of the least of these my brethren, you did it to me" (Mt 25:40). It is not that we, in some isolated manner, increase the sum total of suffering that was originally found wanting in the sufferings that Christ endured. Rather, Christ, in His Paschal Mystery, in a transcendent way, has already taken upon Himself our suffering, and "it is no longer I who live, but Christ who lives in me" (Gal 2:20).

The conversion of St. Paul is a testament to the *economy* of Salvation and of the *grace and mercy* that flow from the Heart of Christ in the Paschal Mystery and out through the lives of the faithful of the Church, who encounter Jesus there. St. Paul himself confessed, "the grace of our Lord overflowed for me with the faith and love that are in Christ Jesus" (1 Tm 1:14). He went on to explain that God had a particular purpose in doing this: "The saying is sure and worthy of full acceptance, that Christ Jesus came into the world to save sinners. And I am the foremost of sinners [for, as he stated just two verses immediately prior to this, "I formerly blasphemed and persecuted and insulted him"]; but I received mercy for this reason, that in me, as the foremost, Jesus Christ might display his perfect patience for an example to those who were to believe in him for eternal life" (1 Tm 1:15-16).

This example of God's patience, grace and mercy displayed in the conversion of St. Paul, follows a pattern that was outlined by St. Luke in the narrative of the *Acts of the Apostles* and theologically developed in St. Paul's letters. St. Stephen, in imitation of his crucified Master, resigned himself to the will of the Father and offered his life for the conversion of those who persecuted him. Though we can assume he wasn't alone in his sufferings and prayer for this intention,

St. Stephen has provided for the Church a prominent example. St. Augustine tells us, "If Stephen had not prayed to God, the Church would not have had Paul."[198]

It is impossible to calculate the impact that the conversion of St. Paul has had on the Church and the world. After Christ, there are few who have assumed a more active role in the foundational formation of the Church and her subsequent development in history. In like manner, it is not possible to know the impact that our own little personal martyrdoms, mortifications and sufferings have, when united to the sufferings of Christ in His Paschal Mystery. But, thanks to the *grace and mercy* given to St. Paul, we have a solid theological foundation upon which to base an understanding of the participation "in Christ's afflictions for the sake of His Body, that is, the Church" (Col 1:24) that we are called to share in. And we can comprehend the imagery of the "two Angels ... [who] gathered up the blood of the martyrs and with it sprinkled the souls that were making their way to God," in the vision of the *third secret*. Though the vision does not include an image of the *triumph of the Immaculate Heart*, we have Mary's assurance in the greater context of the full secret given on July 13, 1917, that, "In the end my Immaculate Heart will triumph ... and a certain period of peace will be granted to the world."[199]

St. John Bosco's Dream of the Two Pillars: A Vision of Triumph

St. John Bosco, who lived in the 19th Century, once related to his community a dream he had. The imagery of the dream bears many thematic parallels to the Fatima visions and message and concludes with the image of a triumph. It is known as St. John Bosco's "dream" of the *Two Pillars*. What follows is the narrative of his dream as it was written down by those who heard him describe the imagery:

> On the whole surface of the sea you see an infinity of ships, all ending in a beak of sharp iron that pierces whatever it hits. Some of these ships have arms, cannons, guns; others

---

[198] *Sermons*, 315, 7: *The Navarre Bible, Acts of the Apostles*, 94.
[199] *Fourth Memoir, Documents*, 440.

have books and incendiary materials. All of them are
thronging after a ship that is considerably bigger, trying to
ram it, set fire to it, and do it every possible sort of damage.
Imagine that in the middle of the sea you also see two very
tall columns. On one is the statue of the Blessed Virgin
Immaculate, with the inscription underneath: *Auxilium
Christianorum* ["Help of Christians"]. On the other which
is even bigger and taller, there is a Host of proportionately
large size in relation to the column, and under it the words:
Salus credentium ["Salvation of believers"]. From the base
of the column hang many chains with anchors to which
ships can be attached. The biggest ship is captained by
the Pope, and all his efforts are bent to steer it in between
those two columns. But, as I said, the other barks try in
every way to block it and destroy it, some with arms,
with the beaks of their prows, with fire from books and
journals. But all their weapons are in vain. Every weapon
and substance splinters and sinks. Now and then the
cannons make a deep hole somewhere in the ship's sides.
But a breeze blowing from the two columns is enough to
heal every wound and close up the holes. The ship again
continues on its way. On the way the Pope falls once, then
rises again, falls a second time and dies. As soon as he is
dead, another immediately replaces him. He guides the
ship to the two columns. Once there he attaches the ship
with one anchor to the column with the consecrated Host,
with another anchor to the column with the Immaculate
Conception. Then total disorder breaks out over the
whole surface of the sea. All the ships that so far had been
battling the Pope's ship scatter, flee, and collide with one
another, some foundering and trying to sink the others.
Those at a distance keep prudently back until the remains
of all the demolished ships have sunk into the depths of
the sea, and then they vigorously make their way to the
side of the bigger ship. Having joined it, they too attach

themselves to the anchors hanging from the two columns and remain there in perfect calm.[200]

Whether the details of St. Bosco's dream refer directly to the *Triumph* promised at Fatima need not be established, for what cannot be denied are the obvious parallels of the basic constituent elements, which both images and messages allude to: the suffering of the pope, errors that promote persecution in the imagery of the "books and journals" used to set fire to the ship, the supernatural interventions coming from Mary and our Eucharistic Lord, and, especially, the great calm that results when the pope finally anchors the ship to the two columns of Mary and the Eucharist. The image of those other boats joining with the great ship in anchoring to the two columns to "remain there in perfect calm" seems to suggest some form of unity in the establishment of devotion to the Immaculate Heart of Mary *in the world*, as is God's expressed intention at Fatima, and the era of peace that will result.

There is good reason to believe that the "certain period of peace" that Our Lady at Fatima promised will be far more enduring than anything that can be accomplished by even the best arrangement of peace treaties between nations. Moreover, the promised triumph of the Immaculate Heart will be far more profound than any mere cessation of political opposition to the Church. What can be expected, from the Fatima promise is a very dramatic transformation of the world's cultures by all that is "good and acceptable and perfect" (Rm 12:2), in forming, shaping and nurturing the hearts of human beings.

The Church has experienced relative triumphs in the past. One very historical triumph took place early in the Fourth Century, when Constantine became the Emperor of Rome and promulgated the Edict of Milan, putting an end to the series of persecutions that had plagued the Church for 300 years. Eventually, what emerged on the continent of Europe was a whole new civilization, never before known in the world. This historic event and what followed can be

---

[200] This testimony was recorded in a letter to a friend by one who heard St. Bosco speak of his dream, taken from *Don Bosco's Dreams*. Translated by John Drury. (New Rochelle, NY: Salesiana Publishers, 1996), 79-80.

viewed, in part, as a foretaste of what might be expected to happen with the coming *triumph of the Immaculate Heart* in the world. In his book *Introduction to Mary*, Dr. Mark Miravalle includes two substantial quotes by non-Catholic historians, which are worthy of our attention. Both historians wrote warmly of the subtle influence of the civilizing effect of devotion to Mary that circulated through the veins of the cultures of Europe during the long incubation period that followed the *triumph* of the Edict of Milan. First, he mentions British historian, Kenneth Clark, who testified that Mary is

> The supreme protectress of civilization. She had taught a race of tough and ruthless barbarians the virtues of tenderness and compassion. The great cathedrals of the Middle Ages were her dwelling places upon earth … in the Renaissance, while remaining Queen of Heaven, she became also the human Mother in whom everyone could recognize qualities of warmth and love and approachability.[201]

The other historian, William Lecky, "a self-professed rationalist," as Dr. Miravalle stated, expounded upon this influence of Mary on Western Civilization in even broader detail:

> The world is governed by its ideals, and seldom or never has there been one which has exercised a more salutary influence than the medieval concept of the Virgin. For the first time woman was elevated to her rightful position, and the sanctity of weakness was recognized, as well as the sanctity of sorrow.
>
> No longer the slave or toy of man, no longer associated only with ideas of degradation and sensuality, woman rose, in the person of the Virgin Mother, into a new sphere, and became the object of reverential homage, of which antiquity had no conception … A new type of character was called into being; a new kind of admiration was fostered. Into a harsh and ignorant and benighted

---

[201] *Introduction to Mary*, 47.

age, this ideal type infused a conception of gentleness and purity, unknown to the proudest civilizations of the past.

In the pages of living tenderness, which many a monkish writer has left in honor of his celestial patron; in the millions who, in many lands and in many ages have sought to mold their characters into her image; in those holy maidens who, for love of Mary, have separated themselves from all glories and pleasures of the world, to seek in fastings and vigils and humble charity to render themselves worthy of her benedictions; in the new sense of honor, in the chivalrous respect, in the softening of manners, in the refinement of tastes displayed in all walks of society; in these and in many other ways we detect the influence of the Virgin. All that was best in Europe clustered around it, and it is the origin of many of the purest elements of our civilization.[202]

What we can expect to emerge from the triumph of the Immaculate Heart is beyond imagining and comprehension. The interminable succession of martyrs in the imagery of the *third secret* is reminiscent of Christ's own prophetic words, spoken shortly after He stated that "unless a grain of wheat falls into the earth and dies, it remains alone" (Jn 12:24). Calling upon his disciples to follow Him, He went on to speak of His Passion and Glorification in inseparable terms (Cf. Jn 12:26-28): "I, when I am lifted up from the earth, will draw all men to myself" (Jn 12:32). At the foot of the cross, with Mary, is the providential destination of all humanity. From this vantage point, to which we are given entry in the sacraments, most especially the Eucharist, we stand as in a basin for holding the fount of "living water" (cf. Jn 7:38), from where *grace and mercy* flow and can be received in such abundance as to "renew the face of the earth" (Ps 104:30). St. Louis De Montfort boldly prophesied that:

> ... at the end of the world and indeed presently, because the Most High with His holy Mother has to form for Himself

---

[202] *ibid.*, 48.

great saints who shall surpass most of the other saints in sanctity as much as the cedars of Lebanon outgrow the little shrubs ...

These great souls, full of grace and zeal, shall be chosen to match themselves against the enemies of God, who shall rage on all sides; and they shall be singularly devout to our Blessed Lady, illuminated by her light, strengthened with her nourishment, led by her spirit, supported by her arm and sheltered under her protection, so that they shall fight with one hand and build with the other. With the one hand they shall fight, overthrow and crush the heretics with their heresies, the schismatics with their schisms, the idolaters with their idolatries, and the sinners with their impieties. With the other hand they shall build (*Esd.* 4:7) the temple of the true Solomon and the mystical city of God, that is to say, the most holy Virgin, called by the Fathers the "Temple of Solomon" and the "City of God." By their words and their examples they shall draw the whole world to true devotion to Mary.[203]

In his commentary on the *third secret,* Cardinal Ratzinger was emphatic that the purpose of the vision was not to show us "a film preview of the future in which nothing can be changed," rather, "to bring freedom onto the scene and to steer freedom in a positive direction."[204] At Fatima, Mary reminded us that the hope of the world lies in the free choices of individuals who make room in their lives for the Spirit of God to freely move and act, so as to bring us ever closer to the Heart of her Son, by implementing and exercising the habits of a particular devotion – devotion to her Immaculate Heart.

O that my people would heed me, that Israel would walk in my ways! At once I would subdue their foes, turn my hand against their enemies. The Lord's enemies would cringe at their feet and their subjection would last forever.

---

[203] St. Louis De Montfort, *True Devotion to Mary.* (Rockford: Tan Books and Publishers, 1985), 26-27.
[204] *Fatima for Today,* 280.

But Israel I would feed with finest wheat and fill them with honey from the rock. (Ps. 81:13-16)[205]

---

[205] *Christian Prayer: Liturgy of the Hours.* (Boston, MA: Pauline Books and Media, 1976), 741.

CHAPTER IV

THE DEVOTION

In the preceding chapters, we have examined the broad foundation for understanding something of God's purpose in wanting devotion to the Immaculate Heart of Mary established in the world. With this background, we are better prepared to recognize the great value of this devotion and consider some of the practical ways in which it can be incorporated into the busy routines of our daily lives.

Our Lady, in many ways, shows us the need we have of imitating her and her Son in their complete and trusting self-surrender to the will of God the Father. We can recognize the direct correlation between the degree to which God's will is "done on earth as it is in heaven" and the degree to which we can expect peace to reign in the world. First, peace is achieved in a person's own heart and soul in their trusting relationship with their Creator and Redeemer, and then that peace is extended to their families, among their neighbors, relatives, friends, even among people who hold opposing philosophical and political views. In this way, a true civilization of love and culture of life might be erected upon the constructive dialogue, debate and diplomacy that is truly "sown in peace by those who make peace" (Jas 3:18).

Every one of us who understands something of the human condition in the face of the moral dilemmas that confront us every day knows that this call to do God's will and its promise of peace reaches far beyond the grasp of human determination alone. And so, Our Lady tells us that in order to accomplish this God wants to establish in the world a devotion that not only helps us better align our hearts and minds with the will of God, but that can enlist hidden forces that are at the beck and call of our heavenly Mother and disassemble the obstacles erected by our common enemy. This devotion has several essential elements, which Sister Lucia has written about in her book, *"Calls" from the Message of Fatima,* published only a few years before her death. The book is an excellent resource for anyone determined to understand and live out the message of Fatima and devotion to the Immaculate Heart of Mary. It was Lucia's mission to make the Mother of Jesus known and loved, and I believe her book can hardly be improved upon. In this chapter, I intend to show how the devotion follows logically from all that has been discussed in the previous chapters and, with that understanding, make a few practical suggestions.

The Rosary

A very central part of the devotion to the Immaculate Heart is the request that Mary repeatedly made to the Fatima children: pray the Rosary every day. Her persistent call for the Rosary was expressed at each of her six appearances in 1917: (May) "Say the Rosary every day to obtain peace for the world and end of the war;"[206] (June) "Say the Rosary every day;"[207] (July) "Continue to say the Rosary every day in honor of Our Lady of the Rosary to obtain the peace of the world and the end of the war;"[208] (August) "Continue to say the Rosary every day;"[209] (September) "Continue to say the Rosary to bring about the end of the war;"[210] (October) *"Let them* continue to say the Rosary every day."[211] However, in October her request for the Rosary went far beyond her merely repeating this directive.

We have seen how at Lourdes Mary's self-identification as the *Immaculate Conception* seemed to bear with it, in what St. Bernadette observed in Our Lady's demeanor and emotion, the tremendous weight of all that those words theologically hold. At Fatima, too, Mary did not casually identify herself. During the months leading up to her October appearance, Mary prepared the children for it. But this self-identification was quite different from that of Lourdes. At

[206] *Fourth Memoir, Documents,* 438.
[207] *ibid.*
[208] *ibid.,* 439.
[209] *ibid.,* 441.
[210] *ibid.,* 442.
[211] *ibid.*

Fatima, you get a sense that she is laying down a spiritual battle plan and is identifying herself with the very spiritual weapon she has been repeatedly encouraging. In July, she didn't just say, "In October I will tell you who I am," but also, "and what I wish."[212] Well, after months of anticipation, she announces her identity this way, "… have them build a chapel here in my honor; I am the Lady of the Rosary." She then went on to make her sixth request that they pray the Rosary each day, "Let them continue to say the Rosary every day."[213]

She then follows up this request by prophetically announcing the fulfillment of the very intention for which she was asking them to pray: "The war is going to end, and the soldiers will soon return to their homes."[214] Initially, this prophecy caused some hardship for Lucia, for the war lasted another thirteen months after Our Lady's October appearance. But the war was already in its fourth year and had become a virtual stalemate. Every attempt by either side to penetrate the fortified lines of their enemy was repelled with disastrous consequences. Our Lady was telling the children and us that despair and fatalism do not belong in the heart that prays. By collectively entering into solidarity with Mary's Immaculate Heart, especially in the praying of the Rosary, the faithful enlist weapons far more potent than anything the great industrial complexes of nations could invent. Seeing that Mary went to such lengths to identify herself precisely with the Rosary, as opposed to a great theological mystery as she did at Lourdes, obliges us to give this devotion serious consideration. But before we take a closer look at the Rosary, we must confront its most formidable intellectual objection.

For some individuals in the Church who have had a bit of theological learning, the powerful efficacy that is attributed to the Rosary in the message of Fatima seems exaggerated and misplaced. The documents of Vatican II were emphatic about the centrality of the Church's liturgy and its efficacy: "No other action of the Church can

---

[212] ibid.

[213] ibid.

[214] ibid.

equal its efficacy ... ."[215] The Rosary, though, is a form of prayer that is not liturgical, formed more than a millennium after the Church's liturgical rites took their form. How can a relatively novel devotional practice make a claim to such dynamic spiritual potency?

This is a good question that has been answered well by both St. Paul VI and St. John Paul II. The answer is that the Rosary does not work some kind of "power" in isolation to the liturgy but, rather, is capable of predisposing human hearts into such correspondence with it that its higher potency can be better realized. As we examine this relationship of the Rosary to the liturgy, it is important that we realize that it is not necessary that those who pray the Rosary be consciously aware of this relationship, though it certainly cannot hurt. As stated in Chapter One, when looking at Our Lady's intervention at the wedding feast at Cana, the intervention which Our Lady is capable of with the Rosary brings all our needs "within the radius of Christ's messianic mission and salvific power."[216] In a sacramental sense, that means the liturgy.

Papal Defense of the Rosary

In St. John Paul II's Apostolic Letter on the Rosary, *Rosarium Virginis Mariae,* his Holiness lamented "a certain crisis of the Rosary," brought on in part by "some who think that the centrality of the liturgy, rightly stressed by the Second Vatican Ecumenical Council, necessarily entails giving lesser importance to the Rosary."[217] This "crisis" the Holy Father refers to had persisted despite the effort made by his predecessor, St. Paul VI, in promulgating his Apostolic Exhortation, *Marialis Cultus,* almost three decades earlier. According to what these two pontiffs wrote in their respective documents, it is clear that the Rosary may just be the most effective instrument for preparing the faithful for a fuller participation in the Eucharistic Liturgy and for allowing the graces of that participation to bear abundant fruit.

The Second Vatican Council certainly did stress the liturgy's cen-

---

[215] *SC* 7.

[216] *Redemptoris Mater,* 21.

[217] *RVM,* 4.

trality. In its very first document, *Sacrosanctum Concilium*, which dealt with the Church's form of worship, the Council fathers affirmed that "the liturgy is the summit toward which the activity of the Church is directed ... [and] also the fount from which all her power flows" and that "especially from the Eucharist, grace is poured forth upon us as from a fountain."[218] But by acknowledging this truth, the Council fathers were not denigrating devotions and other non-liturgical spiritual exercises, for almost immediately following the section of *Sacrosanctum Concilium* just quoted, the Council fathers state, "The spiritual life, however, is not limited solely to participation in the liturgy."[219]

In regard to devotions, the Council simply stipulated that:

> ... such devotions should be so drawn up that they harmonize with the liturgical seasons, accord with the sacred liturgy, are in some way derived from it, and lead the people to it, since in fact the liturgy by its very nature is far superior to any of them.[220]

The principles spelled out here may seem a bit restrictive, and this perceived restrictiveness may have inadvertently contributed to the "crisis of the Rosary." But, especially when it comes to the Rosary, no such scrupulous thoughts should ever impede its exercise. The Rosary lends great support to the Eucharistic Liturgy by facilitating the very ideals mentioned above in a supreme manner. Just as Mary stands at the foot of the cross in the *Paschal Mystery* in perfect submission to the will of the Father, as a catalyst for the communication of the *grace and mercy* which overflow from this source for all of humanity, so too does this devotion draw countless faithful toward contemplation of that same *mystery*, which is presented anew in every Eucharistic Liturgy.

It is significant that the major symbolic visions of Fatima that we have examined in the two previous chapters both affirm the cen-

---

[218] *SC*, 10.

[219] *SC*, 12.

[220] *SC*, 13.

trality of the liturgy. Sister Lucia's vision of the Trinity in Tuy, Spain, clearly depicts the Paschal Mystery and its sacramental / liturgical extension as "the fount from which all [the Church's] power flows,"[221] in the imagery of the Blood of Christ falling upon the Eucharist and into the chalice, and the purifying crystal-clear water flowing out from the left hand of Christ as "grace and mercy." And the vision of the *third secret*, which shows a big cross that is at *the summit* of a steep mountain *toward which* many individuals of the Church make their way, affirms the orientation of those represented as being directed toward the Paschal Mystery.

Thus, despite the explicitly articulated message promoting devotion to the Immaculate Heart of Mary and the Rosary given at Fatima, it is obvious that the promotion of these devotions does not impede on the Church's full understanding of the worship of God in the liturgy and the full *economy* of grace and life in His Spirit. In fact, these images can greatly help our minds better grasp the full reality of what is truly being encountered when we speak of devotion to the Immaculate Heart of Mary in the Rosary and to the Heart of Jesus in the liturgy. By these means we truly draw near and encounter two Hearts that call for our compassion.

Though St. Paul VI lamented the mistaken practice of "recit[ing] the Rosary **during** the celebration of the liturgy"[222] [emphasis added], he wrote in *Marialis Cultus* that,

> The commemoration in the liturgy and the contemplative remembrance proper to the Rosary, although existing on essentially different planes of reality, have as their object the same salvific events wrought by Christ. The former presents new, under the veil of signs and operative in a hidden way the great mysteries of our Redemption. The latter, by means of devout contemplation, recalls these same mysteries to the mind of the person praying ...
> In fact, meditation on the mysteries of the Rosary, by

---

[221] *SC*, 10.

[222] Apostolic Exhortation for the right ordering and development of Devotion to the Blessed Virgin Mary, *Marialis Cultus* (*MC*) (February 2, 1974), 48.

familiarizing the hearts and minds of the faithful with the mysteries of Christ, can be an excellent preparation for the creation of those same mysteries in the liturgical action and also become a continuing echo thereof.[223]

It can be argued that the comparison and contrast made between the liturgy and the Rosary here is the key to understanding the great power handed to us in the Rosary and confirmed by the message given at Fatima. St. Paul VI states that the two exist "on essentially different planes of reality," and understanding this difference is helpful to understanding the dynamic that takes place between the devotion of the Rosary with its "contemplative remembrance" and the "commemoration" that is the liturgy. The *commemoration* that is the liturgy, to a great extent, presupposes the mental activity involved in remembering, where as the *contemplative remembrance* involved in the Rosary is precisely a cultivation of that mental activity done in submission to the movement of the Holy Spirit and the maternal care of Mary.

The liturgy, like Christ, who "had no form or comeliness that we should look at him" (Is 53:2), as a merciful extension of Christ's reach to every generation and place, "presents new," as St. Paul VI states, *"under the veil of signs and operative in a hidden way* the great mysteries of our Redemption." Thus, the liturgy is not self-explanatory. The need persists not only for solid catechesis on *the great mysteries of our Redemption*, but also for meditating and contemplating the content of these mysteries so that their reality encountered at every liturgy may be more fully engaged. Just as Scripture often requires a hermeneutic key to help unlock the hidden treasures of its inexhaustible wisdom, while precluding faulty interpretations, so too the mysteries re-presented in the liturgy are not transparently obvious to every observer, but presuppose a need for catechesis and routine meditation and contemplation upon their truths. As "the New Testament lies hidden in the Old and the Old Testament is unveiled in the New,"[224] the same

---

[223] *MC*, 48.
[224] *CCC*, 129.

can be said about the corresponding relationship of the liturgical mysteries to the "mysteries" of the events of Christ's life:

> A sacramental celebration is woven from signs and symbols. In keeping with the divine pedagogy of salvation, their meaning is rooted in the work of creation and in human culture, specified by the events of the Old Covenant and fully revealed in the person and work of Christ.[225]

A person's encounter with Christ in the liturgy, thus, "must be preceded by evangelization, faith, and conversion."[226] For this reason, St. Paul VI was emphatic that "meditation on the mysteries of the Rosary, by familiarizing the hearts and minds of the faithful with the mysteries of Christ, can be an excellent preparation for the creation of those same mysteries in the liturgical action and also become a continuing echo thereof;"[227] "preparation" and "echo" of the "same mysteries in the liturgical action," which is, "the summit toward which the activity of the Church is directed ... [and] also the fount from which all her power flows."[228] It's difficult to imagine a more suitable means of preparation or daily follow up of the Eucharistic Liturgy than that of meditating with Mary on the Rosary, upon the great mysteries integral to the life and mission of her divine Son.

In reference to this aspect of the Rosary, John Paul II stated in his Apostolic Letter on the Rosary that, "by immersing us in the mysteries of the Redeemer's life, it ensures that what he has done and what the liturgy makes present is profoundly assimilated and shapes our existence."[229] He continues to explain in depth this contemplative dimension of the Rosary that, in praying the Rosary, we enter the "school of Mary" who, as model and Mother of the spiritual life, "teaches by obtaining for us in abundance the gifts of the Holy Spirit,

---

[225] *CCC*, 1145.
[226] *CCC*, 1072.
[227] *MC*, 48.
[228] *SC*, 11.
[229] *RVM*, 13.

even as she offers us the incomparable example of her own 'pilgrimage of faith.'"[230] This example of hers is imbued with a

> ... contemplation [which is] above all *a remembering* ... [which] in the biblical sense ... [is] a making present of the works brought about by God in the history of salvation ... culminating in Christ himself ... [and] comes about above all in the Liturgy.[231]

This *remembering*

> ... is not just a question of learning what He [Christ] taught but of "learning Him" ... Contemplating the scenes of the Rosary in union with Mary is a means of learning from her to "read" Christ, to discover his secrets and to understand his message.[232]

This *remembering,* as we have seen, is the exceptionally unique quality of Mary's Immaculate Heart explicitly highlighted by St. Luke: "Mary kept all these things, pondering them in *her heart*" (Lk 2:19).

The School of Mary

St. Paul has stated that "we do not know how to pray as we ought," and so "the Spirit helps us in our weakness" and "intercedes for us with sighs too deep for words" (cf. Rm 8:26). In the "school of Mary," the Holy Spirit works in tandem with Mary to aid "us in our weakness." She provides us with the supreme example of her "pilgrimage of faith" and the maternal nurturance of her Immaculate Heart. We can say that in this "school of Mary," the Holy Spirit and Mary have worked and continue to work together to bring us closer to that ideal of "know[ing] how to pray as we ought" (Rm 8:26). This is helpful to keep in mind as we consider the structure of the Rosary. "Meditation on the mysteries of Christ is proposed in the Rosary by

---

[230] *ibid.*

[231] *ibid.*

[232] *ibid.,* 14.

means of a method designed to assist in their assimilation ... a method based on repetition."[233] John Paul II goes on to instruct that, "[w]e should not be surprised that our relationship with Christ makes use of a method."[234] We should not be surprised, he says, because this method of repetition is often the target of another complaint commonly raised against its practice. For this reason, he warns that "[i]f this repetition is considered superficially, there could be a temptation to see the Rosary as a dry and boring exercise."[235] He continues: "God communicates Himself to us respecting our human nature and its vital rhythms."[236] This rhythmic dimension of the Rosary is beautifully expounded upon by St. Paul VI:

> By its nature the recitation of the Rosary calls for a quiet rhythm and a lingering pace, helping the individual to meditate on the mysteries of the Lord's life as seen through the eyes of her who was closest to the Lord. In this way the unfathomable riches of these mysteries are unfolded.[237]
> ... the succession of Hail Mary's constitutes the warp [a device used for weaving cloth] on which is woven the contemplation of the mysteries. The Jesus that each Hail Mary recalls is the same Jesus whom the succession of the mysteries proposes to us – now as the Son of God, now as the Son of the Virgin – at His birth in a stable at Bethlehem, at His presentation by His Mother in the Temple, as a youth full of zeal for His Father's affairs, as the Redeemer in agony in the garden, scourged and crowned with thorns, carrying the cross and dying on Calvary, risen from the dead and ascended to the glory of the Father to send forth the gift of the Spirit.[238]

---

[233] RVM, 26.

[234] ibid., 27.

[235] ibid.

[236] ibid.

[237] MC, 47.

[238] MC, 46.

She, who "kept all these things, pondering them in *her heart*" (Lk 2:19), brings with her to the foot of the cross, re-presented in the Eucharistic Liturgy, "the rest of her offspring" (Rv 12:17).

In this contemplation, Mary invites the faithful to the ultimate moral ideal proclaimed by the Council fathers: "Offering the immaculate victim, not only through the hands of the priest but also together with him, they should learn to offer themselves."[239] John Paul II affirms that,

> As we contemplate each mystery of her Son's life, [Mary] invites us to do as she did at the Annunciation: to ask humbly the questions that open us to the light, in order to end with the obedience of faith: "Behold I am the handmaid of the Lord; be it done to me according to your word" (Lk 1:38).[240]

We can thus see that the Rosary is a devotion, not only in "accord with the sacred liturgy, [and] in some way derived from it, and lead[ing] the people to it"[241] – as Vatican II acknowledges devotions need to be – but also we can see it is a devotion which especially empowers Mary, through the grace of the Holy Spirit, to draw her children (and by extension all that falls under their personal authority and concern) into the vortex of the mercy of her Son's Paschal mystery, effectively fulfilling His prophetic words: "I, when I am lifted up from the earth, will draw all men to myself" (Jn 12:32).

This is the transformation we have witnessed in the lives of the children of Fatima and in the lives of all those depicted in the *third secret* going up the mountain to the cross. Through the symbiotic relation between the respective *remembrances* proper to the mysteries of the Rosary and of the Eucharistic Liturgy, we are drawn into the symbiosis of love between the Immaculate Heart of Mary present, active and flowing in that devotion and the Sacred Heart of Jesus truly present and active in the Eucharistic mystery. Jesus, in the lit-

---

[239] *SC*, 48.

[240] *RVM*, 14.

[241] *SC*, 13.

urgy, as on the cross, is as though fixed in place, awaiting the return of the many prodigal children of His Father. Whether that return is an habitual effort or a dramatic new beginning, the Immaculate Heart of Mary is tireless in facilitating that return, by interceding for and dispensing countless, merciful graces from the Holy Spirit to the hearts of "the rest of her offspring" (Rv 12:17).

Liturgy and Devotion: An Authentic Image of the Trinity

In the *American Heritage Dictionary*, the definition of the word *devotion,* which we have mostly been applying to the Rosary to classify its characteristics, is the third one listed: "An act of religious observance or prayer, esp. when private." This is what we mean by calling the Rosary a *devotion.* The second definition listed is, "Religious ardor or zeal; piety." This definition helps us to recognize the spirit of virtue that ought to accompany our prayerful participation in a devotion, the liturgy or any other spiritual exercise. It is most beneficial that when we engage in any of these, we do so with "religious ardor or zeal" or "piety." We remember the angel at Fatima asking the children to make Eucharistic reparation, not only for "outrages" and "sacrileges," but also for the "indifference" that often clouds the hearts of the faithful who are called to make a real devotional encounter with our Lord in His Eucharistic mystery when participating in the Eucharistic Liturgy.[242] By understanding this sense of the term, *devotion* as a virtue of spirit, it can be easier to recognize how the spirit of devotions, such as the Rosary, can overlap and complement that of the liturgy. There is a Trinitarian pattern discernible in the exchange of this virtue of spirit that can move from a *devotion* to the activities involved in a sacramental liturgy and vice versa. Remember what St. Maximilian Kolbe wrote in reference to the Trinitarian pattern in God's work in Creation:

> Everything which exists, outside of God himself, since it is from God and depends on him in every way, bears within itself some semblance to its Creator; there is nothing in any

---

[242] cf. *Fourth Memoir, Documents,* 435.

creature which does not betray this resemblance, because every created thing is an effect of the Primal Cause....[243]

Everywhere in this world we notice action, and the reaction which is equal but contrary to it; departure and return; going away and coming back; separation and reunion. The separation always looks forward to union, which is creative. All this is simply an image of the Blessed Trinity in the activity of creatures. Union means love, creative love. **Divine activity, outside the Trinity itself, follows the same pattern.**[244]

The Holy Spirit, who is the true spirit of any authentically engaged devotion, returns to the Father through the Heart of His Son. Within redeemed Creation, that pattern assumes a very definite form.

In the Church's liturgy the divine blessing is fully revealed and communicated. The Father is acknowledged and adored as the source and the end of all the blessings of creation and salvation. In his Word who became incarnate, died, and rose for us, he fills us with his blessings. Through his Word, he pours into our hearts the Gift that contains all gifts, the Holy Spirit.[245]

Thus, in the liturgy, "Christ now acts through the sacraments he instituted to communicate his grace ... perceptible signs (words and actions) accessible to our human nature. By the action of Christ and the power of the Holy Spirit they make present efficaciously the grace that they signify."[246] As the angel Gabriel responded to Mary's inquiry, "How can this be ...?" (Lk 1:34), by referring to "the power of the Most High" in "the Holy Spirit" (*ibid.*) to take the physical elements of her womb to form within her "the Son of God" (*ibid.*), so we imitate the faith of Mary by confidently accepting God's remedy

---

[243] *Immaculate Conception and the Holy Spirit*, 2.

[244] *ibid.*, 3.

[245] *CCC*, 1082.

[246] *CCC*, 1084.

in the Eucharist formed from the physical gifts of bread and wine. All these blessings in the sacraments and the liturgy are objectively available to humanity through the Church, our Mother. But the work of the Holy Spirit in the liturgy is not limited to that of "artisan of … the sacraments;" that is, the Holy Spirit is not merely limited in His action to making the sacraments truly what they are; the Holy Spirit is also **teacher of the faith.**[247] It is especially in this activity of the Holy Spirit as *teacher of the faith* that we recognize an inseparable overlap of *liturgy* and *devotion*. By the Spirit's power, Christ is made sacramentally present and is encountered in the liturgy; but, by the Holy Spirit's action as "teacher of the faith," we are made capable of recognizing and engaging Christ who is there present, though hidden, under sacramental signs:

> The grace of the Holy Spirit seeks to awaken faith, conversion of heart, and adherence to the Father's will. These dispositions are the precondition both for the reception of other graces conferred in the celebration itself and the fruits of new life which the celebration is intended to produce afterward. [248]
>
> By means of the words, actions, and symbols that form the structure of a celebration, the Spirit puts both the faithful and the ministers into a living relationship with Christ, the Word and Image of the Father, so that they can live out the meaning of what they hear, contemplate, and do in the celebration.[249]
>
> The Church therefore asks the Father to send the Holy Spirit to make the lives of the faithful a living sacrifice to God by their spiritual transformation into the image of Christ, by concern for the Church's unity, and by taking part in her mission through the witness and service of charity.[250]

[247] *CCC*, 1091.

[248] *ibid.*, 1098.

[249] *ibid.*, 1101.

[250] *ibid.*, 1109.

We can recognize here, as described in the activity of the Holy Spirit in the Church and the world, a well-defined mission, where the Spirit "proceeds from the Father and the Son" in the liturgy out into the world and back again, with "[t]he desire ... that we may live from the life of the risen Christ."[251]

St. John Paul II began his Apostolic Letter, *Rosarium Virginis Mariae*, by affirming that the Rosary "gradually took form in the second millennium under the guidance of the Spirit of God." The liturgy, on the other hand, has been handed down to us in its essential form from Christ and His Apostles. The *liturgy* is the work and expression of Christ Himself (though made sacramentally present by the power of the Holy Spirit); whereas, the formation of an authentic *devotion* is better understood as an effect of the activity of the Holy Spirit in the life of the Church over time. What the Church has witnessed in the historical development of the Rosary is precisely what ought to be expected from the centuries-long activity of the Holy Spirit:

> These things I have spoken to you, while I am still with you. But the Counselor, the Holy Spirit, whom the Father will send in my name, he will teach you all things, and bring to your remembrance all that I have said to you. (Jn 14:25-26)
>
> When the Spirit of truth comes, he will guide you into all the truth; for he will not speak on his own authority, but whatever he hears he will speak, and he will declare to you the things that are to come. He will glorify me, for he will take what is mine and declare it to you. (Jn 16:13-14)

Thus, we can be confident that the Rosary was divinely formed to facilitate this activity of the Holy Spirit in a profoundly rich manner. "The Holy Spirit is the Church's living memory" of Christ;[252] the Immaculate Heart of Mary is the living image of a heart that treasures and ponders that memory; and the Rosary is a devotional means ideally and divinely fashioned for awakening and cultivating

---

[251] *ibid.*, 1091.

[252] *ibid.*, 1099.

that memory within us and drawing us ever more profoundly and devoutly to the foot of the cross in the Eucharistic mystery and liturgy.

The Historical Development of the Rosary

During the Middle Ages, the imaginations of faithful Christians in the West had become deeply intrigued with the historical life of Christ. The shrines that memorialized the numerous significant events of Christ's life in the Holy Land, which were often pilgrimage destinations for the well-to-do, especially those who resided in the eastern parts of Christendom, were under serious threat from the rapid expansion and strengthening of the forces of Islam. This threat galvanized that momentous response from western Christendom known as the *Crusades*. Prompted greatly by the preaching that promoted the Crusades and the stories told by those who had returned from these expeditions, "the devotion of the faithful began to focus more and more on various scenes or 'mysteries' of the life of Christ or on the instruments of the passion and death of Christ."[253] The positive spiritual impact of this renewed devotion to Christ's Sacred Life and Humanity upon the lives of those who cultivated it had become obvious to many within the Church. The rapid growth of some of the new mendicant religious orders — the Franciscans, the Dominicans, the Carmelites — were a testament to this positive fruit. These new orders, which budded and blossomed all over western Europe during the 13th and 14th centuries, presented forms of spirituality that were more apostolically active than were customarily found in the eremitical and monastic communities that dominated the landscape of western Europe in previous centuries. The older monastic model was established in the time after the Roman Empire had come to embrace Christianity, and laxity and "worldliness" replaced the threat of persecution as a very present danger and significant temptation for Christians everywhere. At that time, many Christians felt the need to radically separate themselves from the world in the monastic communities in order to adhere more faithfully to the Gospel.

---

[253] Jordan Aumann, *Christian Spirituality in the Catholic Tradition*, (San Francisco: Ignatius Press, 1985),110.

These monastic communities promised a life ordered according to the structure offered by the liturgy.

Along with some of the idealism promoted by the Crusades came a new confidence in the power of Christ to transform and renew the culture by a more aggressive promotion of devotion to His Sacred Humanity. The new orders recognized an optional way for living out a life consecrated to God and found that their apostolic works of drawing greater attention to the life of Christ, as lived out in His Sacred Humanity, was very fruitful in drawing people closer to the liturgy, sacraments and the fullness of life in the Church. Their consecrated lives remained centered on Christ in the Eucharistic Liturgy, but the boundaries that separated them from the mess and chaos of the world were intentionally made more permeable. The new religious orders' communal consecrated life, with their profession of the evangelical counsels of poverty, chastity and obedience, retained the charism "to signify and proclaim in the Church the glory of the world to come,"[254] but these new orders more directly confronted the chaotic and hectic lives of the rest of humanity, who had not the benefit of a community life so well-ordered according to the structure of the liturgy. Many of the devotions promoted were designed particularly for those who struggled to care for their families amidst the unpredictable burdens common to life in the world. Many of these devotions, in their practical simplicity, did not require that a person be sitting still in a quiet place with a reading light and breviary in hand, as is required when praying the Liturgy of the Hours. Many of these devotions, by centering on Christ's Sacred Humanity, helped people to draw a connection between the experiences, burdens and struggles they encountered in their own lives, with those lived out by Christ in His own Sacred Humanity. By making these meditative connections to the common experiences of everyday life, these devotions helped to draw out from the struggles, sufferings and drudgery of common, daily life, meditative anchors for entering into contemplation of the eternal things of God upon which the heart and mind can rest.

---

[254] CCC, 915.

It was especially in these new orders where many of the particular practices of this devotion to Christ's Sacred Humanity became
refined. The Franciscans are credited with giving us nativity scenes,
Stations of the Cross, and Eucharistic adoration; the Carmelites with
consecration to Mary under the sign of the Brown Scapular and
devotion to and imitation of the hidden life of the Holy Family of
Nazareth; and the Dominicans especially with the development and
promotion of the Rosary.

There are several artistic depictions of the Blessed Virgin Mary
supernaturally handing a Rosary to St. Dominic Guzman, founder
of the Dominicans, known as the Order of Preachers. Though this
artistic representation bears some truth, it is an oversimplification of
the origin and development of the Rosary by St. Dominic and his
devotees during the Middle Ages.

St. Dominic, in his missions of preaching to those who had
become confused by the Albigensian heresy of his day, recognized
the apostolic effectiveness of implementing the essential devotional
element of what later developed into the Rosary. This Albigensian
heresy taught that created matter and, by extension, our own human fleshly existence, were evil. To combat their warped views of
Creation and Redemption and their denial of the mystery of the
Incarnation of Christ, St. Dominic found that a meditative form of
preaching, which called upon the intercession of Mary, to be highly
effective. The Dominican theologian Garrigou-LaGrange described
St. Dominic's inspiration this way:

> Our Blessed Lady made known to St. Dominic a kind of
> preaching till then unknown, which she said would be
> one of the most powerful weapons against future errors
> and in future difficulties. Under her inspiration, St. Dom-
> inic went into the villages of the heretics, gathered the
> people, and preached to them the mysteries of salvation
> – the Incarnation, the Redemption, Eternal Life. As Mary
> had taught him to do, he distinguished the different kinds
> of mysteries, and after each short instruction, he had ten

Hail Marys recited – somewhat as might happen even today at a Holy Hour. And what the word of the preacher was unable to do, the sweet prayer of the Hail Mary did for hearts. As Mary promised, it proved to be a most fruitful form of preaching.[255]

The essential devotional element of the Rosary — meditating upon particular "mysteries" of Christ's life in the Gospel, while at the same time calling upon the intercession of Mary when praying ten Hail Marys — is, obviously, already at work in these initial apostolic missions of St. Dominic. The practice of utilizing the instrument of a rosary, grouped by ten beads to separate the various mysteries, became a form of prayer that was especially developed and promoted by countless members of St. Dominic's order. The form of the Rosary we recognize today was complete by the time a spiritual son of St. Dominic ascended to the Chair of St. Peter some three and a half centuries after St. Dominic's death in 1221, Pope St. Pius V. In this pontiff's 1569 Apostolic Constitution, *Consueverant Romani Pontifices*, the Rosary received official papal approval as part of Pius V's effort to promote its practice to the faithful, especially for protection against the growing threat of aggression by the Muslim Ottoman Turks against Western Civilization.

The answer to his prayers and the prayers of those who responded to his pleas came most dramatically on October 7, 1571, in the decisive naval Battle of Lepanto, which turned the tide against that growing threat. On that day, the less experienced Christian naval force confronted its superior enemy in the narrow straits off the coast of Lepanto, Greece, in the Gulf of Corinth. Only minutes before the two forces engaged in the sea battle, the wind shifted direction and handed an unexpected victory to the Christian forces. Military science historian Colonel Melvin Kriesel, U.S. Army (Retired), describes the overwhelming result of the battle that day:

> As the smoke from the cannons and burning galleys cleared it became obvious that the Christians had won

---

[255] *The Mother of the Savior and Our Interior Life*, 255.

an astounding victory. Fifteen thousand Christian galley slaves climbed from the filthy benches of the captured Ottoman war galleys, now free men. The Holy League is estimated to have lost only seven thousand men in the battle. Only twelve war galleys were destroyed; a number were badly damaged and had to be sunk. By contrast, the Christian fleet destroyed or captured more than two hundred Ottoman war galleys and nearly one hundred smaller craft.

It was a staggering defeat for the Ottomans – over thirty thousand were slain that afternoon ... The thirty-four admirals and 120 galley captains who perished, as well as the thousands of trained archers and Janissaries killed in battle, would take years to replace.[256]

Such an overwhelming victory seemed nothing less than miraculous. It indicates something of the providential blessings which this first great Rosary crusade had gained for the Christian forces in this moment of great consequence. The favor of God was so obvious to those who prayed fervently for victory that Pius V determined thereafter that the victory would be commemorated each year on the anniversary date of the battle. October 7 has been celebrated since then under the titles of both the *feast of Our Lady of Victory* and the *feast of Our Lady of the Holy Rosary*. Under these titles of Our Lady, we should rightly recognize the power of her intercession in every whispered prayer we say with her on those beads that we allow to pass through our fingers.

The historian William Cinfici explains how, with the memorable triumph of her victory in 1571, the devotion of the Rosary was then well on its way to becoming a routine part of the daily spiritual diet of devout Catholics everywhere:

Although the political map changed as a result of the Battle of Lepanto, the greatest legacy of the battle is something

---

[256] *Lepanto: With Explanatory Notes and Commentary.* Edited by Dale Ahlquist (San Francisco: Ignatius Press, 2004), 68-69.

that affected the daily lives of millions of Catholics, both across the globe and across the centuries. The feast of Our Lady of the Rosary inspired a more widespread use of this devotional prayer, a prayer that has grown only in significance.[257]

What is the nature of this remarkable power of praying the Rosary about which heaven seems so anxious to convince us? The devotion of the Rosary seems to bridge a spiritual divide between the frailty of our own human hearts, surrounded as they are by chaos, troubles and dangers, and the Heart of Christ, substantially present and waiting for us in the Eucharistic Liturgy. The Rosary seems to be able to do this in a way that is more accessible and expedient than any other at our disposal. In some way, the chasm that separates our hearts from the Heart of God in Christ may be better understood as the proper domain of that current of the Holy Spirit that flows through the Immaculate Heart of Mary.

Five First Saturdays Communion of Reparation

Recall the July 1917 apparition at Fatima, after Mary warned the children of the possibility of an "even worse war" and "persecutions of the Church and of the Holy Father" and other fearful events,[258] she told them that in order "to prevent this I will come to ask for the consecration of Russia to my Immaculate Heart and the Communion of reparation on the first Saturdays." If her requests were heeded, there would be peace, if not, then the moral state of the world would continue to further degenerate, unchecked by acts of reparation, into the terrible conditions about which she was warning and about which we have become so familiar.[259]

As promised, Mary returned later and appeared to Sister Lucia in her cell at her convent in Pontevedra, Spain, on December 10, 1925, to ask for the Communion of reparation on first Saturdays. In a deposition given at the request of her confessor, Sister Lucia wrote

[257] ibid., 75.
[258] July 13, 1917 Apparition, *Fourth Memoir, Documents*, 440.
[259] cf. *ibid.*

down the details of this visit, referring to herself in the third person:

> On December 10, 1925, there appeared to her, the Most
> Holy Virgin, and by her side, on a luminous cloud, a Child.
> The Most Holy Virgin, putting a hand on her shoulder,
> showed her, at the same time, a Heart ringed round with
> thorns, that she held in her other hand. At the same time,
> the Child said, "Have pity on the Heart of your Most Holy
> Mother, that is covered in thorns, which ungrateful men
> at every moment stick in It, without there being anyone to
> make an act of reparation to take them out."
>
> Then the Most Holy Virgin said, "Look, daughter, at
> my Heart surrounded with thorns, [with] which ungrate-
> ful men at every moment pierce me, with blasphemies and
> ingratitude. Let you, at least, strive to console Me, and tell
> all those who during five months, on the first Saturday,
> go to confession, receive Holy Communion, say a Rosary,
> and keep Me company for fifteen minutes, meditating
> on the fifteen Mysteries of the Rosary, for the intention
> of making reparation to Me, I promise to assist them at
> the hour of death, with all the graces necessary for the
> salvation of their souls."[260]

In the previous chapter, we discussed the need expressed by the angel at Fatima in 1916 for Eucharistic reparation to counter the ill effects caused by "outrages, sacrileges and indifference" that offended Our Lord. This form of reparation called for by the angel, is closely related to the form of reparation that our Lord called for through St. Margaret Mary Alacoque in the 17th Century. Our Lord expressed to St. Margaret Mary, the need for making *Communion of reparation on first Fridays to the Sacred Heart of Jesus* and exposed His Heart to her in June 1675, saying,

> There it is, that Heart so deeply in love with men, it spared
> no means of proof – wearing itself out until it was utterly

[260] *Letter of Lucia to Fr. Jose Aparicio, S.J., Documents,* 279-280.

spent! This meets with scant appreciation from most of them; all I get back is ingratitude – witness their irreverence, their sacrileges, their coldness and contempt for me in this Sacrament of Love.[261]

In a vision the year prior, our Lord lamented to St. Margaret Mary that the indifference and ingratitude of so many people caused Him more pain "than all that I suffered in my Passion,"[262] and He pleaded with her, saying "you at least console me by supplying for their ingratitude, as far as you can."[263] In this, we can say, is the essence of reparation: to make a return of gratitude and love, *"as far as* [one] *can,"* for the goodness and love shown to us and others by our good Lord. We can see how similar the reparation requested by our Lord is to that requested by the angel at Fatima to the three children, since both refer directly to our Lord's presence in the Eucharistic mystery.

The devotion of reparation to the Immaculate Heart of Mary is very closely related to that of the Sacred Heart of Jesus. We have already read that our Lord had told Lucia that He wants "to place the devotion to this Immaculate Heart alongside the devotion to my Sacred Heart."[264] Many people often observe first Fridays and first Saturdays together (when they align at the beginning of the month) by an all night vigil, beginning with a Mass on the evening of the first Friday, continuing all night in prayer, and concluding with a Mass on the morning of first Saturday.

Fridays, of course, are a reminder of Good Friday, when Jesus suffered His Passion for love of us. Saturdays have traditionally been dedicated to Mary, in remembrance of the time of anguished surrender to the divine will, which she faithfully endured from the *Hour* of our Lord's Passion until His Resurrection from the tomb. Without interruption, from that *Hour* onward into eternity, the *remembrance* of all that our Lord had accomplished for love of us has been richly

---

[261] Rev. Francis Larkin, SS.CC., *Enthronement of the Sacred Heart.* (Boston: Daughters of St. Paul, 1978), 31.

[262] *ibid.,* 29.

[263] *ibid.,* 30.

[264] *Letter of Sr. Lucia to Fr. Gonzalves, 5/18/1936, Documents,* 324.

preserved, treasured and contemplated in the Sorrowful and Immaculate Heart of Mary. She was the first to make *reparation* to the Heart
of her Son, and she did so in a manner that stands out as a most
perfect model for the Church's life of prayer. The movements of her
heart are the prerequisite dispositions for giving consolation to the
Heart of Jesus and unleashing in abundance the all-consuming fire
of the burning Love of His Spirit (cf. Lk 12:49) upon the Church and
the world.

In the time of St. Margaret Mary, a lingering effect of the heresy of Jansenism in some areas of France, Belgium and Holland had
made the practice of frequent reception of Holy Communion to be
considered a presumptuous act. Jansenism possessed a veneer of rig-
orous religious observance and austerity, but it completely failed to
understand the value of the sacraments. It had become the general
attitude in these areas to view Holy Communion as a reward for virtue, rather than as its means, for which our Lord instituted it: "Truly,
truly, I say to you, unless you eat the flesh of the Son of man and
drink his blood, you have no life in you" (Jn 6:53).

Under Jansenism, a person's readiness for reception of Holy
Communion was taught to be determined by a certain subjective
sense in which the person could claim to recognize within himself
that his attraction toward vice had been subdued sufficiently by the
superior force of God's grace. The Church's teaching on this, rather,
is that a person need only thoroughly examine his conscience and re-
pent of all wrong doing, and, if guilty of having committed a mortal
sin, confess that sin in the sacrament of Confession (prior to reception of Holy Communion), with the intention of not committing
that sin again and performing the penance assigned by the priest in
the confessional. Despite our own weakness in regard to habitual sinful tendencies we may have, God in His mercy waits for us to move
ever more trustingly toward Him in the repeated invitations offered
to us in the sacraments. The grace of the sacraments operates at a
depth far more sublime than we are capable of sensing. Though our
feelings may, as often is the case, share in the joy that radiates from
the depths of our souls as a fruit of God's mercy, such a sense is not

a necessary criterion for determining God's hidden activity. The practice common under Jansenism gave an appearance of piety and reverence, but it was insensitive to the actual Heart of God as expressed by Christ, always full of mercy and waiting for His faithful to come to Him in Holy Communion, that He might refresh them (cf. Mt 11:28).

Today, it is fair to say, that in many places there remains a lack of sensitivity towards God's merciful Heart in Christ, who continuously awaits His faithful in the Eucharist, but this insensitivity manifests itself quite differently from the way it was found under the influence of Jansenism. Among those who attend Mass today, reception of Holy Communion has reached almost universal participation, despite the fact that the practice of sacramental Confession has become almost non-existent. The short lines generally observed for Confession compared to the long lines of those approaching Communion, indicates that the insensitivity towards God has become common and may indicate that the spiritual illness infecting the souls of the faithful today is deeper and wider than that which was common under Jansenism. With Jansenism, it can be argued, there was at least a strong sense of the *justice* of God, however out of balance or distorted it may have been with a true comprehension of the working of His mercy. Under the practice that has become common today, the same claim to a strong sense of God's justice can no longer be made. Communion may not be viewed falsely today as a *reward* for virtue, but neither is it commonly viewed as a *source* of virtue. For many, it can seem that Communion has merely become part of the ritual of the Eucharistic Liturgy, one of the things that is done by all in attendance at the ceremony. This is a dangerous trend which perpetuates the very indifference towards the sacrament of the Eucharist about which our Lord has grievously lamented during these recent centuries.

St. Paul warned Timothy of a future time to come, when people would be "holding a form of religion but denying the power of it" (2 Tm 3:5). This warning sounds eerily indicative of what we so commonly observe today in our parishes. Is the *indifference* that was lamented at Fatima a more current and urgent form of St. Paul's warning to St. Timothy? If it has become common for people today merely to observe the external *"form"* of the Eucharistic Liturgy, while at the same time remaining oblivious or *indifferent* to what is actually being encountered there, then isn't the *"power,"* which is hidden beneath the sacramental signs, being *denied?*

The neglect of the sacrament of Confession seems to indicate that, at the very least, there has been a great loss of a healthy trepidation of the true power we encounter in the Eucharist. Though Holy Communion is truly capable of cleansing an individual of venial sins, it is not the sacrament instituted for the cleansing of mortal sins. For that, Jesus intends to meet us in the sacrament of Confession.[265] These two sacraments work in tandem: Reconciliation restores our communion with God's sanctifying grace, while Holy Communion strengthens and fosters it. Without some sense of God's justice, the truth about His mercy becomes incomprehensible, and the hope of any real communion He wishes to cultivate with us is sabotaged, because the initial steps of seeking reconciliation are never even considered.

Ven. Pope Pius XII addressed this in a radio address to the Eighth U.S. National Catechetical Congress in 1946. In that address he spoke these memorable words: "The greatest evil in the world today is that men have begun to lose the sense of sin."[266] Three decades later, the world-renowned psychiatrist, Dr. Karl Menninger, expressed concern about this growing problem in his book, aptly entitled, *Whatever Became of Sin?* In it, he cited many personal and societal problems that develop if people don't deal adequately with guilt for wrong doing:

> Notions of guilt and sin which formerly served as some restraint on aggression have become eroded by the presumption that the individual has less to do with his actions than we had assumed, and hence any sense of personal responsibility (or guilt) is inappropriate. ...
>
> My proposal is for the revival of reassertion of personal responsibility in all human acts, good and bad. Not

---

[265] cf. *CCC*, 1440.

[266] *Catholic Herald*, 1 November 1946.

total responsibility, but not zero either. I believe that all evildoing in which we become involved to any degree tends to evoke guilt feelings and depression. These may or may not be clearly perceived, but they affect us. They may be reacted to and covered up by all kinds of escapism, rationalization, and reaction or symptom formation. To revive the half-submerged idea of personal responsibility and to seek appropriate measures of reparation might turn the tide of our aggressions and of the moral struggle in which much of the world population is engaged.

We will see our world dilemmas more and more as expressing *internal* personal moral problems instead of seeing them only as *external* social, legal, or environmental complexities.[267]

Though there are many causes that have contributed to the loss of the sense of sin today, one cannot overlook the seismic intellectual shift that resulted from reductionist theories about human origins, based solely on biological evolution from animals. Today, it is common to view our more carnal and base impulses and inclinations as natural, but to forget that our rational and moral capacities are, likewise, natural. The problems identified by Dr. Menninger testify that if we fail to fully appreciate the lofty dignity of the human person, then many problems will build up, while every attempted solution will fall miserably short of curing the ailment. St. John Paul II echoed these concerns, when he lamented the same observation in his Apostolic Exhortation, *Reconciliation and Penance in the Mission of the Church Today,*

This ["eclipse of conscience"] is all the more disturbing in that conscience, defined by the council as "the most secret core and sanctuary of man," is "strictly related to human freedom.... For this reason conscience, to a great extent,

---

[267] Karl Menninger, *Whatever Became of Sin?* (New York, NY: Hawthorn Books, Inc. 1973), 206-207.

constitutes the basis of man's interior dignity and, at the same time, of his relationship to God."[268]

To examine our consciences regularly, go to confession, and follow it up with penance and reparation is the most authentically human thing we can do. All the real power in the world takes place within the secret recesses of the human heart. It is true that we cannot overcome our lower tendencies by mere will power, but God does not expect us to. He has provided for us the means in His own flesh and blood. Within the secret and most deep recesses of our hearts, God is able to clear intimate pathways for the free flow of His grace. Dr. Menninger has stated that, "If the concept of personal responsibility and answerability for ourselves and for others were to return to common acceptance, hope would return to the world with it."[269] The program delineated by Our Lady in the devotion of the First Saturdays of Communion of Reparation begins by helping us to regain our own sense of the full truth about ourselves and of God's desired life for us, and the hope she holds out for us goes far beyond anything that Dr. Menninger could have imagined. For very good reason, we are asked in this devotion to make a good confession on, or some time near, the First Saturday of each month.

Confession

Going to Confession was the first requirement mentioned by Our Lady for faithfully fulfilling the request for Communions of Reparation on the First Saturdays. In the oldest known document we have that deals with the First Saturday Devotion, Sister Lucia relates the incident occurring on February 15, 1926, where Jesus appeared to her as a young boy outside her convent when she was fulfilling her duty of taking out the garbage for her community. In this appearance, she confided to Jesus that, "Many souls have difficulty in going to Confession on Saturdays," and she asked Him if He would "permit that a confession within eight days be valid?" Our Lord responded by

---

[268] *Reconciliatio et Paenitentia (R et P)*, (Boston, MA: Pauline Books & Media, 1984), 18.
[269] *Whatever Became of Sin?*, 219.

providing great latitude: "Yes. It can even be many more days, as long as they are in the state of grace on the first Saturday, when they receive Me; and, in this previous confession, have formed the intention during it to make reparation to the Sacred Heart of Mary."[270] Sister Lucia went on to express her concern "about those who forget to form this intention?" Again, our Lord responded with characteristic latitude: "They can form it immediately in the next confession, availing of the first opportunity they have of going to confession."[271]

We will look more closely at the *intention* of making reparation to the Immaculate Heart of Mary and all that it means later. It is enough for now to recall that Our Lady told the children in her July 1917 appearance to, "Sacrifice yourselves for sinners and say many times, especially when you make some sacrifice: '**O Jesus, it is for love of You, for the conversion of sinners, and in reparation for the sins committed against the Immaculate Heart of Mary.**"[272] Confession is one such sacrifice that our Lord asks of us to make in order that we might draw closer to Him. Apart from hearing the words of absolution of our Lord spoken through the lips of the priest, there is little that is pleasant about going to confession. The sacrifices we are called upon to make are meant especially to make reparation for sin; therefore, the prayer above is also, and especially, applicable when making the sacrifices necessary for making a good confession. Let us give some further practical consideration regarding this much neglected sacrament.

Those who have been away from this sacrament for a long time will need to take a little time to prepare for it by making a thorough examination of conscience. Helpful tips for making an examination of conscience can be found and downloaded off the internet from a number of Catholic websites, and clarification of many details can be obtained from the *Catechism of the Catholic Church*, Part Three, Section Two. Keep in mind, however, that scrupulosity should be

---

[270] *Letter of Sr. Lucia to Mons. Pereira Lopez*, (the oldest known document dealing with the devotion of the First Saturdays, *Documents*, 274.

[271] *ibid.*

[272] *Her Own Words*, 254.

avoided; if it has been a long time since the last confession, it is likely that you will not be able to remember every sin you've committed, let alone every relevant detail. Also, as already mentioned, Holy Communion is capable of absolving us of venial sins. After making a thorough examination of conscience, you may want to make an appointment with a priest and ask him to guide you through a *general* confession, where time can be devoted to cover all the main areas of moral concern and an effort made to identify any major areas of weakness; this is especially appropriate if you have taken down notes in your examination of conscience and, maybe, have written some questions.

Most important is that a person not attempt to *deliberately* hide anything from the confessor. It is likely there is nothing you can say that the priest has not already heard confessed by someone else before, and the priest is bound by a very serious solemn oath, called the *seal of confession,* never to reveal anything he has heard in confession. Do not be too concerned about how to engage the sacrament with the priest; priests are normally more than happy to help a penitent who has long been away from the sacrament to fumble his way through it. Additionally, I have often found posted in the confessional a formula for the Act of Contrition visibly displayed for recitation by the penitent at the conclusion of the sacrament. No one should allow any negative thoughts to prevent them from making this vital sacrifice of reparation to the Immaculate Heart of Mary. The evil one will do all he can to inflate in our minds any negative thoughts or feelings to keep us away from reconciling our consciences with God, but there is nothing that compares with the removal of the burden of guilt that can result from a good confession; the weight that is lifted is a true restoration of interior harmony and balance.

People who have been regularly going to confession for some time, are often tempted to become discouraged and embarrassed that they seem to be confessing the same sins over and over again, feeling that little or no progress is being made in their lives. It should be understood that this is not uncommon and is, in fact, the way most of us become more familiar with our own tendencies and weaknesses. If one makes confession a regular habit, the examination of conscience normally becomes more particular over time. As you become more aware of your weaknesses and sinful habits and patterns of vice, you must take more account of particular circumstances and situations that become for you the *near occasions of sin*. How you handle those moments of temptation in the near occasions of sin then becomes the more particular content of your self-examination. It is a general principle of the spiritual life that this concentration on pinpoint areas of weakness does not result in a broader neglect of all the other areas; rather, it has the opposite effect of strengthening the virtues of the whole person. A good testimony of this is the moral success that has been witnessed by those who have loyally attended the meetings and followed the guidance of a twelve-step program for avoiding the pitfalls of an addiction. As people take courageous and honest audits of their behavior, they grow in humility and learn more clearly the truths about themselves, their solidarity with the rest of sinful humanity, and their continued need and reliance upon the grace and mercy of God.

A general growth in humility is foundational for the broader reception of all other graces and virtues (cf. Lk 18:9-14) and, thus, plays a vital role in preparation for the reception of Holy Communion. The seeming lack of improvement in areas of weakness despite long years of struggle can reap a wide range of benefits in our spiritual lives in ways that we do not recognize. Beyond this personal benefit, we have the expressed promise of Mary of the great benefit she is able to make in the lives of others because of the hidden sacrifices we make in our own moral struggles. Combined with these benefits, we will gain a greater freedom of conscience and be more open in our hearts to offer the time asked of us to meditate on the mysteries of the Rosary.

Fifteen Minutes Meditation

We have examined the topics of reception of Holy Communion and the practice of praying the Rosary, both of which are included in the requirements for fulfilling the Communion of reparation on the first Saturday. We will now examine more closely Mary's request to meditate for fifteen minutes on the mysteries of the Rosary, something Sister Lucia explained "will be more perfect to do," as an act separate from the meditations we are already asked to do *while* praying the Rosary.[273]

The expression Our Lady chose when asking that we meditate for fifteen minutes on the mysteries of the Rosary is very enlightening. She said, "keep me company for fifteen minutes, meditating on the fifteen mysteries of the Rosary ..."[274] The implication here is that by meditating upon the mysteries of the Rosary, we, in truth, draw near to Mary in a way that she actually finds comforting and consoling, as a mother would feel consolation from a child who, recognizing the value of the gift of her maternal love, spends time with her to listen to her and better understand the thoughts that her heart treasures. She is truly our spiritual mother who moves in response to us, her children. Our meditation is an action which, in some way, reciprocates her love and expresses gratitude to her for her benevolence. Again, we are reminded of the Gospel's characterization of Mary as the one who "kept all these things, pondering them in her heart" (Lk 2:19). Where Mary's treasure is, there her Immaculate Heart is also (cf. Lk 12:34; Mt 6:21). Her treasure is the memory of her Son.

When we enter into meditation upon the life of her Son and all that corresponds to it, we enter into a real communion with her Immaculate Heart. She is able to communicate with us the treasure that fills her own heart; and we, consoling her heart in this manner, *keep her company.* We commune with her at a level deeper than a mere conveyance of words spoken to us by a prophet. And there is no telling of the wonders she is able to perform in response to this communion of hearts.

Meditation is an essential human action that strives to fulfill, in part, what Christ called "the great and first commandment:" "You shall love the Lord your God with all your heart, and with all your soul, and with all your mind" (cf. Mt 22:38, 37). As the *Catechism of the*

---

[273] cf. 12/3/1939 letter from Sister Lucia to Very Rev. Fr. Aparicio da Silva, S.J., her confessor in Tuy, *Documents*, 370.

[274] cf. Document written at the request of Fr. Aparicio, *Documents*, 280.

Catholic Church tells us, "Meditation engages thought, imagination, emotion, and desire. This mobilization of our faculties is necessary in order to deepen our convictions of faith, prompt the conversion of our heart, and strengthen our will to follow Christ."[275]

Meditation is a demanding, sacrificial, spiritual exercise, which, like any exercise, can require some effort and practice before a person reaches some proficiency; which is likely the reason Our Lady is asking us to spend fifteen minutes in meditation over and above the time spent in the praying the Rosary. It is unlikely that she is expecting us to meditate on all the mysteries within a single fifteen minute period, since so little time could be devoted to any one of the mysteries. She is asking for at least five Saturdays of fifteen minutes each, a total of seventy-five minutes of meditation. If divided up carefully, all of the now twenty Rosary mysteries could be covered in this amount of time by devoting between three and four minutes to each particular mystery. This could be sufficient for gaining at least a rudimentary exposure to these mysteries and, thus, better prepare us for the efforts of meditation that we will make while praying the Rosary. It should be understood that growth in knowledge and understanding is not the only purpose for meditating upon the mysteries. Meditation is meant to become a daily reinforcement of the truths of the Gospel, allowing us to relate everything that we daily experience, or try to make sense of, to the revelation of the mysteries of Christ, so that our entire lives might then become better rooted and anchored in the solid rock foundation of His revelation.[276]

Often, a little preparation is needed for arranging the undisturbed time and space needed for the fifteen minutes of meditation. In addition, some prep time may be needed for calling upon her intercession and the graces of the Holy Spirit to help inspire and guide the meditation, and to gently quiet the heart and the mind of all the worries and distractions that can so easily preoccupy any time set aside for meditation. Despite the incessant annoyances of worries and distractions, one should not become scrupulous or discouraged

---

[275] *CCC*, 2708.
[276] cf. Mt 7:24-25.

in the efforts made at meditation. We should keep in mind some proverbial advice of G.K. Chesterton when we might become frustrated: "If something is worth doing, it is worth doing badly." Like an athlete or musician who hones his craft, only in time can we hope that the practice of meditation become more like second nature to us. A golfer will often spend some time at a driving range, practicing his or her swing over and over again before getting out on the actual course to play a real game. So it seems in this particular request of Our Lady, that she would like us to become more familiar with and adept at meditating upon the mysteries of the Rosary so that when we do pray the Rosary, we will ponder its mysteries more easily and fruitfully.

Styles and methods of meditation vary from one person to the next, and it is up to each individual to discover for him or herself what works best. We live at a time when many resources are available to aid us in our meditations. Certainly a person ought to become familiar with those scriptural passages that help capture some content of the mysteries. There are books available designed to accompany the Rosary which draw upon scriptural references and other sources to aid in the meditations. Free materials can be found on the internet, including written meditations and artistic images that depict various Gospel scenes. There are also resources, such as apps and audio/video materials that can be very valuable for guiding one's prayer time alone or with a group of family and friends. These same technologies that are so often used as instruments of distraction and sin can easily be harnessed to help us center our hearts and minds on the great mysteries of God, and help us to pray, make reparation and console the Hearts of Jesus and Mary.

The value of this devotional time cannot be overestimated. On October 16, 2002, St. John Paul II launched the Year of the Rosary and released his apostolic letter on the Rosary. That date marked the 24th anniversary of his election to the papacy, and he wanted to prepare for the commemoration of his 25th by this means. On Holy Thursday during the Year of the Rosary, he release his Encyclical Letter on the Eucharist, *Ecclesia de Eucharistia*. In that letter he summarized the overarching goal of his papacy in a single sentence: "To contemplate the face of Christ, and to contemplate it with Mary, is the 'program' which I have set before the Church at the dawn of the third millennium ...."[277] This summation may sound like abstract mystical jargon, but it is really the exact opposite. In his letter on the Rosary he details, in very practical terms, just what he means by contemplating the face of Christ with Mary:

> To look upon the face of Christ, to recognize its mystery amid the daily events and the sufferings of his human life, and then to grasp the divine splendor definitively revealed in the Risen Lord, seated in glory at the right hand of the Father: this is the task of every follower of Christ and therefore the task of each one of us. In contemplating Christ's face we become open to receiving the mystery of Trinitarian life, experiencing ever anew the love of the Father and delighting in the joy of the Holy Spirit...
>
> The contemplation of Christ has an incomparable model in Mary. In a unique way the face of the Son belongs to Mary. It was in her womb that Christ was formed, receiving from her a human resemblance which points to an even greater spiritual closeness. No one has ever devoted himself to the contemplation of the face of Christ as faithfully as Mary. The eyes of her heart already turned to him at the Annunciation, when she conceived him by the power of the Holy Spirit. In the months that followed she began to sense his presence and to picture his features. When at last she gave birth to him in Bethlehem, her eyes were able to gaze tenderly on the face of her Son, as she "wrapped him in swaddling cloths, and laid him in a manger" (Lk 2:7).
>
> Thereafter Mary's gaze, ever filled with adoration and wonder, would never leave him. At times it would be *a questioning look,* as in the episode of the finding in the

---

[277] *Ecclesia de Eucharistia,* 6.

Temple: "Son, why have you treated us so?" (Lk 2:48); it would always be a penetrating gaze, one capable of deeply understanding Jesus, even to the point of perceiving his hidden feelings and anticipating his decisions, as at Cana (cf. Jn 2:5). At other times it would be *a look of sorrow,* especially beneath the Cross, where her vision would still be that of a mother giving birth, for Mary not only shared the passion and death of her Son, she also received the new son given to her in the beloved disciple (cf. Jn 19:26-27). On the morning of Easter hers would be *a gaze radiant with the joy of the Resurrection,* and finally, on the day of Pentecost, *a gaze afire* with the outpouring of the Spirit (cf. Acts 1:14).

Mary lived with her eyes fixed on Christ, treasuring his every word: "She kept all these things, pondering them in her heart" (Lk 2:19; cf. 2:51). The memories of Jesus, impressed upon her heart, were always with her, leading her to reflect on the various moments of her life at her Son's side. In a way those memories were to be the "rosary" which she recited uninterruptedly throughout her earthly life.

Even now, amid the joyful songs of the heavenly Jerusalem, the reasons for her thanksgiving and praise remain unchanged. They inspire the maternal concern for the pilgrim Church, in which she continues to relate her personal account of the Gospel. *Mary constantly sets before the faithful the "mysteries" of her Son,* with the desire that the contemplation of those mysteries will release all their saving power. In the recitation of the Rosary, the Christian community enters into contact with the memories and the contemplative gaze of Mary.[278]

The face of Christ, which the whole Church is called upon to contemplate, is the *matter of the heart,* the Immaculate Heart of Mary. In the sentence where John Paul II summarizes the "program" which he

---

[278] RVM, 9 – 11.

"set before the Church," I left out, in ellipses, what he expects will be the fruit of such a program: He said it is "summoning [the Church] to put out into the deep on the sea of history with the enthusiasm of the new evangelization." This, we can say, is the *heart of the matter*, the *metanoia*, the change of heart that will result from such contemplation. I am personally convinced that the papacy of John Paul II is the one best depicted in the imagery of St. John Bosco's *dream of the two pillars*, that we looked at in the previous chapter. During his more than quarter-century papacy he strove tirelessly to anchor the Church to the two pillars of the Eucharist, *the Salvation of believers*, and Mary, *the help of Christians*. St. John Bosco stated that the immediate result of the pope's efforts was not peace but "total disorder" that broke "out over the whole surface of the sea." We should not be surprised by the present condition of the Church and the world. I believe what we are witnessing is truly a great global exorcism, where frantic and violent acts of desperation now typify the actions of many who hold positions of power. But we can be confident that "the light shines in the darkness, and the darkness has not overcome it" (Jn 1:5).

Sister Lucia told her confessor, Father Gonzalves, in 1930, that in response to the transformation in Russia that would result from the collegial consecration, the pope "is to promise to approve of and recommend the practice" of Communions of reparation to the Immaculate Heart of Mary on five consecutive first Saturdays.[279] What John Paul II has done is provide the theological and devotional foundation of such an approval, and he has lived out its essence. As the Church continues to assimilate the "program" that has been set before it, we will witness and anticipate the completion of the great exorcism that has begun and will consummate in the triumph of Mary's Immaculate Heart.

Intentions of the First Saturdays

Recall the vision that Sister Lucia had when Our Lady asked for the devotion of the Five First Saturdays of Communion of Reparation. Mary appeared with the boy Jesus and showed Sister Lucia her

[279] cf., *Documents*, 284.

"heart ringed round with thorns," which she held up in the palm of her hand. The boy Jesus was the first to speak, saying, "Have pity on the Heart of your Most Holy Mother, that is covered in thorns, which ungrateful men at every moment stick in It, without there being anyone to make an act of reparation to take them out." Then, Mary spoke similarly, "Look, daughter, at my Heart surrounded with thorns, which ungrateful men at every moment pierce me, with blasphemies and ingratitude. Let you, at least, strive to console Me ...."[280]

We have already recognized the direct relationship between devotion to the Immaculate Heart of Mary and devotion to the Sacred Heart of Jesus, and how devotion to Mary helps us to better appreciate what is given to us in the Eucharistic mystery, *the source and summit of the Christian life.* We have seen that this connection between the Hearts of the Son and His Mother corresponds to the *procession* of the Holy Spirit, both in time and in eternity. Keeping all this in mind, we have concluded that by cultivating devotion to the Immaculate Heart of Mary, we most ideally allow the Holy Spirit to cultivate within us a more authentic relationship with the Heart of Jesus in the Eucharist and, through Him, with His heavenly Father.

For this reason, at Fatima, Our Lady is right in telling the children that in order "to save [poor sinners] God wishes to establish in the world the devotion to my Immaculate Heart," and that "she alone will be able to help."[281] These words, in the context of all we have learned and come to understand about Mary's relationship with her Son, make perfect sense. We can thus understand why there is now a need, not only to make spiritual, heart-to-Heart reparation for "outrages, sacrileges and indifference" given to our Lord in His Eucharistic presence, but also for an even more rudimentary level of reparation for "blasphemies and ingratitude"[282] directed against the heart of His Mother and ours; offenses akin to breaking the Fourth Commandment, which states, "Honor your father and mother," which St. Paul states, "is the first commandment with a promise,

---

[280] cf., *ibid.* 279.
[281] *Third Apparition, Fourth Memoir, Documents,* 439.
[282] *Documents,* 279.

'that it may be well with you and that you may live long on the earth"
(Eph 6:2-3; cf. Dt 5:16). Is it a mere coincidence that the hope for
a future era of peace in the world is dependent upon the establishment within the world of devotion to the Immaculate Heart of Jesus'
Mother? The first three commandments of the Decalogue are duties
we owe directly to God; the rest are duties we owe to our neighbor.
The commandment which makes the transition from duties owed
to God toward those owed to our neighbor is the Fourth. It is in the
Heart of our Blessed Mother that earth is joined to heaven, and it is in
devotion to her that we may hope for the coming of a new era when
the Father's will might be done "on earth as it is in heaven."

A few years after the appearance of the Child Jesus and Mary,
Sister Lucia received some insightful details about those "blasphemies and ingratitude" that she saw piercing the heart of Mary. Sister
Lucia was asked to answer a series of questions posed to her by her
spiritual director, which included the question, "Why does it have to
be 'five Saturdays,' and not nine or seven in honor of the Sorrows of
Our Lady?" Sister Lucia received an answer in a moment of prayer,
which she later related in writing to her spiritual director:

> Remaining in the chapel, with Our Lord, part of the night
> of the 29th – 30th of that month of May, 1930, and talking to
> Our Lord about the fourth and fifth questions, I suddenly
> felt possessed more intimately by the Divine Presence; and
> if I am not mistaken, the following was revealed to me:
> "Daughter, the motive is simple: There are five kinds of
> offenses and blasphemies spoken against the Immaculate
> Heart of Mary."
>
> 1st: Blasphemies against the Immaculate Conception.
>
> 2nd: Against Her Virginity.
>
> 3rd: Against the Divine Maternity, refusing, at the
> same time, to receive Her as the Mother of mankind.
>
> 4th: Those who seek publicly to implant, in the hearts
> of children, indifference, disrespect, and even hate for this
> Immaculate Mother.

5th: Those who revile Her directly in Her Sacred Images.

Here, dear daughter, is the motive that led the Immaculate Heart of Mary to petition Me to ask for this small act of reparation. And, out of regard for her, to move My mercy to pardon those souls who have had the misfortune to offend her. As for you, seek endlessly, with your prayers and sacrifices, to move Me to mercy in regard to these poor souls.[283]

There are four dogmatic teachings about Mary proclaimed by the Church: The Immaculate Conception, defined by Pope Bl. Pius IX in 1854; the Perpetual Virginity of Mary, commonly held throughout the Church from its inception and explicitly defended at the Lateran Council of 649, convened by Pope St. Martin I; the Assumption of Mary, celebrated as the *Dormition* among eastern Christians, defined by Pope Ven. Pius XII in 1950, but celebrated liturgically throughout the centuries; finally, the Divine Maternity, the teaching that Mary is the Mother of God, defended at the Council of Ephesus in 431. Teachings that oppose three of the four Marian Dogmas are explicitly mentioned in our Lord's lamentation to Sister Lucia quoted above (at the time Sister Lucia received the above locution from our Lord in 1930, the Assumption had not yet been defined as a dogma, though it is a teaching about Mary that was received from antiquity). Our Lord also laments, in connection with blasphemies against the Divine Maternity, teaching that opposes Mary's maternal spiritual mediation in the lives of the rest of humanity. This in particular seems to be the real crux of the concern expressed by our Lord above in the list of five types of offenses. It is the third in the list. Hinging upon it is the fourth, which expresses a concern for "[t]hose who seek publicly to implant, in the hearts of children, *indifference, disrespect,* and even *hate* for this Immaculate Mother," an interesting parallel to the angel's concern in 1916 for "outrages, sacrileges, and indifference" given to our Lord's presence in the Blessed Sacrament. Following upon the

---

[283] *Notes of Fr. Gonzalves from questions posed to Sr. Lucia, Documents,* 284.

fourth is a concern for "those who revile Her directly in Her Sacred Images." Just like with indifference toward our Lord's presence, so too with indifference to Our Lady, the communication of the grace of God is hampered, or maybe even all together frustrated, by such neglectful attitudes of indifference paid to them both, who are the only real hope for the regeneration of such a degenerate culture.

We have already seen how false interpretations of the meaning of the Second Vatican Council led to significant abandonment of the practice of praying the Rosary. This abandonment of devotion to Mary was not confined, though, merely to neglect of the Rosary. Before the Council, general devotion to Mary within the Catholic Church appeared to be practically universal. There was, though, a fairly significant recognition that the teaching on Mary was still yet incomplete. In preparation for the Council, Pope St. John XXIII had sent out an inquiry to the Church's bishops and faculties of Catholic Universities to gather opinions about what ought to be included in the Council's agenda. In 382 of the replies there was included a request that a clear statement about Mary's mediation be made, and among these, 266 requested that the statement carry the weight of a dogmatic definition.[284] Though we know that the Council chose not to make any such dogmatic statement, the Council did speak significantly about Mary's mediation and helped to explain the special prerogatives granted Mary in reference to her maternal relationship to the whole Church.

Following the Council, however, there emerged a new season, where many pastors and teachers had become seemingly overly self-conscious of the Church's already well-defined and established teaching on Mary and hyper-critical of some of the appropriate devotions that were already then commonly observed. Though this general reaction does not follow logically from any clear reading of what is so beautifully written about Our Lady in the Council documents, an inadvertent development occurred when many developed the false

---

[284] cf. Frederick M. Jelly, O.P., *The Theological Context of and Introduction to Chapter 8 of Lumen Gentium*, (Proceedings of the Thirty Seventh National Convention of the Mariological Society of America, *Marian Studies*, Volume XXXVII, 1986), 45.

impression that the Council fathers were intentionally downplaying the Church's understanding of the position Mary holds.

Mary and the Second Vatican Council

As mentioned above, the teaching about Mary in the Council documents is beautifully written. A sampling of the Eighth Chapter of *Lumen Gentium*, the Dogmatic Constitution on the Church, and the chapter of that document that focuses on the Church's teaching on Mary, confirms that there is nothing in the document itself that can be construed as undermining what the Church has always taught about Mary:

> The Virgin Mary ... is acknowledged and honored as being truly the Mother of God and of the redeemer. Redeemed in a more exalted fashion, by reason of the merits of her Son and united to him by a close and indissoluble tie, she is endowed with the high office and dignity of the Mother of the Son of God ...[285]

> ... It was customary for the Fathers to refer to the Mother of God as all holy and free from every stain of sin, as though fashioned by the Holy Spirit and formed as a new creature. Enriched from the first instant of her conception with the splendor of an entirely unique holiness, the virgin of Nazareth is hailed by the heralding angel, by divine command, as "full of grace" (cf. Lk 1:28) ... [286]

> This union of the mother with the Son in the work of salvation is made manifest from the time of Christ's conception up to his death ... [and notably] the birth of Our Lord ... did not diminish his mother's virginal integrity but sanctified it ... [287]

> ... The Blessed Virgin advanced in her pilgrimage of faith, and faithfully persevered in her union with her Son unto the cross, where she stood, in keeping with the divine

[285] *LG*, 53.
[286] *LG*, 56.
[287] *LG*, 57.

plan, enduring with her only begotten Son the intensity of his suffering, associated herself with his sacrifice in her mother's heart, and lovingly consenting to the immolation of this victim which was born of her.[288]

In the words of the apostle there is but one mediator: "for there is but one God and one mediator of God and men, the man Christ Jesus, who gave himself as redemption for all" (1 Tm 2:5-6). But Mary's function as mother of men in no way obscures or diminishes this unique mediation of Christ, but rather shows its power. But the Blessed Virgin's salutary influence on men originates not in any inner necessity but in the disposition of God. It flows forth from the superabundance of the merits of Christ, rests on his mediation, depends entirely on it and draws all its power from it. It does not hinder in any way the immediate union of the faithful with Christ but on the contrary fosters it.[289]

… In a wholly singular way she cooperated by her obedience, faith, hope and burning charity in the work of the Savior in restoring supernatural life to souls. For this reason she is a mother to us in the order of grace.[290]

This motherhood of Mary in the order of grace continues uninterruptedly from the consent which she loyally gave at the Annunciation and which she sustained without wavering beneath the cross, until the eternal fulfillment of all the elect. Taken up to heaven she does not lay aside this saving office but by her manifold intercession continues to bring us the gifts of eternal salvation. By her maternal charity, she cares for the brethren of her Son, who still journey on earth surrounded by dangers and difficulties, until they are led into their blessed home. Therefore the Blessed Virgin is invoked in the Church under the titles

---

[288] LG, 58.

[289] LG, 60.

[290] LG, 61.

of Advocate, Helper, Benefactress, and Mediatrix. This, however, is so understood that it neither takes away anything from nor adds anything to the dignity and efficacy of Christ the one Mediator.

No creature could ever be counted along with the Incarnate Word and Redeemer; but just as the priesthood of Christ is shared in various ways both by his ministers and the faithful, and as the one goodness of God is radiated in different ways among his creatures, so also the unique mediation of the Redeemer does not exclude but rather gives rise to a manifold cooperation which is but a sharing in this one source.

The Church does not hesitate to profess this subordinate role of Mary, which it constantly experiences and recommends to the heartfelt attention of the faithful, so that encouraged by this maternal help they may the more closely adhere to the Mediator and Redeemer.[291]

Devoutly meditating on her and contemplating her in the light of the Word made man, the Church reverently penetrates more deeply into the great mystery of the Incarnation and becomes more and more like her spouse. Having entered deeply into the history of salvation, Mary, in a way, unites in her person and re-echoes the most important doctrines of the faith; and when she is the subject of preaching and worship she prompts the faithful to come to her Son, to his sacrifice and to the love of the Father.[292]

The sacred synod teaches this Catholic doctrine advisedly and at the same time admonishes all the sons of the Church that the cult, especially the liturgical cult, of the Blessed Virgin, be generously fostered, and that the practices and exercises of devotion towards her, recommended by the teaching authority of the Church in the

---

[291] LG, 62.
[292] LG, 65.

course of centuries be highly esteemed, and that those decrees, which were given in the early days regarding the cult images of Christ, the Blessed Virgin and the saints, be religiously observed.[293]

Clearly, there is nothing lamentable in the teaching that is expressed here, yet what is expressed here and what the document "admonishes all the sons of the Church" to do seems in stark contrast to what actually followed in the wake of what was to be the implementation of the Second Vatican Council. So where did some people, immediately after the Council, find the rationale for undermining the Church's Marian teaching and devotional practice?

The answer to this question seems to be in the common impression that was developed by the general approach to the presentation of the Church's Marian teachings, decided on by a very slight majority of the Council fathers in the parliamentary proceedings that anticipated that presentation. The Council fathers decided that the Council could more effectively present the Church's Marian teachings, not with a separate document devoted solely to Church doctrine on Mary, but as a final chapter of the Council's Dogmatic Constitution on the Church. Some bishops that advocated for a separate document warned of the possible false impression that could be construed that the Church was intentionally demoting Mary by seemingly confining the Council teaching about her to a single chapter of *Lumen Gentium*. In hindsight, the concerns that their warnings raised seem to have been accurate. The secular media, at the same time, ever sniffing for whiffs of controversy, exploited the situation with their own distorted impressions of the debate.[294] For almost a week prior to the final vote on October 29, 1963, the Council fathers debated the merits of the two proposals. The final vote was decided by less than a two percent margin, with 1,114 voting for placing the schema within the document on the Church and 1,074 voting for a

---

[293] LG, 67.
[294] cf. ibid., 60.

separate document.[295] This was the narrowest majority that had determined anything during the Council, where most things were decided with over a ninety percent majority.[296] Although it was not at all the intention of the majority of the Council fathers to impress upon the Church a pastoral directive to suppress or neglect expressed devotion to Mary, many interpreted this move as an effort to downplay the role of Mary in the Church in order to foster greater unity with Protestant communions. This impression was conveyed by the media and everywhere that it became common to reference a nebulous "spirit of Vatican II", rather than implement a careful study of the Council documents. The broad application of this approach within the Church resulted in its tragic pastoral outcome. This application was especially recognizable in the removal of images of Mary from places of prominence near sanctuaries within churches. By removing the mother's image in the family home, her distracted children too easily forgot her importance within the family and became oblivious to her continuous, but subtle, activity in their own lives.

This same thing happened very rapidly in the various Protestant communions, in the iconoclasm [aggressive removal of religious images] that accompanied the Reformation. Many people would be very surprised to learn of the exalted veneration that the reformers retained for the Mother of our Lord, though their thoughts are readily available to anyone with internet access. The best explanation for "the break with the past must be attributed to the iconoclastic passion of the followers of the Reformation and the consequences of some Reformation principles," especially "their rejection of all human mediation."[297] Thus, *out of sight, out of mind*, the faithful end up becoming less aware of their spiritual Mother and less equipped to defend the teachings, which the Church has never shed and which remain sticking points in conversations between ordinary Catholics and their non-Catholic neighbors.

---

[295] cf. *ibid.*, 60.

[296] cf. *ibid.*

[297] *The Protestant Reformers on Mary*. Accessed August 1, 2015. www.catholicapologetics.info/apologetics/general/mary.htm.

Since it is now more than fifty years since the implementations of Vatican II decisions were set in motion, it is helpful to become aware of some of the false interpretations of the Council, interpretations that have taken on lives of their own. We have done so, not in order to wring our hands and say, "If only the Council fathers had decided differently ...," but in order to better understand the distortions that the "father of lies" is ever capable of promoting in his effort to protect his dark fiefdom of human servitude, and to help us form right intentions in our own observation of the First Saturdays of Communion of Reparation. Now we can focus more clearly on dispelling Satan's wiles and defusing all the snares that he has set to foil the relationship Our Lady longs to have with every member of the human race. Knowing that there are today many, even within the Catholic Church, who are confused about the Blessed Virgin Mary's position and role in our salvation, and still many more who have become indifferent, we are better prepared to form right intentions of concern for making reparation and anticipating with prayer the beginnings of a new springtime in renewed devotion to Our Lady and her Immaculate Heart.

We do not have to confine our offerings of reparation to the Immaculate Heart of Mary only to first Saturdays, nor should we restrict it to only *five* first Saturdays. The *five* is the bare minimum that Our Lady asks for in order that we might hope to gain the benefit of her promise: "To the souls who in this manner seek to make reparation to Me, I promise to assist them, at the hour of death, with all the graces necessary for salvation."[298] We should always keep in mind what Our Lady told the children in July of 1917, "Sacrifice yourselves for sinners and say many times, especially when you make some sacrifice: 'Jesus it is for love of You, for the conversion of sinners and in reparation for the sins committed against the Immaculate Heart of Mary.'"[299] Our Lady would like this intention to become a permanent sentiment within our own hearts, as it is in hers. This permanent sentiment to console the Heart of Mary should lead us to abandon ourselves completely to her maternal care.

---

[298] *Documents*, 284.
[299] Third Apparition, *Fourth Memoir*, 439.

Consecration: An Implicit Element of the Devotion

There is no explicit message about personal consecration to Mary at Fatima, but this message can be found implicitly, particularly in two places: first, in an implicit extension of Our Lady's request for the consecration of Russia to her Immaculate Heart, and second, by the symbolism proposed in the vision of Our Lady of Mount Carmel to the three children in the final apparition on October 13, 1917.[300] We know that Our Lady did ask for all the bishops in the world to unite with the Holy Father in the consecration of "Russia"[301] and "the world"[302] to her Immaculate Heart. Recall that Sister Lucia believed she received an answer during prayer to the question of why our Lord would not convert Russia without the fulfillment of the collegial consecration. She said that she heard our Lord say to her, "Because I want my whole Church to acknowledge that consecration as a triumph of the Immaculate Heart of Mary, in order to later extend its cult and to place the devotion to this Immaculate Heart alongside the devotion to my Sacred Heart."[303]

Consecration to Mary is a total entrustment of something that falls under our authority and care to the greater spiritual authority and maternal care of the Mother of God. If the *cult*, or manner of devotion, to the Immaculate Heart of Mary spoken of above includes *consecration* to her, then the extension of that devotion implies that national conferences of bishops ought also to consecrate their nations to the care of Mary; local ordinaries, the jurisdictions of their own dioceses; pastors, that of their own parishes; heads of households, their own families; and, certainly, each individual, his or her own life and vocation.

Sometime after the events at Fatima, the bishops of Portugal recognized this implication and on May 13, 1931, and again on May 13, 1938, united in consecrating the care of their nation to the Immaculate Heart of Mary. In a letter addressed to Pope Pius XII on

---

[300] cf. *Fourth Memoir, Documents*, 443.

[301] *ibid.*, 440., cf. *Letter of Sr. Lucia to Pope Pius XII, 10/24/1940, Documents*, 378.

[302] *Letter of Sr. Lucia to Fr. Aparicio, 12/16/1940, Documents*, 387.

[303] *Letter of Sr. Lucia to Fr. Gonzalves, 5/18/1936, Documents*, 324.

October 24, 1940, and written under obedience from her bishop, Sister Lucia referenced the Portuguese bishop's national consecration:

> Most Holy Father, if in the union of my soul with God I have not been deceived by some illusion, our Lord promises a special protection to our little nation due to the consecration made by the Portuguese Prelates to the Immaculate Heart of Mary, as proof of the graces that would have been granted to other nations, had they also consecrated themselves to Her.[304]

Thus, we can see that the cult of consecration is not reserved exclusively for the pope in union with all the bishops of the world, but should be considered for all smaller societies and institutions as well.

The Brown Scapular: A Sign of Personal Consecration

Personal consecration to Mary is an ancient tradition promoted, particularly, in the spiritual tradition of the Carmelite Order. The brown scapular of Our Lady of Mount Carmel is recognized as a *sign* of personal consecration to her maternal spiritual care, which, by being enrolled in the confraternity of the Order, can be fruitfully worn by all the baptized of the Church. Our Lady of Fatima implicitly promoted the wearing of the brown scapular in her final apparition to the three children on October 13, 1917, in the final image of the visions the children witnessed. While the people were witnessing the great miracle of the sun, the children saw a series of three symbolic visions. Lucia describes them thus:

> When our Lady disappeared in the immense distance of the sky, next to the sun we saw Saint Joseph holding the Child Jesus and our Lady dressed in white with a blue mantle. Saint Joseph and the Child seemed to be blessing the world, making the sign of the cross. Shortly after this vision had vanished, I saw our Lord and our Lady who reminded me of our Lady of sorrows. Our Lord was

---

[304] *Letter of Sr. Lucia to Pope Pius XII, Documents,* 378.

blessing the world just the same way as Saint Joseph. This vision vanished too, and it seemed to me *I again saw our Lady dressed as our Lady of Mount Carmel.*[305]

Sister Lucia later explained that she was familiar with the image of *Our Lady of Mount Carmel* because this image was represented in her local parish church. She stated that, "In my view, the apparition of Our Lady of Mount Carmel means total consecration to God."[306] This "total consecration to God" is, of course, perfected by a total consecration to His Mother. We can include in this consecration a daily self-offering in imitation of Our Lady's *fiat* and our Lord's surrender to His Father's will. The image of *Our Lady of Mount Carmel* is a depiction of how Our Lady appeared on July 16, 1251 to St. Simon Stock, the head of the Carmelite order. He and other members of the Order had to flee from Mount Carmel in the Holy Land to England, to escape from the advancing Muslim forces regaining possession of the Holy Land. While St. Simon was deep in prayer about the survival of his religious order, Our Lady appeared to him and assured him of its survival, took into her hand the scapular of his habit and promised, "This shall be to thee and to all Carmelites a privilege, that whosoever dies clothed in this shall never suffer eternal fire."[307]

Mary's promise to St. Simon Stock cannot be separated from the charism of the Carmelite Order that the scapular represents. The scapular is the part of the habit that drapes like an apron over the shoulders down the front and back of the body. As part of this habit, the brown scapular is indicative of the particular charism of the Order that emphasizes consecration to and imitation of the hidden life of the Blessed Virgin of Nazareth. Nazareth is located only 44 km (27 miles) from Mount Carmel in the Holy Land. Carmelite tradition holds that the Blessed Virgin and the Holy Family visited the hermits

[305] October 13,1917 Apparition, *Fourth Memoir, Documents*, 443.

[306] *"Calls" from the Message of Fatima.* (Coimbra Carmel and Fatima Shrine, 2000), 180.

[307] Viridarium Ordinis B. Virginis Mariae de Monte Carmelo per Johannem Grossi, reproduced in the Analecta Ordinis Carmelitarum, VIII (1932, Rome) from the Spec., t. I, Danielis a V. M., taken from *Sign of Her Heart*, 10.

living in the caves of Mount Carmel. These hermits and their spiritual descendants, the Carmelites, always treasured a very close affinity
to the hidden life of the Blessed Virgin and the Holy Family of Nazareth, and they sought in prayer, contemplation and humble labor the
salvation of others, in imitation of that exemplary life of humility.
The Church, by its authority, has extended the blessing granted to
St. Simon Stock and the Carmelites, to all the faithful who willingly
enter the *confraternity* of the Carmelite Order.

This entrance or *enrollment* in the brown scapular is a blessing
that can be performed by any priest or deacon, and has been commonly done in the past at First Holy Communion ceremonies. If an
individual has already been enrolled, then it is only necessary for that
person to begin wearing the brown scapular again. Like an investiture
ceremony of a religious habit, the blessing of enrollment extends to
all future brown scapulars the individual might use to replace the old
one. If one is not certain of having been enrolled, a priest or deacon
can perform the enrollment. The brown scapular that non-Carmelites
wear is a tiny, inconspicuous version of the habit and is normally worn
underneath the clothing. It should be understood that the brown
scapular does not work like a lucky charm or talisman; rather, it is a
sacramental, and as such, it should be worn with a conviction of what
it signifies. By putting on the brown scapular, one is entrusting oneself
to the maternal, spiritual protection of the Mother of God and seeking to live in a manner that she has modeled and offered for us.

Today, one cannot speak about consecration to Mary without
mentioning the name of the great apostle of consecration to Mary,
St. Louis de Montfort (1673-1716). His classic book on *True Devotion
to Mary* and his program, *Preparation for Total Consecration to Jesus
through Mary*, are ideal follow-ups for anyone who wants to begin to
live out most completely the devotion spoken of at Fatima. Like St.
Maximilian Kolbe, St. Louis de Montfort long anticipated the future
triumph of the Immaculate Heart of Mary:

God wishes that His holy Mother should be at present
more known, more loved, more honored than she has ever

been. This, no doubt, will take place if the predestinate enter, with the grace and light of the Holy Ghost, into the interior and perfect practice which I will disclose to them shortly. Then they will see clearly, as far as faith allows, that beautiful Star of the Sea. They will arrive happily in harbor, following its guidance, in spite of the tempests and the pirates. They will know the grandeur of that Queen, and will consecrate themselves entirely to her service as subjects and slaves of love. They will experience her sweetness and her maternal goodness, and they will love her tenderly like well-beloved children. They will know the mercies of which she is full, and the need they have of her help; and they will have recourse to her in all things, as to their dear advocate and Mediatrix with Jesus Christ. They will know what is the surest, the easiest, the shortest and the most perfect means of going to Jesus Christ; and they will give themselves to Mary, body and soul, without reserve, that they may thus belong entirely to Jesus Christ.

They shall be the ministers of the Lord who, like a burning fire, shall kindle the fire of divine love everywhere.[308]

St. John Paul II, while he was yet a clandestine seminarian during the Nazi occupation of Poland, treasured this work of St. Louis de Montfort and openly read his writings when on break from his work in the quarry. Though by this time in his life he was alone in the world, as all the members of his immediate family had passed away, he found great consolation in the refuge of Mary's Immaculate Heart. His hallmark motto, *Totus Tuus*, "I am totally yours [Mary]," expressing a devotion spiritually forged in the crucible of national suffering and humiliation, emerged within him from coal dust and ashes to provide an incalculable abundance of fruit for the Church and the world, while living out his personal consecration in a very public way.

---

[308] *True Devotion to Mary*, (Tan Books and Publishers, Inc. Rockford, IL), 33.

Conclusion

In the Introduction, we discussed Sister Lucia's belief that the mission that God had given her was "not that of a prophet, but rather that of a voice in the desert where only God hears,"[309] and "that God intended to use me only to remind the world of the necessity of avoiding sin and making reparation to God by prayer and penance."[310] We have also seen that, although Mary appeared to three children at Fatima, it is clear from Sister Lucia's own words that she believed God had singled her out for an important work. This self-awareness is especially made clear in her *Second Memoir,* where she was asked by the bishop of Leiria (which includes Fatima) "to write the history of her life and the Apparitions just as they happened."[311] There she shows that from her infancy, she was already being prepared with natural and supernatural gifts and graces for fulfilling the mission to which God was leading her. In that memoir, she speaks about an even earlier experience of being visited three times by a mysterious presence while praying the Rosary in 1915, when she first became a shepherdess and was with different companions. She explained that on the first occasion,

> Shortly after we had begun [the Rosary] we saw, in front of us, something hanging in the air over the grove of trees. It was a figure like a statue made of snow that the rays from the sun had turned somewhat transparent.
> "What is that?" asked my companions a bit frightened.
> "I don't know."
> We continued our prayer, our eyes always fixed upon that figure which disappeared when we finished praying.[312]

This very same thing, she said, happened two more times.[313] We can only speculate that this mysterious presence was the angel who

---

[309] *Letter of Sr. Lucia to Fr. Aparicio, 12/16/1940, Documents,* 387.
[310] *Third Memoir, Documents,* 408.
[311] *Second Memoir, Documents,* 331.
[312] *Second Memoir, Documents,* 337-338.
[313] *ibid.,* 338.

appeared to her three times the following year, when she was tending sheep with her two younger cousins.

When we read in the same memoir about Lucia's childhood life and upbringing, and especially all that converged in her preparation and experience of First Holy Communion, we should have no doubt that God intends, by her life, to highlight a marvelous example of a life well cultivated for eternity with Him, and the manner in which He intends to open the floodgates of His divine *mercy and graces* upon a world so in need. Her biography, *A Pathway Under the Gaze of Mary* (World Apostolate of Fatima, USA/Blue Army), has been written most beautifully by the Carmelite sisters of Coimbra, who knew her best. It is worth reading the story of her childhood, as we reflect on all that God has sought to remind us of through her, while keeping in mind our Lord's words, "Truly, I say to you, whoever does not receive the kingdom of God like a child shall not enter it" (Mk 10:15; Lk 18:17; also, cf. Mt 18:3):

> The first thing I learned was the Hail Mary because my mother used to hold me in her arms, while she taught my sister Carolina, who was five years older than I.
>
> … My mother used to teach catechism to her little children at siesta during the summer. In the winter our classes were at night after supper at soiree near the fireplace where we roasted and ate chestnuts and sweet acorns.
>
> It was then approaching the day the parish priest had scheduled for the children of the parish to make their first solemn Communion. My mother then thought that, since her little child knew all the catechism and was already six, she could perhaps receive her first Holy Communion. With this goal in her mind she ordered me to go with my sister Carolina to assist in the explanation of the catechism given to the children by the Rev. Pastor as preparation for such an event. I went then, very happy, with the hope of shortly receiving my God the first time.

The Rev. Pastor made his explanations sitting in a chair on a platform. He called me near him, and when any child didn't know the answers to his questions, to make them ashamed he ordered me to tell them the answer. Finally, the day before the feast arrived and he ordered all the children to go to church in the morning and he would tell them definitely who was going to receive the Holy Communion. What grief I felt when the Rev. Pastor called me near to him, and making caresses to me, he said I would have to wait until I was seven years old! I then began to cry, and just as I would have done with my own mother, I laid my head on his knees and sobbed.

I was in this condition when one priest, who the Reverend Pastor had invited to help in hearing confessions, entered the church. He asked why I was crying, and when he was told the reason, he took me to the sacristy and tested me with questions from the catechism, especially about the mystery of the Eucharist. Afterwards he took me, holding my hand, to the Reverend Pastor and said, "Father Pena, you may let this child receive the Holy Communion. She knows what she is going to do, better than many others who are going to receive their Holy Communion."

"But she is only six years old!" objected the good priest.

"It doesn't matter. I will assume the responsibility, if you wish."

"All right," the good priest told me, "Go and tell your mother that you will receive your first Communion tomorrow."

My happiness knew no bounds. I went running all the way, very glad, and clapping my hands, to tell my mother the good news. She immediately began to prepare me to go to confession that afternoon. When we arrived at the Church I told my mother I would like to make my confession to that priest who came from the other place. He was sitting in a chair hearing confessions in the sacristy. My mother then knelt near the door in front of the high altar close to the other mothers who were waiting for their children's turn. There, before the Holy Sacrament, she made her last recommendations.

When my turn came, I went to kneel down at the feet of our good Lord, represented there by His minister, to implore the pardon for my sins. When I finished, I noticed all the people were laughing. My mother called me and said, "My daughter, don't you know that the confession is a secret and must be made in a low voice? Everybody heard you. Only in the end did you say something they couldn't understand." All the way home, my mother tried over and over to discover what she called the secret of my confession, but she didn't get any other answer than complete silence.

Now I'll try to explain the secret of my first confession. The good priest, after he had heard me, said these short words, "My daughter, your soul is the temple of the Holy Spirit. Keep it always pure, so that He can carry on His divine action in it." Listening to these words, I felt penetrated by respect for my inner being, and asked the good priest what I should do to keep it pure.

"On your knees, there, before our Lady ask her with a great confidence and she will take care of your heart and prepare it to be worthy of receiving Her beloved Son and to keep it for Him alone." In the Church there was more than one statue of our Lady but as my sisters used to arrange the altar of our Lady of the Rosary, I therefore used to pray before her statue and so I went there to ask her, with all the fervor I could to keep my poor heart for God alone.

As I repeated this humble prayer, gazing at the statue, it seemed to me that she smiled, and with a kindly look and gesture, told me she would. I was so deeply happy that I could scarcely articulate a word. My sisters stayed home all night working to get my white dress and the garland of flowers ready. Filled with happiness, I couldn't sleep, and it seemed to me that the time would never pass. I got up every now and then to go to where they worked and asked if it was not yet dawn or if they wanted me to try on my dress and the garland, etc. At last the happy day dawned, but what that time of nine o'clock had cost me coming! When I was dressed my sister Maria took me to the kitchen so I could ask my parents' pardon, to kiss their hands and ask for their blessing. When all this was finished, my mother gave me her last recommendation. She told me what she wanted me to ask our Lord when I received Him in my heart and she said good-bye with these words, "Above all, ask our Lord to make you a saint." Those words were so impressed in my heart that they were the first I told our Lord when I received Him. And even today, it seems to me I can hear the echo of my mother's voice repeating those words to me.

So I went to church with my sisters, and lest I get dirty with the dust on the road, my brother took me in his arms.

As soon as I arrived at the Church, I ran to the altar of our Lady to renew my request. I stayed there contemplating her smile from the day before until my sisters went looking for me to put me in the designated place ...

High Mass then began and as the time approached, my heart beat faster and faster with the expectation of the visit from the Great God who was coming down from Heaven to join Himself with my poor soul. The Reverend Pastor came through the ranks to distribute the Bread of Angels. I had the chance of being the first one. When the priest was coming down over the steps of the altar my heart seemed to jump from my chest. But, as soon as the

Divine Host touched my lips I felt an unalterable serenity and peace. I felt I was surrounded by a supernatural atmosphere and the presence of our good Lord became so sensitive that I could see Him and hear Him with my corporeal senses. Then I addressed my prayers to Him, "Lord, make me a saint, keep my heart always pure, for You alone!" At this point, it seemed to me that our good Lord said to me, in the depths of my heart, these distinct words, "The grace that I grant you today will remain living in your soul producing fruits for eternal life."

When the religious service was over ... I felt so transformed to God that when my worried mother came looking for me, thinking I was going to fall down from hunger, I felt so satiated with the Bread of Angels that it was impossible for me to take any food.

After this I lost the inclination and attraction that I had begun to feel for the things of this world and I only felt well in some solitary place where I could, alone, remember the delights of my first communion ...

I don't know whether or not the facts I wrote ... about my first Communion are a reality or a little girl's illusion. All I know is, that they always had, and even today have a great influence in uniting my soul with God.[314]

Sister Lucia's story of her First Holy Communion summarizes so well the devotion we have studied in the pages of this book, which God "wishes to establish in the world." It is difficult to imagine a child more ideally prepared for encountering her Lord in the sacraments. Though Portugal was undergoing political upheaval, life in Fatima in the first years after the revolution had continued much as it had for centuries. The daily routines of their simple, peasant lifestyle were woven organically with meaningful devotion. Everything and everybody in Lucia's immediate circle of family, friends and acquaintances reinforced all that she had learned in her catechetical lessons.

---

[314] ibid., 333-337.

Throughout her book, *"Calls" from the Message of Fatima*, Sister Lucia repeatedly makes reference to the loss of the many supports that once so readily helped to instill and sustain faith within society. She, thus, points out the need for parents and others to be vigilant in regaining some of these supports and formation within the refuge of their homes, a sanctuary for the cultivation of faith and virtue. The Second Vatican Council highlighted this need in its Declaration on Christian Education, *Gravissimum educationis,* and affirmed that the role of parents

> ... as educators is so decisive that scarcely anything can compensate for their failure in it. For it devolves on parents to create a family atmosphere so animated with love and reverence for God and others that a well-rounded personal and social development will be fostered among the children. Hence, the family is the first school of those social virtues which every society needs.[315]

We know in our consecration to Mary that she promises to "be [our] refuge and the road that will lead [us] to God."[316] She loves and cares for those we love and care for, greater than we ourselves are capable of doing, and she will enlighten and strengthen us in our efforts to secure for them homes that effectively preserve innocence and cultivate virtue and faith. We can proceed in confidence that, despite the many developing trends in the world that contradict the Gospel, God is doing something that will not ultimately be frustrated. But we also must keep in mind that we, in the most intimate depths of our hearts, are, by both nature and grace, God's agents of change and transformation in the world.

The message of Our Lady of Fatima is especially an emphatic reminder of this truth. As the Church and individual Christians draw ever nearer to the Immaculate Heart of the Mother of Jesus, they will

---

[315] Taken from John Paul II, Apostolic Exhortation *Familiaris Consortio,* "The Role of the Christian Family in the Modern World," (Boston, MA: Daughters of St. Paul, 1981), 36.

[316] Second Apparition, *Fourth Memoir, Documents,* 439.

become increasingly more aware and comprehending of this latent potency at the disposal of all. We can be confident that the current of this hidden trend proceeds unabated in the hearts of all those who have abandoned themselves without reserve to the Hearts of Jesus and Mary, where it may seem that they are but "a voice in the desert where only God hears."[317]

In 1985, the Italian journalist Vittorio Messori conducted an interview on the state of the Church with Joseph Cardinal Ratzinger, then Prefect for the Congregation of the Doctrine of the Faith, who later became Pope Benedict XVI. Messori compiled the content of that interview into the book *The Ratzinger Report*. Many of the observations of the former prefect remain very relevant today, especially much of what he observed about devotion to Mary, the impact of the Second Vatican Council, and a new trend toward recovering what, at that time, had only shortly been forgotten. The prefect stated,

> By inserting the mystery of Mary into the mystery of the Church Vatican II made an important decision which should have given a new impetus to theological research. Instead, in the early post-conciliar period, there has been a sudden decline in this respect - almost a collapse, even though there are now signs of a new vitality.[318]

He then went on to describe the dramatic deflation of enthusiasm and change from thinking that had originally reigned after the 1950 dogmatic declaration of the Assumption of Mary:

> The fundamental orientation which guided our lives in only a few years has so changed that today we find it difficult to understand the enthusiasm and the joy that then reigned in so many parts of the Catholic Church ... Since then much has changed, and today that dogma which at that time so uplifted us instead escapes us. We

---

[317] Sr. Lucia, *Letter to Very Rev. Fr. Aparicio from Tuy, Spain, 9/1/1940, Documents*, 387.

[318] *The Ratzinger Report*, (San Francisco: Ignatius Press, 1985), 104.

ask ourselves whether with it we may not be placing unnecessary obstacles in the way of a reunion with our evangelical fellow Christians, whether it would not be much easier if this stone did not lie on the road, this stone which we ourselves had placed there in the so recent past. We also ask ourselves whether with such a dogma we may not threaten the orientation of Christian piety. Will it not be misdirected, instead of looking toward God the Father and toward the sole mediator, Jesus Christ ...?[319]

Humbly, he goes on to confess his own conversion of thinking on this whole essential matter:

As a young theologian in the time before (and also during) the Council, I had, as many did then and still do today, some reservations in regard to certain ancient formulas, as, for example, that famous *De Maria nunquam satis*, "concerning Mary one can never say enough." It seemed exaggerated to me. So it was difficult for me later to understand the true meaning of another famous expression (current in the Church since the first centuries when – after a memorable dispute – the Council of Ephesus, in 431, had proclaimed Mary *Theotokos*, Mother of God). The declaration, namely, that designated the Virgin as "the conqueror of all heresies." Now – in this confused period where truly every type of heretical aberration seems to be pressing upon the doors of the authentic faith – now I understand that it was not a matter of pious exaggerations, but of truths that today are more valid than ever.

Yes it is necessary to go back to Mary if we want to return to that "truth about Jesus Christ," "truth about the Church" and the "truth about man"... [320]

If Mary no longer finds a place in many theologies and ecclesiologies, the reason is obvious: they have reduced

[319] *ibid., 104-105.*
[320] *ibid., 105-106.*

faith to an abstraction. And an abstraction does not need a Mother.[321]

The remarks above, especially the last phrase, from one of the greatest theological minds of present and recent memory, sum up beautifully the current state of the Church regarding its relationship to Mary and our great need for the coming triumph of her Immaculate Heart. Even though most of us are not theologians, we still regularly engage in theology, for as was mentioned earlier, theology is simply *faith seeking understanding.* We will understand Jesus, the Church, and the meaning of our own lives better, the more we take Mary "to [our] own home" (cf. Jn 19:27) as our own mother. In the vortex of the love that flows between and radiates from the Hearts of Jesus and Mary, we will lose all sense of alienation and abstraction, not only in matters of theology, but also in all the existential questions that perplex us in our daily lives. The common errors, which have so successfully migrated from a formerly atheistic Russia, will dissipate like fog in the heat of the rising sun. The conversion of thought, so beautifully articulated by Pope Benedict XVI when he served as Prefect of the Congregation for the Doctrine of the Faith, will come like a renewed awakening, a new springtime in the Church, the effect of which will only be suitably described as a great *Triumph* of heart, the Immaculate Heart.

We should not become discouraged by any former or current setbacks that have so often occurred within the Church. As Sister Lucia prayed and sacrificed longingly for the fulfillment of the collegial consecration, she remained confident that God allowed the long delay, in order "to prepare [the world] for a more complete turn toward Him."[322] We can fortify ourselves with the same confidence in divine providence, as we anticipate with our own prayers and sacrifices a greater ecclesial promotion of the Five First Saturdays of Communion of Reparation, the fuller extension of the cult of devotion to the Immaculate Heart of Mary throughout the Church, and its establishment in the world according to God's expressed desire at Fatima.

---

[321] *ibid.,* 108.

[322] *Letter of Sr. Lucia to Fr. Gonzalves, 8/18/1940, Documents,* 374.

For as the rain and the snow come down from heaven, and return not thither but water the earth, making it bring forth and sprout, giving seed to the sower and bread to the eater, so shall my word be that goes forth from my mouth; it shall not return to me empty, but it shall accomplish that which I purpose, and prosper in the thing for which I sent it. (Is 55:10-11)

A new heart I will give you, and a new spirit I will put within you; and I will take out of your flesh the heart of stone and give you a heart of flesh. And I will put my spirit within you and cause you to walk in my statutes and be careful to observe my ordinances. ... and you shall be my people, and I will be your God. (Ez 36:26-28)

For still the vision awaits its time; it hastens to the end – it will not lie. If it seem slow, wait for it; it will surely come, it will not delay. (Heb 2:3)

BIBLIOGRAPHY

ELECTRONIC MEDIA SOURCES:

5 October 1910 Revolution. Accessed July 11, 2015 from Wikipedia https://en.wikipedia.org/wiki/5_October_1910_revolution.

Congregation for the Doctrine of the Faith. *The Message of Fatima*. Accessed July 11, 2015 from http://www.vatican.va/.../ rc_con_cfaith_doc_20000626_message-fatima_en.html.

Breen, Stephen. *"Lourdes and Bernadette."* Taken from *Recent Apparitions of the Blessed Virgin Mary*. The Scapular Press, 1952. EWTN Online Library. Accessed August 2, 2015. http://www.ewtn.com/library/mary/lourbern.htm.

Delany, Joseph F. "Sacrilege." *The Catholic Encyclopedia*. Vol.13. New York: Robert Appleton Company, 1912. Accessed July 27, 2015 from New Advent: http://www.newadvent.org/ cathen/13321a.htm.

Fortescue, Adrian. "Liturgy." *The Catholic Encyclopedia*. Vol. 9. New York: Robert Appleton Company, 1910. Accessed August 1, 2015 from New Advent: http://www.newadvent.org/ cathen/09306a.htm.

Kolbe, St. Maximilian. *Act of Consecration*. Accessed February 25, 2019 from https://saintmaximiliankolbe.com/consecration/.

Sacraments Today: Belief and Practice among U.S. Catholics – Center for Applied Research in the Apostolate (CARA). Accessed July 31, 2015. www.cara.georgetown.edu/sacraments.html.

The Protestant Reformers on Mary. Accessed July 21, 2015 from www.catholicapologetics.info/apologetics/general/mary.htm.

PRINTED SOURCES:

American Heritage Dictionary, 2nd College Ed. Boston, MA: Houghton Mifflin Company. 1985.

Andrew, Christopher, and Vasili Mitrokhin. *The Sword and the Shield: The Mitrokhin Archive and the Secret History of the KGB.* New York, NY: Basic Books, 1999.

Apostoli, Fr. Andrew, C.F.R. *Fatima for Today: The Urgent Marian Message of Hope.* San Francisco: Ignatius Press, 2010.

Aumann, Jordan, O.P. *Christian Spirituality in the Catholic Tradition.* San Francisco: Ignatius Press, 1985.

Brown, Colin. *The New International Dictionary of New Testament Theology*, Vol. 2. Grand Rapids, MI: Zondervan Publishing House, 1976.

Campbell, Fr. Dwight, "Mary: Universal Mother in the Order of Grace." *Homiletic and Pastoral Review,* May, 1998.

Catechism of the Catholic Church, 2nd Ed. English Trans. Washington, D.C.: United States Catholic Conference, 1997.

Chesterton, G.K. *Lepanto: With Explanatory Notes and Commentary.* Edited by Dale Ahlquist. San Francisco: Ignatius Press, 2004.

Christian Prayer: The Liturgy of the Hours. Boston: Pauline Books and Media, 1976.

Chrysostom, St. John. *Catechesis 3, 13-19,* in *The Liturgy of the Hours according to the Roman Rite*, Office of Readings for Good Friday. New York: Catholic Book Publishing Company, 1976.

De Margerie, Fr. Bertrand, S.J. *Heart of Mary, Heart of the Church.* Translated from French by Sr. Mary Thomas Noble, O.P. Washington, NJ: AMI Press, 1991.

Documents on Fatima & Memoirs of Sr. Lucia. Edited by Fr. Antonio
    Maria Martins, S.J. 2nd English ed. Hanceville, AL: Fatima
    Family Apostolate, 2002.

Dubay, Fr. Thomas, S.M. *Fire Within: St. Teresa of Avila, St. John of the
    Cross, and the Gospel – on Prayer.* San Francisco: Ignatius Press,
    1989.

Garrigou-Lagrange, Fr. Reginald, O.P. *The Mother of the Savior and
    Our Interior Life.* Rockford, IL: Tan Books and Publishers,
    Inc., 1993.

Haffert, John M. *Her Own Words to the Nuclear Age.* Asbury, NJ: The
    101 Foundation, 1993.

_____. *Meet the Witnesses.* Asbury, NJ: 101 Foundation,
    2002.

_____. *Sign of Her Heart.* Washington, NJ: Ave Maria Insti-
    tute, 1971.

Ignatius Catholic Study Bible, New Testament, Revised Standard Version,
    2nd Catholic ed. San Francisco: Ignatius Press, 2001.

Ignatius Holy Bible, Old and New Testament, Revised Standard Version,
    Catholic ed. San Francisco: Ignatius Press, 1966.

Jelly, Frederick M., O.P. *Madonna: Mary in the Catholic Tradition.* Eu-
    gene, OR: Wipf and Stock Publishers, 1986.

_____. *The Theological Context of and Introduction to Chap-
    ter 8 of Lumen Gentium,* Proceedings of the Thirty-Seventh
    National Convention of the Mariological Society of America,
    Marian Studies, Volume XXXVII. 1986.

John of the Cross, *The Collected Works of St. John of the Cross,* Translat-
    ed by Kieran Kavanaugh and Otilio Rodriguez. Washington,
    D.C.: ICS Publications, 1991.

John Paul II. Encyclical Letter, *Dominum et Vivificantem, On the Holy Spirit in the Life of the Church and the World*. Boston, MA: St. Paul Books and Media, 1986.

_____. Apostolic Letter *Rosarium Virginis Mariae, On the Rosary of the Virgin Mary*. 2002.

_____. Apostolic Letter *Salvifici Doloris, On the Christian Meaning of Human Suffering*. Boston, MA: St. Paul Books & Media, 1984.

_____. Encyclical Letter *Redemptoris Mater (Mother of the Redeemer)*. Eugene, OR: Wipf and Stock Publishers, 1987.

Kowalska, M. Faustina, *Divine Mercy in My Soul: Diary*. Stockbridge, MA: Marian Press, 1987.

Larkin, Francis, SS.CC. *Enthronement of the Sacred Heart*. Boston, MA: Daughters of St. Paul, 1978.

Lucia dos Santos. *"CALLS" from the Message of Fatima*. Coimbra Carmel and Fatima Shrine, 2000.

_____. *Fatima in Lucia's Own Words: Sister Lucia's Memoirs*. Edited by Fr. Louis Kondor, SVD. Translated by Dominican Nuns of Perpetual Rosary. Fatima, Portugal Postulation Centre, 1976. .

Manteau-Bonamy, H. M., O.P. *Immaculate Conception and the Holy Spirit: The Marian Teachings of St. Maximilian Kolbe*. Translated from French by Br. Richard Arnandez. Liberyville, IL: Prow Books / Franciscan Marytown Press, 1977.

Mariology: A Guide for Priests, Deacons, Seminarians, and Consecrated Persons. Edited by Dr. Mark Miravalle. Goleta, CA: Seat of Wisdom Books Queenship Publishing, 2007.

Marmion, Dom. *Christ the Life of the Soul*. Leominster, UK: Gracewing Publishing, 2005.

McFadden, Charles J., O.S.A., PhD., *The Philosophy of Communism*. New York: Benzinger Brothers, Inc. 1963.

Menninger, Karl. *Whatever Became of Sin?* New York, NY: Hawthorn Books, Inc. 1973.

Miravalle, Mark. *Introduction to Mary: The Heart of Marian Doctrine and Devotion*. Santa Barbara, CA: Queenship Publishing Company, 1993.

Mlodozeniec, Br. J., OFM Conv. *I Knew Saint Maximilian*, rev. ed. Washington, NJ: AMI Press, 1979.

Montfort, Louis de. *True Devotion to Mary*. Translated from French by Fr. Frederick Faber. Tan Books and Publishers, Inc. Rockford, IL, 1985

Navarre Bible, Gospel of St. John: Texts and Commentaries, 2nd ed. Dublin, Ireland: Four Courts Press, 1992.

Navarre Bible, Romans and Galatians: Texts and Commentaries, Dublin, Ireland: Four Courts Press, 1990.

Newman, John Henry. *An Essay on the Development of Christian Doctrine*. London, England: Basil Montagu Pickering, 1878..

Pacepa, Lt. Gen. Ion Mihai, and Ronald J. Rychlak. *Disinformation: Former Spy Chief Reveals Secret Strategies for Undermining Freedom, Attacking Religion, and Promoting Terrorism*. Washington, DC: WND Books, 2013.

Paul VI. Apostolic Exhortation for the right ordering and development of Devotion to the Blessed Virgin Mary, *Marialis Cultus*, February 2, 1974.

Ratzinger, Joseph Cardinal with Vittorio Messori. *The Ratzinger Report*. San Francisco: Ignatius Press, 1985.

Sheen, Fulton J. *The Worlds First Love: Mary the Mother of God*. San Francisco: Ignatius Press, 2010.

Stella, Pietro. *Don Bosco's Dreams*. Translated by John Drury. New Rochelle, NY: Salesiana Publishers, 1996.

Teresa of Avila. *The Way of Perfection,* in *The Collected Works of St. Teresa of Avila, Volume II*. Translated by Kieran Kavanaugh and Otilio Rodriguez. Washington, DC: ICS Publications, 1980.

Vatican Council II: The Conciliar and Post Conciliar Documents. Edited by Austin Flannery. Collegeville, MN: The Liturgical Press, 1975.

CPSIA information can be obtained
at www.ICGtesting.com
Printed in the USA
LVHW012157071021
699833LV00010B/870